THE TREE OF LIFE & THE ORIGIN OF THE SPECIES

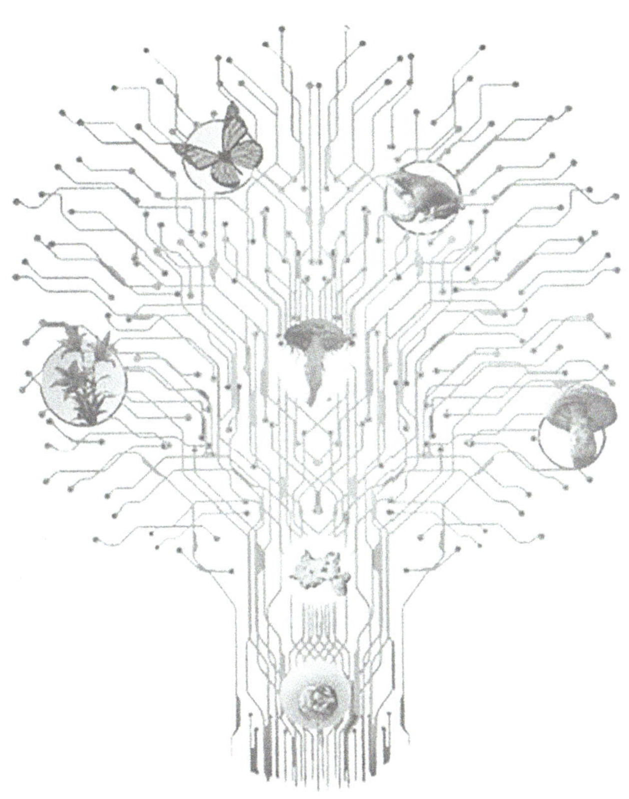

PHILIP BRUCE HEYWOOD

ISBN: 9798869286185

I. TABLE OF CONTENTS

About The Author

Philip Bruce Heywood B. Sc (*hons*), an Australian geologist, set out to teach Origins, and finds himself announcing a range of developments - including the end of the controversy! Science and education are within his fields of interest.

Preamble

Every scientific controversy has finally been laid to rest through application of fact and observation. Sometimes the controversy itself, to the modern mind, has been bizarre. The concepts of dust transmutation into lice and beef transmutation into maggots were put to bed by the microscope. Faraday, the experimenter, at one time was mired in controversy because political radicals were asserting that life equals electricity - electricity therefore explains God, government, law! Once it was experimentally proven that frogs could not power electric circuits and corpses could not be resurrected through electric shock, radicalism surrendered electricity to electricians!

Pursuing truth in all its varied contexts has benefitted Mankind. Everyday devices such as the microscope and the telescope changed our world view. Bloodletting, for example, was abandoned. Hygiene as a means of combating disease was embraced. The telescope and microscope have figuratively been upgraded, and the revolution continues....

.... At the turn of the new millennium we need assurance in answering questions about our planet and ourselves. Science, applied within the relevant parameters, is up to the task....

I. ANSWERING QUESTIONS ABOUT OUR PLANET AND OURSELVES, PAST, PRESENT AND FUTURE.

We need certainty in answering questions of global significance.

Burning fossil fuels as we have in the past – right or wrong?

Solar and nuclear power may throw light, whilst leading to another question:

The by-products of solar and nuclear, accumulating over thousands of years – won't they become an environmental hazard?

What should we do?

Attempt to consult the manufacturer?

Sir Francis Bacon, an advocate of scientific thinking, observed that God has written two books – the scriptures, and creation. The word of God and the 'word' of science.

If you are a geologist, as is the author, you will know that the bible, especially but not exclusively the early chapters, as a technical reference, is reminiscent of some sort of divine jigsaw puzzle.

Change the ***is*** to ***was.*** Past tense. Recent advances in science research have closed gaps in the technical thread running through the Bible.

Introducing Climate.

Drawing on the word of God and the 'word' of science, we cast light on carbon and climate, *instanta*. Don't worry about ruining the planet by lighting that candle during power saving blackouts.

Quoting professor K.B. Krauskopf, Stanford University, 1967, *Introduction to Geochemistry,* McGraw-Hill International Student Edition, 720pp., p. 618: "A rough calculation of the carbon balance indicates that CO2 in air will fall to a level too low to support plant life within a few centuries, unless some other source of the gas is available."

We were saved from disaster by the industrial revolution.
Further: ScienceAlert. *Ancient Ice has Revealed the CO2 Cycle of Earth going back Nearly 2 Million years*, by Carly Cassella, 1/10/2019, accessed 1/11/2020: "Ancient air bubbles trapped in the Antarctic ice sheet .... dating back roughly 1.5 million years .... contain 'amazingly low' CO2 levels, according to paleoclimatologist Yige Zhang from Texas A&M University ... who told *Science* Magazine he found the results "quite interesting". These are the first direct observations of atmospheric greenhouse gases before the ice ages on Earth began to grow longer, and they suggest something other than a long-term decline in CO2 was at play to shift our planet's entire ice age cycle."

Geerts, B. & Linacre, E. 2002, *'Ice Cores, CO2 Concentration & Climate'*. Accessed 23 June 2007 from URL: http://www-das.uwyo.edu/~geerts/cwx/notes/chap01/icecore.html. "Carbon dioxide and methane (main greenhouse gases) occur in higher concentrations during warm periods; the two variables, temperature and greenhouse gas concentration, are clearly consistent, yet it is not clear what drives what. The correlation coefficient is 0.81 between CO2 content and apparent temperature, on the whole. During deglaciation the two varied simultaneously, but during times of cooling the CO2 changed after the temperature change, by up to 1000 years. This order of events is not what one would expect from the enhanced greenhouse effect."

Not a shred of evidence gives greenhouse gases, of which carbon gases are but one component, overall control of global climate. They merely play a necessary part.

How does the word of God chime in with the measurements? It gives the sun the leading role in moderating our temperature whilst pointing to the involvement of magnetism. No, we shan't find the word, magnetism, in the bible. We shall, however, find the phrase, light parted. Refer Zeeman and Faraday Effects. We shall also find phraseology implicating quantum physics, quantum entanglement, evolution as an outcome of information signalling -- the whole box and dice.

Is there in fact a thermostat built into the system? Consult this book and/or ancillary websites. One of the keys is a fact only first proved by observation, 2013 – stellar magnetic fields can transmit heat. Another is evidence published, 2009, by U.S. geophysics prof. G. Ryskin -- our magnetic field has to be directly influenced by ocean circulation ..... .

Background to Our Own Origins.

En route to discovering our thermostat; discover how we started out on the planet? Essential components of our body were here 550-odd million years ago. ....

.... The Authorized Version, exact transliteration from the original Hebrew *etc.*, creates *ex nihilo* all complex life *in totality* at a moment of geologic time, long after plant category or simple life -- the Cambrian 'Explosion'. In four concise English sentences (not all in the same chapter) and a qualifying side-note, this most reliable of all English translations without fear or favour originates *all* complex organisms, Man's physical body presumably included(?), brings in subsequent secondary modification (make, form, not create *ex nihilo*) for those which go on land; gives precedence to aquatics (which the waters brought forth) over and above the land dwellers (which the earth brought forth -- a modification to latent life-forms already brought forth by the waters); associates the flying insects (fowl that may fly, which the waters brought forth) with the aquatics; associates the flying reptiles, mammals, and birds proper (which the waters brought forth, subsequently formed out of the ground) with the land animals. .....

...... We might clear the mind, here, by factoring in quantum chemistry. Water, which, as part of the 550 million yr creative action, brought forth complex life, has an amazing property. Water is specifically designed to be signalled so as to .... bring forth life. This attribute is finely engineered. H2O is absolutely essential in every living organism, being intimately involved with DNA. Replace H2O with a chemical of the same formula -- heavy water, H2O – every complex organism dies. The only difference is an extra neutron – a quantum -- making a barely perceptible difference in the hydrogen bond. In other words – DNA, RNA & co. , and water, are a team – fine tuned. Water is akin to combined communicator, servant and nurse.

The bible is talking ultra-sophisticated quantum technology. Being formed out of the ground, or, 'which the earth brought forth', is an octave lower than being 'brought forth' by 'the waters'. The basis of all complex or animal life has to do at least in part with the hydrogen bond and H2O. Evolution over the following 550 million years never altered the basics. It was pre-arranged for information to be written in over the top – at least in part through a created, natural mechanism. Information is timeless. Man's body essentially existed back at the Cambrian......

.... Speciation the hands-on event can no longer be observed because we can no longer access the tree of life – but we can certainly make an attempt. Lamarck, unlike Darwin, pursued the obvious: If an organism is constantly attempting something, wouldn't it make sense if it turned into an organism that could succeed? A short necked Something reaching for leaves turns into a – giraffe. It makes sense. What if, say, in one female, the Something's memories became so urgent and pressing, they were to trigger a now non-functioning bio-technical capacity which flipped the organism back to a form of asexual reproduction? Some vertebrates display variants of asexual reproduction to this day. Natural hybridization, although not an engine of speciation, nevertheless gives a hint of autoimmune tolerance in near-identical species. True cloning, of course, is humanly engineered asexual reproduction, not remote. Shut down the autoimmune rejection, give embryo(s) re-programmed DNA – the re-adjustments being emplaced courtesy of the accumulated memories. This is info. tech., plus – but it is theoretically possible. Mother and offspring are close to identical, but not the same species. Repeat the process if need be until we have two offspring of the new species, opposite sex. A newly revealed species with all its genetics in entirety! Launching forth in an environment to which it is at least partly suited. Guess which book gives us without equivocation but one mother and father, the mother having been derived by supernatural (in this case) genetic engineering from what was originally the father-mother body -- -- and the virgin birth to boot. ....

Guidance for Government.

This corporation is going to be wound up – today, in terms of geologic time. People will be alive at the end. The Creator gives specific permission to utilize buried resources. "Out of whose hills thou mayest dig brass" *Deut. 8:9.* Therefore he gives the clear go-ahead to go on using fossil fuels and uranium. So either God the Creator of the world gets it right, or the present god (or prince) of this world – Satan, to whom Adam (myself;

Man) sold out, gets it and us as twisted as we allow him. Is the problem with the world, sin, originating in Adam, i.e., myself – or do we blame something else – get politically correct, run a revolution, get 'progressive'? And if people have been so delusional as to embrace what amounts to Animism/Spiritism and give pondscum and even lumps of rock or even nothing at all creative powers in the face of all science fact, what becomes of our Constitution? Our Constitution anathematizes State quasi-religion. Shun superstition! The founding fathers gave clear guidance. ...... *Honour thy father and thy mother, that thy days may be long on the earth, Eph. 6:2.*

Science Symphonizing with the word of God.

In the beginning, God created the heaven and the earth. The heaven and the earth were not created at a point in time: rather, their creation was the beginning of time. The embryonic universe, initially no thing, destined to become every thing. "Without form .... void ... darkness ... the deep ... ." Words fail! What latent potential is this! No object could have been travelling below light speed. No object existed! According to the known laws of physics, nothing with mass can travel at the speed of light. And this indescribable void initially emitted no light. "Darkness ... upon the face of the deep ... ."

Thanks to Thomas Edison & co., we can close the switch and observe light in action. Light may readily be generated from matter. But initially there was no matter! How did something akin to weightless pure energy transform into substance?

The year 2012 witnessed verification of what has been jocularly tagged, the 'big bang'. It seems that the big arrival of every thing was accompanied by commensurate mathematics. It was a case of the big bang and the bigger math formulae. To the distress of all of us who felt we were drowning during mathematics lessons, every thing, it appears, is an outcome of that dread brain torment.

An expression of mathematics dubbed 'Higgs Field', theoretically testifies to a detectable expression of itself, namely, Higgs's Boson. It seems the 'big bang' came with mathematics that resulted in energy becoming 'quantized' as discreet units or quanta. Finding themselves in Higgs's Field, whether or not they actually 'collided' with a boson therein(?), these quanta were imbued with mass potential. In co-relating with each other, quanta form atoms. Because of the effect of the Higgs Field on the quanta, atoms in turn are imbued with mass. Higgs is essentially mathematics, quanta are mathematics and in a sense particles, an atom is a particle – the smallest integral component of solid matter.

How did physicists in 2012 manage to capture Higgs's boson? They did not. The boson exists only on the borderline between matter and information or intelligence. A mathematical formula is not an object. It may, however, produce an object by taking effect. In breaking down matter to its finest components, researchers proved that an atom's finest components rely upon having mass imbued in them by a process or power which left evidence of its real existence. They captured the certainty of this mathematical effect. Its ultimate and perhaps only purpose could be to trigger mass?

The universe is an expression of information or intelligence.

The revelation of the species was the miracle of life, combined with totally sophisticated information technology.

Gen. 2: 4: .... in the day that the Lord God made the earth and the heavens, and every plant of the field before it was in the earth ...

Ps. 19: 2-4: Day unto day uttereth speech, and night unto night sheweth knowledge._There is no speech nor language, where their voice is not heard. Their line is gone out through all the earth, and their words to the end of the world. In them hath he set a tabernacle for the sun ..... .

Gen.1:14: And God said, Let there be lights in the firmament of the heaven to divide the day from the night; and let them be for signs.... .

Signs store and transmit information.

After two or more centuries of concentrated research and debate, the origin of species can now be put to bed - not because of debate, but because science has advanced. The origins hens are finally coming home to roost, after almost two centuries of audible cackle. Lice do not transmute from dust; electricity does not vivify the dead; and Grandfather was not a chimpanzee. Grandfather was a human—one hundred percent.

Keep in mind, though, when reading this, that wheat is wheat, rye is rye, and triticale is triticale, yet triticale is a recent breeding outcome of wheat and rye. While reading this, what appear to be new species of simple, single-celled organisms will seemingly come into existence and no one will know exactly where to place them. Snakes are generally acknowledged to be reptiles somehow bereft of their legs, and viruses are morphing every minute yet have no life of their own. Darwinism has a point. The confusion has a reason.

"The scientific evidence shows clearly that early . . . genetic relationships among bacteria cannot be accurately represented by a single tree. The proper relationship is a net, network, or a web. Again, this is not controversial among those scientists who are aware of the data. The facts and the conclusion have been around for over a decade. There is no 'tree of life' representing the early evolution of life on Earth."[1]

In claiming "there is no 'tree of life' representing the early evolution of life on Earth," modern biologists are implying that descent from a common ancestor does not agree with observation. The old "tree of life" with its simplistic

1 Laurence A. Moran, *"Sandwalk: Strolling with a Skeptical Biochemist,"* 31 July 2009

trunk growing out of the first living cell in the primordial soup, is in the process of reconstruction. The diagram below visualizes modern thinking.

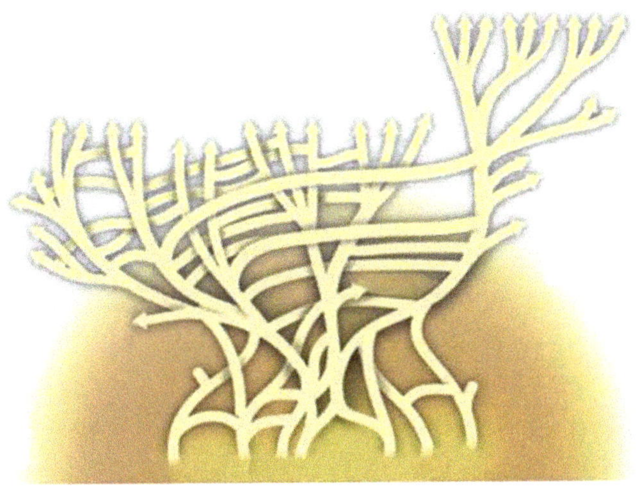

Source: W. Ford Doolittle, 'Uprooting the tree of life.'
Scientific American, 282(2):90-5, modified, 2000

The newer tree of life suggested by modern biologists for earliest, simplest life is a complex, multiple-stemmed vine with aerial roots and many lengthy cross-branches. Life, indeed, flowed along various stems, but the branches also represent something not forward in Darwin's writings - information technology.

The source of information and of life is unknown to science. The roots are hidden, once we get down to ground level.

The equation of species with units of information married with life is not new. Darwin's superior and advisor, Sir Richard Owen, highlighted pre-programming and information-driven transformers before Darwin had published his theory! Owen's notion, presented to the leading scientists of England, was titled *The Law of Progression from the General to the Particular.*

Owen long pre-dated DNA and the prospect of superior or "quantum" information technology, so could not provide specifics. Today, the specifics are beginning to come into distant view.

And God said, Let the waters bring forth abundantly the moving creature that hath life, and fowl that may fly above the earth in the open firmament of heaven. -- The accurate English translation of ancient Hebrew involves equal concurrent meaning. *Gen.1:20:* "And God said, 'Let the waters bring forth abundantly the moving creature that hath life, and fowl that may fly above the earth in the open firmament of heaven.'" (Equal concurrent) "And God said, Let the waters bring forth abundantly the moving creature that hath life, and let fowl fly above the earth in the open firmament of heaven." Now, reproducing *Gen.2:19:* "And out of the ground the LORD God formed every beast of the field, and every fowl of the air; and brought them unto Adam to see what he would call them: and whatsoever Adam called every living creature, that was the name thereof." Verse *20* translates the Hebrew as, "fowl that may fly."

These fowl were brought forth abundantly by the waters. This of course is a direct reference to the Cambrian so-called 'explosion', Day 5, approximately 500 million years past. If we take only the equal concurrent listed first, we have a problem with accuracy. "Fowl that may fly" means exactly what it says. Fowl that may fly include birds, bats, flying reptiles - and the most prolific and ancient of all - the insects. Herein the potential contradiction if the equal concurrent is ignored.

According to the literal meaning of *1:20*, all complex life (i.e., above plant level) leaped into existence on Day 5 -- all of it. Yet it was water- generated and by implication water-based and waterdwelling. This is exactly as the fossil record shows. Large portions of it had not yet appeared, but, excluding (in some vital sense), Man, every species was effectively created, and alive, at that point in time. That is exactly what the Bible demands. On Day 6, already created divisions of life were merely modified, or formed (in the sense of over-formed) of earth. Again, this is precisely as the fossil record shows. The 'over-forming' of earth did not cancel the water base.

Which division of fowl that may fly was not formed (over-formed) of earth? Squash one! And the insects are far older than the earthy fliers, and first appeared in conjunction with aquatic and amphibious species — long before even the gliding reptiles. Birds, bats, flying reptiles appeared in conjunction with the land animals — Day 6. Comparing now *2:19* against *1:20.* Note the changed wording referring to flight— 'fowl of the air'. Real fowl of the air; species that fly strongly and rule the skies.

Like all complex life, they are water based, but birds, bats and reptiles are formed out of the ground. They are earthy, as distinct from insects. Where were they at the 'Cambrian Explosion', Day 5? They were in existence, as living species, as information, pre-programmed to automatically be transmitted into a living cell. Hence, they were all alive, as the Bible implies of all species. See *Gen.2:4 & 5.* Man, of course, is exceptional. *Genesis* could be taken to suggest he more-or- less preexisted in an embryonic way with God himself. He was 'put' (*Gen.2:15*) in the garden. Not all creatures capable of flight or of the flying category leaped into visible view during the earliest outbreak of complex life. This is the testimony of the fossil record.

Gen.1:20 informs the reader that some fowl that may fly, were 'let fly', but it is an unspecified generality. As we have learned, there was a category of flying life that the waters brought forth but which was not subsequently brought forth 'out of the ground', or 'formed of earth' — the old and ubiquitous insects. *Gen.2:19* goes on to explain that earthy fliers are associated with the land animals. Thus, the text of *Genesis* in co-operation with geology gives the origin of all complex (including flying) life at the Cambrian Day 5, says that watery water related flying creatures were a definite aspect of that far-off 'explosion,' gives precedence to the insects, and allows for future appearance of the birds, bats, and reptiles, giving them future rule of the air and association in time with land animals.

Not all varieties simultaneously were found on earth at once is evident from the fossil record; but as has already been shown (*Gen. 2:4-5*), the God who made "every plant of the field **before it was in the earth"** is equally able to make every fish of the sea or fowl of the air or beast of the field **before it is in the earth.**

How was this accomplished?

The long-term storage of species is not science fiction.

It may be helpful in this matter to consider the words - especially the action words - employed in *Genesis.* A remarkable combination of action words and phrases is employed in the biblical narrative. Under our current level of technical understanding, these words are a little cloudy, but in future they may well be pivotal to answering the question of how species can exist without being physically manifest on earth.

There are three superlative creation events: three times a strong, significant expression, translated *create,* is employed:- when God called the heavens and earth out of nothing; when he formed the great sea creatures; and when he made Man. Superlative indeed; to create all matter from nothing; to create complex animal life; and to create Mankind in the image of God. These are unique events, foreign to our understanding, impossible to duplicate. God created out of nothing; he created in a way impossible to duplicate, and he created a species embodying an element of himself, in his own likeness.

The three master works are high peaks in a chain of peaks. The lesser peaks - the other creative works - are described under words neither so strong nor climactic.

The lesser word most often employed is translated *make.* From its usage in the text, it overlaps in meaning with *create,* but is also different from it. This is best shown by an equal concurrent in *Gen.2:3* "...God created and made": equally and concurrently, "God created to make". God created and made, whilst he created "to make".

It is obvious that God *created* matter before he *made* it into its final product - such as the sun, or the stars, or the oceans, or the landscape - and that some things God made, man can also make. But does this apply to living matter? The text implies as much.

God *created* Mankind, before He *made* or *builded* one-half of mankind! (The word describing Eve's physical origin is unique in the whole account, being translated *made,* or, literally, *builded.* Eve was made or "builded", although Womankind already existed, being one-half of Mankind, Mankind already existing in fullness and perfection, created in the image of God.)

God made all vegetation before it grew or was in the earth (*Gen.2:4, 5*). It should prove relatively easy to replicate plants, since a lesser word - *made* - is employed in describing their genesis. God made all vegetation before it was in the earth (*Gen.2:4, 5*). He created Mankind before Mankind was in the Garden of Eden. Twice we are advised: "The Lord God took man and **put** him into the garden" (*Gen.2:8, 15*). The Garden of Eden did not grow until God "planted a garden eastward in Eden", and "made to grow every tree that is pleasant..." He certainly did not plant these trees with a spade, and it would perhaps be adventurous to suggest he planted them from seeds. Simply, "...Out of the ground [he] made to grow every tree..." *Gen.2:9.* Although all vegetation already existed!

All winged life was generated on the fifth day; under the strong term rendered *create.* In *Gen.2:19,* the birds are associated with the land animals, creatures of the sixth day, under a lesser expression translated *formed.*

Did God create all winged life on the fifth day and then form or make it into an active, reproducing, physically obvious life division on the sixth? Did he create with a trigger and a time-delay mechanism?

He made all plants before they grew.

He created Mankind before he placed Mankind in the ecologic niche he was to occupy.

He created Mankind, placed him in his ecologic niche, set him to rule in his own environment, and yet did not make him immediately able to reproduce. Until Eve was "builded" from Adam, Mankind was incapable of reproduction.

To follow up on the topics listed below, please consult the comments under the Genesis verses such as these listed beside the topic.

Expanding Universe: 1:6 & 7

Solar System: 1:14-19

Species Origin: 1:11, 20-27

Tree of Life Mechanism: 2:9

Origin of Man: 1:24-27, 2:7-18

The great Flood: chapters 6-9

Climate Change: chapters 6-9, following on from flood comments.

The Geologic Column and the History of Life Revealed in it.

(Not to Scale)

Quaternary	- man epoch of gigantism, long life mammals common
Tertiary	- apparent extinction of the dinosaurs
Cretaceous	- 1st flowering plants giant reptiles common
Jurassic	- 1st known birds
Triassic	- 1st flying reptiles - 1st mammals
Permian	- 1st reptiles - 1st conifers
Carboniferous	- 1st fems
Devonian	- 1st mosses - 1st insects - 1st amphibians
Silurian	- 1st fish
Ordovician	- 1st corals
Cambrian	{ 1st shells/skeletons Complex life "explodes" Every division of animal life may be traced back to this level
Pre-Cambrian	- 1st simple (aquatic) plants

Earth History According to Radiometric Dating

Event	Age (millions of years)
Man	**Present**
Advent of fruit-bearing trees.	
Advent of birds.	
Advent of true land animals.	
Advent of abundant insects, amphibians, ferns & conifers.	**300**
Earth more active, fundamentally different.	
Complex life "explodes".	
— Worldwide land-planning event followed by the greatest of all submergences by sea. —	**600**
Advent of aquatic pseudo animals -- perhaps akin to organised seaweed.	
	1,000
Earth seemed to "sleep".	
Plants remaining simple.	**2,000**
Gold and valuable ores a feature of these ancient times.	
	3,000
The ancient earth's structure permitted formation of diamonds, necessitating very fast lava-movement from great depth direct to the surface.	
Advent of ultra-simple plant-like life, and plants. Advent of rain - exact time uncertain.	**4,000**
Earth rapidly warmed internally & began to differentiate into core, crust, oceans etc..	
Earth coalesced.	**4,600+**

The History of Life, Simplified

(Not to scale)

Plants		**Animals**
	Present	

1st flowering plants - prolific		
		1st birds
		1st mammals
		1st reptiles
1st conifers (pines)		
1st ferns		1st insects
1st mosses		
		1st amphibians
		1st fish
		1st corals
		1st shells - complex aquatic life, abundant varieties
Simple Plants		

II. BELIEVE IN HIM

The great labour that God has given to men is to believe in Him.

This believing is a far greater matter than mere intellectual assent. Even the devils believe with intellectual assent (*Jam.2:19*). Their intellectual knowledge avails nothing. Intellectual belief is only of benefit if it leads on to heart belief. "For with the heart man believeth unto righteousness . . ." (*Ro.10:10*). The satisfying way to prove the truth of everything God says is at the coal-face of day-to-day existence!

"Try me, try me, put me to the test today," says the Lord, "and see if I am not everything I say I am, and abundantly more besides!"

The foundation of all true belief is truth itself. A love of all truth automatically leads us toward faith.

A love of all truth automatically leads us toward God: for God is truth. All truth - not intellectual truth alone, but heart-truth as well - the truth that says, "I see the truth of my own shortcomings and I am going to act to bring my problems into the place where God's answer to those shortcomings can take effect."

God is not a cosmic Santa Claus, or a dispenser of magic. He ever and only acts in harmony with logical, factual principles. He only ever does that which is possible. By faith, all things are possible (see *Matt.17:20*). Faith is productive belief in God and in his words. So all things are possible - but only as they become a realization in this world dimension of that which is reality in the higher world dimension. All things are ours by faith - those things which align with God's will.

Faith is *substance*: faith is *evidence* (*Heb.11:1*). It is God's word, and our heart-belief in that word, that proves these things to us in real life.

So God's words are paramount, and our belief in God is paramount. There is nothing complicated in believing. Nothing more complicated than the young child, launching itself into space content in the assurance of its parent's spoken directive.

Belief is based on truth: God is truth and God's words are truth: understanding the words God speaks assists us in believing. True understanding comes through humble faith. "For it is written, I will destroy the wisdom of the "wise," and will bring to nothing the understanding of the "prudent," *I Cor.1:19.* "For the Jews require a sign [spiritual pride tries to get God to do as we demand], and the Greeks seek after wisdom [intellectual pride tries to bend God to fit its notions]: but we preach Christ crucified, unto the Jews a stumbling block, and unto the Greeks foolishness; but unto them which are called, both Jews and Greeks, Christ the power of God, and the wisdom of God" *1 Cor.1:22-24.* Christ, the power of God and the wisdom of God, the eternal Word, vibrant communication, or *Logos;* revealed in all his multiple facets through every word of scripture.

The key to getting benefit from the scriptures is *humble faith.*

In the Beginning, God...

Gen.1:1

The word of God attributes man with reasoning ability. A material world surrounds us. Our reason tells us laws governing this material world cannot explain its origin. We may take two paths.

One: we may step outside reason, and postulate a time or place where these laws of physics change. This means they are not laws at all, and our physical world is ultimately irrational, capricious, and nonsensical. This approach denies observed fact and cannot explain the universe logically.

Two: we may take the rational approach, and postulate a higher or a super-natural dimension from which our natural worlds originated. Because this higher or super-natural dimension is outside and above natural physical laws and time, its existence logically and reasonably accounts for everything. Even the most primitive of peoples understood this.

The Almighty credits man with intelligence. He does not say, "The fool hath said in his head, 'There is no God'," for such reasoning is no reasoning at all: rather, he says, "The fool hath said in his *heart,* 'There is no God' - the fool *ignores* God, but cannot logically disprove him *(Ps.14:1).* At some time or other in our lives, most of us have been fools, even if we did not rule God out of our reasoning. We ruled him out of our *actions.*

"In the beginning God . . ." In the beginning, God; and God is the beginning and the ending. We live in a temporal dimension, created out of an eternal dimension. He who "inhabiteth eternity" *Isa.57:15,* who is "from everlasting to everlasting," *Ps. 90:2,* even he who "changes not" *Mal.3:6,* "formed all things" *Pro.26:10.* The question is sometimes asked, "How can eternity go on forever?" Eternity does not go on. It is not temporal - not measurable by a clock. "Before Abraham was, I am." *John 8:58.* "Before the mountains were brought forth, or ever thou hadst formed the earth and the world, even from everlasting to everlasting, thou art God." *Ps.90:2.*

Thus we have the origin of good, and the eternal God. But can we also explain the origin of evil?

God is of the eternity dimension. He was at the beginning, and he is the beginning. He is also the ending, and the ending is the beginning. Was anything else present at the beginning, as an integral part of the eternity dimension? Is there anything else which, like God, simply exists? Something that can only be rationally explained if it is defined as an integral and inescapable aspect of eternity?

Yes. One such pre-existent aspect of eternity is the *possibility of evil.* God himself is righteous; He is clothed with majesty. He is light, and in him is no darkness at all. He cannot be tempted with evil; neither does he tempt any man. "Righteousness and judgment are the habitation of his throne." *Ps.97:2.* "Shall not the Judge of all the earth do right?" *Gen.18:25.* He shall certainly do right, for he is perfect. "I am the Lord, and there is none beside me." *Isa.45:5.*

Evil exists, but it cannot have come from the perfect God. If God were to create evil, the divine purpose would be divided against itself and would come to nothing. Therefore the possibility of evil must simply exist in its own right, like an inbuilt antithesis. We have height: we also have depth. We know of Christ: we also hear of Anti-Christ. Science has lately discovered anti-matter. It was first deduced to exist by mathematically-based theory, and then shown to exist by experiment. If a particle of matter encounters its equivalent in anti-matter, they cease to exist! Science is trying to deduce why there is anything here at all! It seems there happened to be more matter than antimatter produced back "in the beginning."

We need not concern ourselves in regard to anti-matter destroying matter. The universe is not about to dissolve by mixing of these antitheses. There is more matter than antimatter. Likewise, the divine purpose is not about to be thwarted by encountering evil. The perfect God, who sees all things, has perfect knowledge and has met every danger before it eventuates. The existence of evil here on the earth is not a result of divine oversight, but of human disobedience; even so, divine providence has made a way for overcoming this evil - through faith.

A logical view of all things leads to the assumption of a higher or eternity dimension, of an eternal, perfectly virtuous, totally powerful God - and the possibility of evil. This evil does not originate in God. It can only do real harm to those who are apart from God, who have not become part of the divine plan and purpose.

In the beginning God . . . and where God is, evil can have no real power. The evidencing of evil became possible in God's subsequent creation - angels and men - but only through intentional and unprovoked disobedience. Angels were created before man, and are of a profoundly different nature to him; yet both angels and men possess a feature in common - a free will. They have built into them an element of the eternity dimension itself, and it seems that a being can only exist in the eternity dimension if it does have, in some way, this attribute of free will. This is perhaps a little akin to breathing, or respiration, in our temporal dimension. Nothing can live in our natural world unless it can breathe, or transpire in some way. Perhaps the "air" of that higher dimension is composed of moral attributes such as faithfulness, endurance, charity, and so on, and life in that dimension requires free will to enable "breathing." It follows that if the higher dimension is a realm of moral virtues, then the antithesis of virtue - vice, or evil - could be a possibility. If there is height, by definition there must be depth.

Thus if we postulate an eternity dimension, a perfect, all-powerful God, free-will as an aspect of existence in that eternal time-frame, and moral virtues (with the possibility of their antitheses) as an integral part of that dimension; we have a logical explanation of the world around us. Our world was created out of a timeless dimension; and man was created perfect, with free will, which he exercised counterproductively, allowing evil into our world.

In the beginning there was perfection. At man's beginning there was perfection; we have marred that perfection, but it can be re-attained.

The Beginning is the Ending, and the Ending is the Beginning, and God is Both

If we assume God *is*, and if we assume the possibility of evil, but that evil cannot thwart the divine purpose, then we have a very reassuring view of Time and the Cosmos. It is a view fully harmonious with both the scriptures and Science. As St. Paul quoted certain Greek thinkers, "In him we live, and move, and have our being" *Acts 17:28.* An understanding of the mathematical basis of Einstein's Theory of Relativity may not be within our reach, but two simple conclusions of that theory are within everyone's reach.

One: space and time are the same, and are curved, so the beginning comes back to itself, and the beginning and the ending are the same. **Two**: everything is relative: something only exists in terms of its speed, weight, path of travel, etc., measured relative to something else. Unless there is a standard against which to measure something: unless something can be described *relative to something else,* it has no real substance or meaning. This means the Earth, and the physical worlds, only really exist if there is an unchanging, eternal Being giving them reality. Temporary matter (such as the universe) only exists *relatively* - relative to the eternal, unchanging *fixed point.*

Like Kepler, Einstein "thought God's thoughts after him." Kepler placed the sun at the centre of the solar system, and he knew and acknowledged that a Creator must have put it there. Einstein mathematically demonstrated an eternal Creator or ultimate reference point at the centre of everything. The Theory of Relativity is only complete if the Eternal is made an integral part of it.

We have demonstrated the existence of an eternal Creator by mathematical and logical reason. Every aspect of human thought and endeavour eventually leads toward the same conclusion. Ancient peoples understood this quite clearly. "In him we live, and move, and have our being." Only in him can we live, or move, or have any being. All things only exist relatively - relative to an eternal, unchanging reference, The Beginning, The Ending, *I Am, I Am that I Am.*

Good and reassuring it is to logically prove the existence of the great God, the eternal Father. How much better to prove the existence of the Divine by experience! To be able to say, "I deduce there must be a higher Power," is good. To be able to say, "I understand this higher Power has the attributes of a perfect Father," is better. To be able to say, "Father!" and experience that relationship more certainly than a relationship to any earthly parent - this surpasses. This is superlative. This is life. This is eternal life. This is "joy unspeakable and full of glory." To be able to say, "Father, my Father!" and to know it more certainly than any physical family tie! This is the pearl of great price. This is the field with hidden treasure, which a man sells everything to attain.

Gen. 1:1

In the beginning God created . . .

The existence of the eternal, the "in the beginning" God, may be proved by science and logic. But what is this being like? What is the nature and essence of Divinity?

Whilst it is true that no man can fully see or understand God, for his ways are "past finding out" *Ro.11:33,* and he dwells in "the light which no man can approach unto" *I Tim.6:16;* even so, the gracious invitation is, "come near, ye nations" *Isa.34:1,* and "learn of me" *Matt.11:2.* "For the earth shall be full of the knowledge of the Lord" *Isa.11:9.*

The eternal God is not static; he is dynamic. No sooner do we learn of him than we find him in action. Self-sustained action, dynamic action, universal action, multiple actions. God is *spirit.* The Spirit "moved upon the face of the waters." Like the wind, the Spirit is simultaneously active or potentially active everywhere, and can be seen to be so by the results of its actions.

The beginning (and ending) God is eternal, and he is Spirit; he is ever and always dynamic, vibrant, ever new, yet always the same. He is "the Lord; and changes not" *Mal.3:6;* his mercies are "new every morning" *Lam.3:23.* The originator of the kaleidoscopic variety around us is infinitely varied, perfectly stable, and altogether self-energizing. Yet He is more.

Gen.1:1

In the beginning God created the heaven and the earth.

God is the first, the perfect, self-sustaining society. He is the 'In the beginning' God - the eternal God. God, the Godhead.

He is the 'In the beginning' God who creates - the eternal God the Spirit, a God of action who is everywhere.

He is the 'In the beginning' God, the communication into the physical realm - the eternal God the *Logos* (Word). *John 1*: "In the beginning was the *Logos,* and the *Logos* was with God, and the *Logos* was God . . . All things were made by him; and without him was not anything made that was made . . . And the *Logos* was made flesh, and dwelt among us . . ." God, the *Logos,* the communication or translator between the eternal and the temporal. Not only does he translate the heaven and earth into physical reality; in a figure, he is the heaven and earth, for he is both Heaven (God) and Earth (Humanity). It is he himself who translates vibrant energy into matter (the heavens and the earth); and he is both Heaven (God) and Earth (Humanity). He is both these, in totality and perfection, *concurrently.* He is God, and he is man, *concurrently.*

God is three persons. Each of those three persons is God, in totality and perfection, at the same time!

This is no simple concept; but it can be more easily understood by considering substances of the natural worlds. Of all natural substances, light was the first to be manifest in its finished state. It is the closest substance of our world to the substance of that other world. In many ways, it points to the other world.

Light is Both Matter and Energy at the Same Time

A light beam is made up of a stream of speeding "energy packets" called photons. These photons can act as though they are nothing but invisible, weightless energy, and they can also act as though they are particles of matter. They are a single entity, yet they can act as though they are two distinct entities. For example, when a beam of light is shone through a line of fine slots, beams come out the other side of all the slots; when *a single photon* of light is isolated and "shone" on a series of slots, light energy still comes out the other side of all the slots - even though only one particle was directed toward them. This means we are dealing with something that is one, whilst it is more than one! The closer man comes to breaking matter into its smallest components, the closer he comes to producing particles which behave as these light photons. Particles are detected which can become invisible and undetectable under certain conditions. They are present, but they cannot be detected. Others behave as multiples, whilst they are one.

Human technology is borrowing terminology from religion to explain the basis of matter; terminology describing invisible powers and entities that are more than one whilst remaining one.

Far from being static or inactive, God is a society of perfect fellowship within himself. And Man (in a figure, *the earth*) features in this fellowship.

The opening sentence of Holy Writ declares, "God. God the timeless creator of time, the Source, the Beginning and the Ending. God the ever-active creator, everywhere in space and time, everywhere present and always present. God the communicator, constantly translating vibrant pure energy into the material worlds around us, who is Himself pointed to by the physical heaven and earth as being both God and Man himself. God, God the Godhead, God the Spirit, God the Word *[Logos]*. God is all things. Acknowledge Him!"

Having learned a little of the existence of God, and the essential divine Nature, can we learn anything of the way in which the divine Wisdom operates? Of the way in which He communicates to us via the written word? Of the way in which he achieves His purposes, and of the way in which, through faith, we can enter into those purposes?

"*In the beginning God created the heaven and the earth*." This sentence has two distinct meanings, both of which are true, and both of which are equally important. Like our light photon, this verse is one, whilst it is two - yet it is one. Light photons? "Thy word is a lamp unto my feet, and a light unto my path" *Ps.119:105*. In the beginning God created the heaven and the earth, finished and complete. In the beginning, God created *all the materials* of which the heaven and earth consist, but the heaven and earth were then unfinished.

Like the photon, this verse is one, yet it is two, yet it is one.

One: Everything was created, finished, perfected and complete, in the beginning. And can God create anything, without it being finished, complete, and perfect, as soon as it is created?

Two: Everything was created in its unformed state, and awaited completion in our temporal or time dimension, over time.

We know the latter to be true, because it goes on to say, "The earth was without form, and void . . ." We know the former to be true, because it goes on to say, "The works were finished from the foundation of the world" *Heb.4:3*. Finished, yet awaiting physical manifestation in our temporal dimension.

A little analysis of the universe and of history reveals both sides of *Gen.1:1* to be true - equally. When we study some events - and the scriptures abound in such events, whilst our own personal experience will also reveal them - the only way to make sense of some occurrences is to suppose everything is pre-planned and pre-destined. All but the most determined sceptics acknowledge occurrences in their personal lives that were beyond the scope of blind chance. For even one event to occur other than by blind chance necessitates fore-planning of the entire universe. Cause and effect tie into each other as we go back in time, and would become hopelessly entangled were it not for complete fore-planning. The scriptures assume such pre-destination.

As an example, take the culmination of events surrounding the birth of Christ. It is impossible to call up astronomical events (the star), a crowded inn (necessitating birth in a stable), a decree to tax the world, and fulfilment of a pregnancy, without pre-planning. And pre-planning necessitates other pre-planning - all the way back to the beginning. So it is with the lives of people such as Ruth, Esther, Jonah, and innumerable others. Divinely-appointed coincidences occur that can only be accounted for by pre-planning. As *Gen.1:1* has it, "*In the beginning God created the heaven and earth,*" perfect, finished, complete.

Everything has already been done! And if everything has already been done, here lie grounds for hope.

The other aspect of this photon informs us, "*In the beginning God created the heaven and the earth,*" and that work was not finished, but went on, step-by-step, over time, here in our physical dimension. There was an earthly manifestation of that work, even though it had already been done in the Heavens. The only way we can possibly hope to understand this concept is to consider Christ, who is both heavenly and earthly at once. He is all of Heaven, being God; He is all of earth, being Man. And Christ is God. So when God creates, there is a heavenly or timeless creation, and equally an earthly creation. The heavenly is first, and the earthly is a manifestation of that which already exists in the Heavens.

So, although we know of coincidences that can only be the product of complete pre-planning, we equally recall instances of our destiny being governed by our own personal responses and actions. The innkeeper pointed Joseph and Mary to the stable. The wise men determined to follow the star. Jonah commanded the storm-tossed sailors to throw him overboard. Our destiny is in our own hands. Our destiny is in God's hands. It is impossible to logically reconcile the two, other than by looking at Christ. All things are reconciled in him.

Here Lie Grounds for Hope upon Hope

"If God be for us, who can be against us?" *Ro.8:31.* All is pre-destined and pre-planned. "My sheep hear my voice, and I know them, and they follow me: and I give unto them eternal life; and they shall never perish, neither shall any man pluck them out of my hand. My Father, which gave them me, is greater than all; and no man is able to pluck them out of my Father's hand" *John 10:27-29.* Assurance! "No man is able to pluck them out of my Father's hand." Since our future depends entirely on us, we have grounds for even greater confidence: "Him that cometh unto me I will in no wise cast out" *John 6:37.* Do we but stir ourselves, and come to Christ, he has given us assurance he will in no wise reject us.

The point is then raised; "No man can come unto me, except it were given unto him of my Father" *John 6:65.* Well then; call upon God, and do not spare ourselves in repenting, in searching ourselves, in seeking God by humble faith, and he has given us the assurance he will not cast us out. Just as he made the Heaven and Earth in a moment, yet caused it to evidence as our Heaven and Earth over time, so he has the power and provision to reveal his new creation in man, for it already exists; "All spiritual blessings in heavenly places" *Eph.1:3-5.* We enter into it and evidence it in our own lives by "the faith of the operation of God" *Col.2:12.* We may have confidence in his work - for it is already done, and faith will reveal it!

You have no faith? Fear not: it is all of God; he will accomplish the work. You need help from God? Call on him, trust in him, look to him, believe his words, conform to his will, and see his loving provision! This provision already exists, in completeness. It is revealed in the physical dimension over time, in the lives of people. The two aspects of creation; complete, yet awaiting completion. All of Heaven, all of earth. In a sense, the first verse of the Bible is Christ himself.

The first sentence of the Bible lays the groundwork for understanding the workings of divine Wisdom, for understanding Christ himself, for understanding the language and pattern of creation, for seeing the infinite care and love of God, and for understanding the scriptures. Those same two principles of pre-existence in a higher dimension on the one hand, and manifestation in our temporal dimension over time on the other, flow through the creation account and indeed are an integrated part of the Bible. It is already ours: the Spirit will bring it to fruition: believe God!

Gen.1:2

And the earth was . . .

As at the present day; so in the past; some insist nothing could have given rise to the universe. Yet these same theorists cannot invent a perpetual motion machine, merely to show that the universe can self- perpetuate without external assistance - leave alone bring itself forth from nothing. There are two fundamental laws, basic to all of science and technology. The whole of industry, technology, and science stands upon them. They have been proven in a thousand ways, they can be proven mathematically, and they are proved by observation. No departure from them has ever been observed in the entire universe.

The first implies *that it is impossible to create something from nothing.* The second implies that *the universe is constantly becoming more disordered.* Yet theorists have stood forth in the name of technology and learning and claimed to have proof not only that the universe originated from a preexisting universe or from absolutely nothing, but the heavenly bodies and the Earth as we know them achieved their present status without any assistance whatsoever, and then went on to produce the diverse and complex life forms we see today - without any help!

Brayings such as these under the guise of light and learning prove nothing except that we have indeed sold out to the Prince of Deception, who disguises himself as the light whilst promulgating lies and ruin. Man in general has become so alienated and estranged from his Creator, he will find ways to twist and cover over truth, rather than honour Him to whom all honour must eventually come. Assertions of self-creation have nothing to do with learning or truth, except to show the truth that

"A fool hath no delight in understanding" *Pro.18:2,* and that "God has given them over to a mind void of judgment" *Ro.1:28.* Howbeit, we most of us have been fools at some time, and becoming a fool - a fool awakened to his own foolishness - is often the first step toward mending. If a man whom the Almighty himself described as "perfect and upright" was obliged to confess "I abhor myself, and repent in dust and ashes" (*Job 1:1* & *42:6*) when God but spoke to him at a distance, what hope is there for we who are sinners? Our hope is Christ, who came into the world to rescue sinners - and there is no man who really knows himself to be a sinner, who does not know himself to be the worst and most comprehensive of such.

Life and beauty no more sprang up of their own power than a man can cease to be a fool and a sinner by his own power. Spontaneous generation of the universe, the planets, and life is not science but superstition. When we hear of the invention of a perpetual motion machine, or of the extraction of matter from a bottle of nothing, then we may heed these impossibilities.

"Worthy is the Lamb . . . to receive power, and riches, and wisdom, and strength, and honour, and glory, and blessing . . . for thou hast created all things, and for thy pleasure they are and were created" *Rev.4:11 & 5:12.* Give God the honour!

Gen.1:2

And the earth was without form, and void; and darkness was upon the face of the deep. And the Spirit of God moved upon the face of the waters.

If the Spirit of God had not moved upon the face of the waters (or fluid-like disorder), the earth would be yet "without form, and void." And if the Spirit that moved upon the waters - "the Spirit of him that raised up Jesus from the dead - dwell in you, He that raised up Christ from the dead shall also quicken [give vital life to] your mortal bodies by his Spirit that dwelleth in you" *Ro.8:11.* Man alone cannot make something good of himself; the universe did not order itself. There is a higher power at work.

Physicists have formulated a mathematical framework, by which rapidly expanding energy/matter could be spread into a pattern not unlike our present galaxies. The formulations cannot explain the origin of this energy/matter (energy and matter are interchangeable, the same thing), but they do show the likelihood of its spreading from a point-source of initial, vibrant energy. By measurement it has been deduced that there were slight temperature variations throughout these expanding "waters," meaning that as matter realized from the energy, its distribution was slightly "lumpy," These "lumps," where the concentration of matter was slightly greater, became centres of greater gravitational attraction that eventually became the galaxies. The regions between the "lumps" were eventually "sucked dry" by the gravitational pull of the regions with more matter, and became empty space.

The agents at work giving the heavenly bodies and the Earth substance and stability, are those everyday forces such as magnetism, electrical attraction and repulsion, and gravity. Of these, gravity is the most significant and the most mysterious. The nature and cause of each of these three forces is but dimly perceived, and gravity is the most enigmatic of all. Its cause and its nature defy all attempts at explanation. Above all else it gives the created worlds their form and stability, yet above all else, by its universal and inexorable urge, it has the power to draw all created substances back into a swirling confusion of "waters," and ultimately reconvert them to nothing but almost infinite energy.

A power that gives all things form and stability, and can convert all matter back into invisible pure energy, is surely a power from God himself? Is gravity, in a sense, God at work?

Gravity is Even Closer

Of all natural created things, light comes closest to the Infinite and Eternal. Gravity is even closer. It is of the Eternal, whilst having its effects in the Temporal. Small wonder the world's most clever minds have wearied themselves with finding a mathematical formulation of it! It can be used to give the physical worlds stability, and it can be used to make them dissolve. It profoundly affects the physical realm, whilst its nature and origin are outside the physical realm.

Along with the other forces such as electricity and magnetism, it gives the Earth substance and stability; yet it has the potential to override both these forces and reconvert all things to darkened confusion and ultimately, emptiness. It is God at work, now, giving stability to his creation, *Ps.75:3:* "The earth and all the inhabitants thereof are dissolved [speaking of fluidity]: I bear up the pillars of it [God is now giving all things substance]." If God bears up the pillars of the earth, one end of those pillars is evidencing in the physical universe, and the other end of them is in the supernatural. Small wonder gravity and the other stabilizing forces are so difficult to comprehend. They are in a sense God himself at work, giving all things stability.

Thus the scriptures are effectively saying, "The universe was once dissolved, without any stability. It was waters. Forces such as gravity, *etc.* were employed in giving it stability. These forces can only satisfactorily be explained as originating in the supernatural. A day will come when that stability shall be withdrawn, and everything shall again be dissolved." So immediately we see one of the ways in which the Spirit moved upon the waters. He lent all things their form and stability. He lends all things stability even now; and if anything of beauty or of variety or of life exists in the universe, it is entirely of him.

The world's cleverest minds have been unable to show how the universe began to expand and flower from nothing but pure energy, although they have deduced it must have done so. The world's best mathematicians continue to be baffled in their attempts to encompass gravity within mathematical formulae. The scriptures tell us that this expansion and flowering under the formative influence of forces such as gravity led to the existing heavens and earth. Therefore the world's best technologies are proclaiming the greatness of God, as the Heavens declare his glory. Truly, God created the Heavens and the Earth, and God the Spirit formed and beautified the Heavens and the Earth - at his leisure, and for his pleasure and purpose. Their origin is and always will be beyond human technology, and the forces giving them stability always will be beyond human technology.

Light was created. It can be understood. Gravity, in a sense, is God at work, and therefore was not created. It cannot be fully understood nor confined entirely to a mathematical system. It is God himself, "bearing up" the "pillars" of the Earth.

God *is*. He is one, yet he is more than one. He is the first perfect society, self-sustaining, self-energizing, self-harmonizing. He is perfectly stable, "upholding all things by the word of his power," a person; yet he is dynamic, Spirit, everywhere in time and action. He "dwells in light, which no man can approach unto," "It is he that sitteth upon the circle of the Earth, and the inhabitants thereof are as grasshoppers; that stretcheth out the heavens as a curtain, and spreadeth them out as a tent to dwell in" *Isa.40:22;* yet his "tabernacle is with men" *Rev.21:3,* and his name is "Emmanuel, . . . God with us [men]" *Matt.1:23.* He and he alone created the Heaven and the Earth and in a figure is both Heaven (God) and Earth (Man). It is he who garnishes the Heavens with diamond light, whose Spirit shapes and upholds the far-flung worlds, who gives breath to all living, who lifts men "out of the miry clay, and sets their feet upon a rock, and establishes their goings" *Ps.40:2.* He establishes all the laws of the natural world, employing them as he sees fit; and those who follow these laws can only demonstrate his greatness, and speak of his majesty, whether they mean it or no.

Shall we proceed through the early chapters of the Bible, hopefully learning a little of how man, by following the principles of science, has, advertently or inadvertently, heaped honours upon the creator of Science?

III. UNDERSTANDING THE TIME FRAME

Before going step-by-step through the progressive creative sequence we need first to understand the time frame within which the sequence fits.

In the eternal dimension, of course, time has little meaning; but the creative manifestation into our temporal dimension can only be fully appreciated if an understanding of the time frame into which it fits can be gained. Do the scriptures give any hint of the time it took to realize in our dimension the Heaven and the Earth as we now experience them?

The first chapter of the Bible comprises a step-by-step account of creation in time sequence. Six times in this account is repeated a most unusual phrase: "And the evening and the morning were the first day," "And the evening and the morning were the second day," "And the evening and the morning were the third day." And so on, until the completion of work on the sixth day. This persistent repetition of an unconventional phrase is significant.

Six times this strange configuration of time-indicative words is repeated. Six times, once for each day of work, as though to build into our minds by way of repetition some significant feature of the days of work. What is the message this divinely-appointed repetition is building into the reader?

The evening and the morning were the day. The evening and the morning were the day. The evening and the morning were the day.

Evening as employed here means a later, a concluding part of something.

Morning similarly refers to an earlier and an opening part.

An *evening* and *a morning* of work refers to a later and a closing period of work activity, and an early or opening period of work activity. Perforce it also compasses all the work done between the opening and the closing.

By mentioning *evening* first, the text is reinforcing the importance of the work of each day being a *finished* work. An opening and earlier period of creative accomplishment; a later and closing period of creative accomplishment; and all the work done between the two - a complete, finished work. It was these periods of creative accomplishment that *were* each day. The work of each day was finished, complete. When evening came to an end, and the day of work was finished, it came to an end only *because the work was finished.*

The Creator did not work to the sun (it did not illumine the earth for the first three days!) or a clock; he concluded each day at his own leisure when his purposes for that day were fully complete. This is why the *evening* and *morning were the day,* rather than the *day being a morning and an evening!* Measured time did not define those mornings and evenings. The morning (work accomplishment) and evening (work accomplishment) *were* the day. A clock and the passage of time did not define those days. It was creative achievement that was purposed, which was accomplished, which was perfectly completed, which made those days.

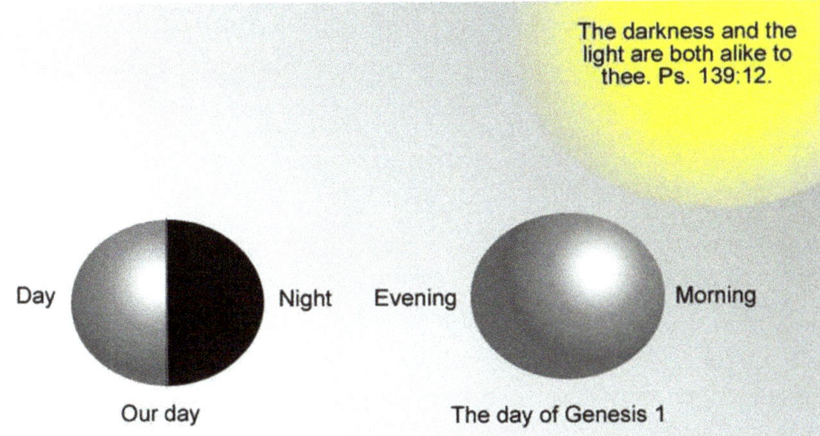

So, in this Day of Grace, a clock does not govern the Divine Purpose. The doors are not going to slam shut at some arbitrary hour, leaving the Spirit's work unfinished. Do we know we need more, much more, of the work of God's Spirit? Does the thought of God closing his works today leave us perplexed, lost, perhaps undone? Do we sometimes tend to despair at the slowness with which we advance? There are no grounds for complacency. Howbeit, although birth is more-or-less instantaneous, it does not just *happen* without foregoing events and preparation; and although character maturity, and the overcoming of sin are likewise a gift from God, they may require time.

No matter how far away from hope and from holiness we may be, no matter how desperate and lost our situation, this is the Day of Grace. Christ did not accomplish his works in vain. He is bringing many sons unto glory, and he will bring every one of them to glory (*Heb.2:10*).

He will not fail. Our situation may well be hopeless, but we can at least cast ourselves upon the grace of Christ, and not turn back. One may say, "I have gone too low: there is no hope; I am rejected of Divine Love, and I am no longer one of God's elect."

The only person going about telling people they are not of God's chosen election is the Devil; and since he is not privy to the divine counsel, he has no reliable advice to give. The prodigal son turned his back on his father and his inheritance, yet even from starvation amongst swine he was given courage to "arise, and go to his father." The banqueting hall will be filled, and the door will not be shut until the last person is safely inside. Yet there is room! (*Luke 14:22*). "I beheld, and, lo, a great multitude, which no man could number, of all nations, and kindreds, and people, and tongues, stood before the throne, and before the Lamb, clothed with white robes . . ." *Rev.7:9.*

Only when the Spirit's work is accomplished will the Day end. Whilst ever there is a person with a heart to seek God, who has not yet found him, with a heart to know him, who does not yet know him to satisfaction, the "Sun of righteousness"(*Mal.4:2*) will not set from over mankind.

The evening and morning are the day; the Spirit will bring to fruition all the wonders of the divine purpose; and although the time taken to bring all this beauty to full flower will be measurable by a clock, God is not beholden to calendars. The days of creation were as long or as short as the time taken to accomplish the works described in them. This is the literal meaning of the word of God. Since various events, such as the growth to maturity of trees, and the receivership on earth of light from distant stars, took substantial time, some or all of these days were of great duration. This is the literal intent of the language employed. The God who "is from everlasting to everlasting" no more required our twenty-four hour day to tell him when to begin and cease work, than the God to whom "the darkness and light are both alike" required the sun to give him light to see what he was doing.

The Events in Sequence

The time frame was suited to the works: now to the events in sequence.

Calendar Date: Zero (fifteen thousand million years + before present).

Location: Unless evidence to the contrary is forthcoming, quite possibly Earth's present general location.

Event: Beginning of the universe. Initial visible evidence: Little or none!

"And the earth was without form, and void." A void is empty. Something without form cannot be described. Yet it was something. It was the heaven and the earth. What was it like?

"It is like a grain of mustard seed, which when it is sown in the earth, is less than all the seeds [it is of no size or apparent significance] . . . but when it is sown, it groweth up, and . . . shooteth out great branches . . ." *Mark 4:31, 32.*

It has been suggested that the universe at its inception was no larger than a pinhead, yet this "seed" was our entire temporal dimension. The mathematical formulae point to it. No sooner did this "seed" exist, than it began to expand, or "grow." Initially this embryo was nothing but energy - or, in equivalent terminology, information, ready to take effect. This inherent excitement and vibrancy meant that, as the initial point grew, it would have been either invisible or opaque; unable to be seen into. As it grew further, its vibrancy began to convert into matter; not the full variety of matter we now know, but unrefined matter of various simple types.

As this happened, a veritable "ocean" of these simpler, lighter elements - fluid in nature - began to "synthesize" from the energy. This "ocean," or *deep,* was as yet so weighty and compact within itself that its totalized gravitational pull would not permit the escape and the display even of light. "And darkness was upon the face of the deep."

Gen.1:3

And God said, Let there be light: and there was light.

Human minds and human technologies are straining to comprehend how the various substances, of which light is one, were created. They have reached an understanding that all substances are nothing but pure energy, acting according to instructions. Here they have stalled. The ancient Greeks seem to have come to almost the same conclusions. They coined the term *Logos.* All substance is nothing but vibrant pure energy being communicated or translated into material substance - this communication being the *Logos,* God. All substance is energy, obeying a Word! That is why God *said,* "Let there be light."

Words made the worlds

The words we use with intent and meaning today make our world in which we live tomorrow.

"...with the mouth, confession is made unto salvation." *Ro.10:10.*

If God is love, and God can be in control if by faith I put him in control: why do I speak words of complaint? Why fret and worry? Why am I afraid? Why do I curse and not bless? If the situation appears miserable: God is not miserable. Do my words bring the truth of divine sufficiency onto the scene - or do my words formulate a lie - that God is not all he says he is? Do I believe in God? Do I believe in divine ability? If I believe in God, then I with my mouth will be giving thanks in every situation - because I believe in God. I believe in the miraculous. I am not to be governed by feelings.

I believe, therefore I speak. I mean what I say. In all things I give thanks. In all things I oblige my mouth to agree with faith. A key is in the words we speak. His mercies endure forever. His loving kindness is from generation to generation. His truth will stand when heaven and earth have passed away.

Are we speaking God-kind of words?

Hope where there is no hope?

Health where there is no health?

Safety where there is no safety?

Cheer in the face of depression?

Light where there is only suffocating, impenetrable darkness?

God did not make any no-hopers. Believe it, say it!

Words make the worlds.

Concurrently with God speaking, "The Spirit of God moved upon the face of the waters." These waters were initially without self-illumination. Then, through agencies such as gravity, electricity, and magnetism - agencies themselves beyond man's full comprehension - the Spirit of God ordered those materials so that light not only began to be emitted, but it began to shine and display in the new, expanding universe. Thus, of all objects, light-sources - but not exactly our modern stars - were formed first, and it is measurements of the ages of certain ancient radiation-sources that give the proposed date of origin of the worlds.

Gen. 1:4

And God saw the light, that it was good . . .

In the divine reckoning the "light . . . was good." Everything that was created was likewise reckoned to be "good." In one sense, *good* means *perfect.* "None is good, save one, that is, *God" Luke 18:19.* God is perfect, therefore *good* means *perfect.* In another sense, *good* falls *short of perfection.* As employed in *Genesis, good* means *perfect for the present purpose, but nevertheless wanting something or awaiting an event to make it ultimately complete.* Light, and all other things created, are altogether suitable for the purpose intended for them, yet they await a fuller purpose, a final consummation.

A question now being asked is whether or not the universe is destined to go on expanding forever. This question is not readily answered, for at least two reasons: no one knows exactly how much energy was expended at the beginning, to set it expanding; and since matter and energy are interchangeable, matter as such is not always readily detected in space, so the total mass of matter remains unknown. If the sum of the mass of the universe is unknown, the total gravitational pull working against the expansionary forces is unknown. Hence, future continued expansion and future contraction are both possibilities on the basis of existing knowledge. Whether it goes on expanding or no, we do know it is awaiting something - fulfilment!

The creation is *good* - perfect for the current purpose. It is destined to become *better* - perfect and complete. "For the creature was made subject to vanity [seemingly empty pointlessness - such as retrogression and decay] not willingly, but by reason of him [God] who hath subjected the same in hope [for an ultimate, unseen purpose]; because the creature [creation] itself also shall be delivered from the bondage of corruption [disorder and decay, seen in the natural worlds] into the glorious liberty of the children of God. For we know that the whole creation groaneth and travaileth [as though bringing something to birth] until now" *Ro.8:20-22.* Whether by contraction or in some other way, the universe as we experience it is destined to be put away, withdrawn, and renewed.

The laws of ever-increasing disorder and the presence of death are "vanity" to which this physical dispensation has been subject. A time will come when the hidden purposes of this subjection to "vanity" are fulfilled. These physical worlds will then be renewed, set free into a dimension where decay and death are unknown.

Gen.1:4

And God saw the light, that is was good: and God divided the light from the darkness.

Light is designed so that it cannot dissolve or dissipate itself in any way into darkness. A light photon cannot be consumed by darkness. It travels on forever, untouched, unfaltering, unheeding of the void gulf around it. In the end, it triumphs. The two cannot be mixed.

As a living illustration of this, we need only consider Jesus Christ, against whom all the powers of darkness were arrayed, and who not only was untouched by them, but scattered them and spoiled their powers. "I am the light of the world . . ." *John 8:12.*

Gen.1:5

And God called the light Day, and the darkness he called Night. And the evening and the morning were the first day.

The first day comprised the nurturing and growth of the heaven and earth from something unable to be described or properly seen, to an "ocean" or "deep" of unrefined, active, hot, dense fluids (probably mostly pressurized simple gases), that were sufficiently developed to emit and display light. Illumination was termed *Day,* or daylight; darkness was termed *Night.* The length in time of this first day is not precisely known, for the obvious reason that He whose work defined it has not recorded the starting date.

The most ancient time-indicators are themselves semi-defunct, one- time, light-sources, and we cannot be certain that those of calculable age are the oldest that existed. Advice from physicists makes the first day no more than one thousand million years duration, and probably much less: the enquirer could do no better than consult a learned discourse in such matters. (Such as Filkin, D. *Stephen Hawking's Universe.* London: BBC Books, 1997, 144-151, and elsewhere.) We do know that light has been shining for fifteen thousand million years at the very least, so the first Day was ended by then. And fifteen thousand million years is less than a *moment when it is gone* to him who *inhabits eternity.*

The Existence of Space

Gen.1:6

And God said, Let there be a firmament in the midst of the waters . . .

The original "seed," the almost infinitely small point of almost infinite content, has been expanded into a compact, energy-filled "deep," a veritable ocean of fluidity, energy, and formative simple matter now beginning to emit and display light. These waters are tightly compact, without any one part appearing any different to any other. But now observe a process of separation and differentiation. Separation: "Let there be a firmament [expansion, volume, or space] in the midst of the waters." Expansion, in the midst of the waters. A general volume, or space, begins in the early universe.

This expansion was general: as yet there is no specialist grouping together of waters according to type or location. But for the first time, space exists.

Gen.1:6

And God said, Let there be a firmament in the midst of the waters, and let it divide the waters from the waters.

The first refinement was a general infusion of volume or space: "A firmament in the midst of the waters." The second refinement was a grouping according to type and location. "Let it divide the waters [a specific group of waters] from the waters [another grouping of waters]." Waters became divided from waters, as to produce groupings. This is as deduced by physics: the early spreading cosmos had areas within itself slightly richer in matter than other areas, and these became galaxial groupings. "Let it divide the waters from the waters." Let it divide water group from water group.

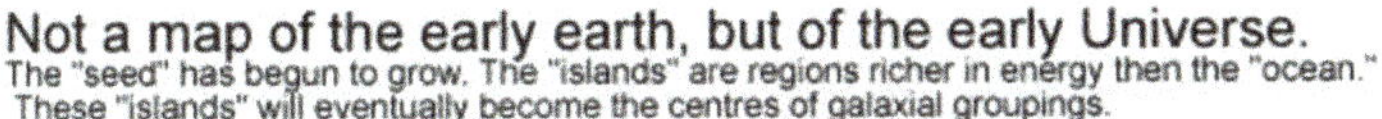

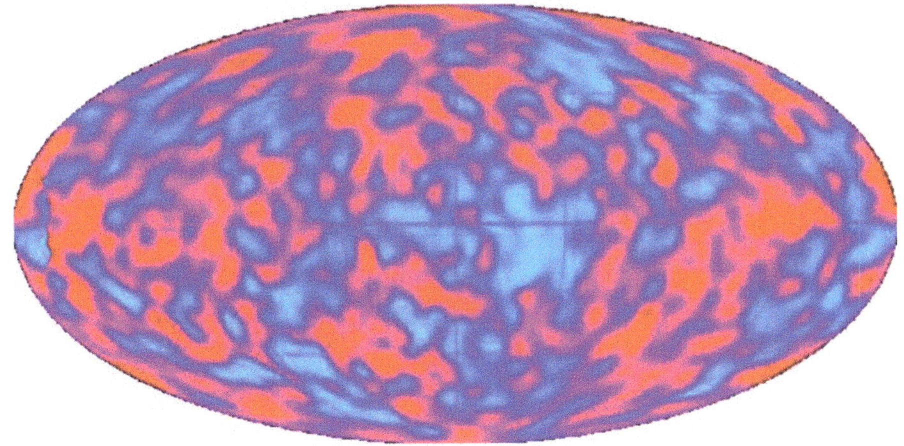

And now observe a yet more specialized differentiation process within a specific group of waters:

Gen.1:7

And God made the firmament, and divided the waters which were under the firmament from the waters which were above the firmament: and it was so.

In the preceding verse (v. *6*) we have **a** firmament - that is, a general expansion, spreading throughout all the waters in general. Following this general expansion is a more specific differentiation, leading to the galaxies. Finally there comes a particular expansion targeting one specific set of waters, and it divides that grouping of waters into two. This particular expansion is not a general, expansion, but **the** firmament, the specific expanse we recognize as the firmament, the expanse above the Earth - our own sky. The sequence is as follows:

- **A firmament in the midst of the waters**: a generalized gaining of volume, the beginnings of space.

- **A firmament dividing the waters from the waters:** this same expansionary process, but carried on in a deliberate manner, leading to generalized groupings of matter according to location and composition - the beginnings of the galaxial groupings within space.

- **The firmament: the firmament as we know it, above our heads**, dividing one specific grouping of waters into two, the part beneath the expansion subsequently going to make up the earth, and *the part above the expansion not being used to make the earth, but of close compositional affinity with it.*

Three distinct differentiating and refining steps are being alluded to: A general infusion of volume in the early, growing universe, a differentiation of the early universe into clumps rich in matter, a subsequent division of one specific body of matter into two, of which one part is from then on referred to as "the waters under the firmament," and the other, "the waters above the firmament." This division into parts of one specific body or grouping of waters implies some affinity of composition between the parts.

Although water, proper, occurs throughout space, it is a minor component of it; by contrast, water, H_2O, is by no means a minor component of the Earth itself. It may therefore be reasoned that the body of waters that was divided into those above and below the firmament ("sky") was relatively rich in this compound. Therefore, the biblical account suggests the existence of vast quantities of water, H_2O, along with other atmospheric gases and vapours, and mineral matter, "above the sky," in space, but not far distant from the "building site" of Earth itself. This material could be quite distinct from the materials utilized in forming the bulk of the heavenly bodies.

What objects of space are relatively close to the Earth, consist of atmospheric-type gases, H_2O, and mineral matter, and, like the Earth itself, seem to be almost unique strangers amongst the myriad barren and waterless objects of space?

From almost infinitely small "seed" to almost infinitely great "branches". The story of our universe.

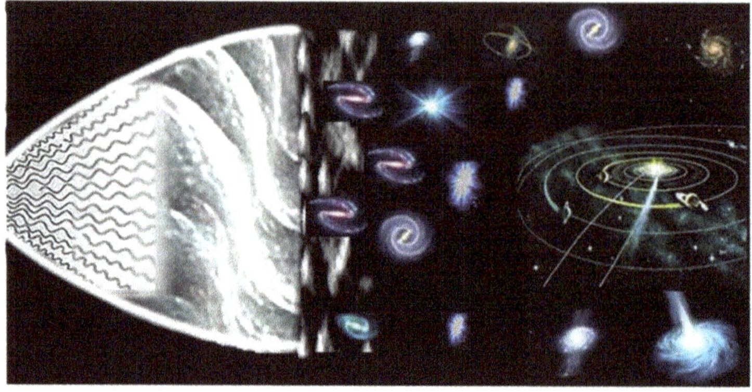

Comets

Countless millions of tons of frozen materials not dissimilar to a mixture of the Earth's atmosphere and crust, rich in water, H_2O, regularly course through our solar system following the most inexplicable of orbits.

These are part of the remnants of that specific grouping of waters, actually rich in water itself, that was employed when "God made the [our familiar] firmament," and divided the waters above it from those below. Both these sets of waters doubtless played a vital part in the subsequent nurturing and sustaining of life.

Gen.1:8

And God called the firmament heaven. And the evening and the morning were the second day.

The second day comprised the activity implied in growth and formation of the early universe from a compact "deep" of waters newly illuminated by the first natural light to the development of protogalaxies, galaxies, and the materials of which the Earth was to be formed. Since the whole range of elements of the Earth had to be smelted, refined, and assembled at the site, this was indeed a day of intense activity. Divine Creativity enlisted multiple nuclear power outputs, galaxies for refineries, and stars for furnaces. The heat and pressure necessary to the manufacture of some of the elements which make up the Earth are almost beyond comprehension. These pressurized infernos have long since expired or moved on; yet it seems the sparks from some of them are even now shedding their brilliance into Earth's telescopes, lending a lustre and a realism to those events of long ago, and reflecting in some small way the refulgent glory of him whose "hair is white like wool; his eyes are a flame of fire; his feet are like fine brass, as if they burned in a furnace; and his voice as the sound of many waterfalls" *Rev.1:15.*

The student of scripture may now be wondering at how the Almighty could employ stars for his purposes, if they were not yet made (*Gen.1:16*). At least some stars as astronomers and modern science define them had been made; it was stars as the great body of humanity and especially pre-twentieth century man understood them that had not yet been made. The discrepancy is entirely one of terminology. Modern technology defines a star as a massive body in space that is or in the past has been a source of intense heat and radiation. This new definition of a star brings our own sun into the fold, and excludes planets and meteors. The older definition, the biblical meaning, is of a point source of light in our sky. It takes in meteors, which are falling stars, it includes planets, and it emphatically disowns the sun. Whilst the sun is up, the stars do not exist! Stars in the biblical sense of the term are an optical phenomenon, visible to the naked human eye, usually only at night.

Gen.1:9

And God said, "Let the waters under the heaven be gathered together unto one place . . ."

For obvious reasons, divine Revelation does not side-track itself into complex technical explanations. As employed in *Genesis,* the term *waters* encompasses within its fold a host of shades of meaning of fluidity and instability, from almost infinitely hot and active energy-waves, through hot, simple gases so compressed they are effectively solid, to fragmented, cool solids. It can also mean what it obviously suggests, H_2O. It therefore takes in water, ice, and snow. And it encompasses any combination of all these!

The same God who "maketh a path in the mighty waters" *Isa.43:16,* who "rebuked the winds and the sea, so that there was a great calm" *Matt.8:26,* spoke to the instability that was the early Earth, which, in obedience to his command, coalesced or was "gathered together" into stability. The agency most implicated in this settling of the waters and attaining of stability was, of course, gravity. Partly reduce gravitational pull downward, and the seas - the H_2O waters - will again cover the land, as they now attempt to do in response to the upward pull of the moon and sun - the tides. Completely reduce gravitational pull, and the entire Earth will reconvert to waters - fragmentation and instability.

As the new-born Earth coalesced, particles came together with some force, elements reacted to form various compounds, and radioactive elements produced heat as they decayed. The interior of the new planet gained and retained heat and, as a result, various processes of refinement and differentiation could take place within it, and not only within it.

Gen.1:9, 10

And God said, "Let the waters under the heaven be gathered together unto one place, and let the dry land appear" and it was so. And God called the dry land Earth; and the gathering together of the waters called he Seas: and God saw that it was good.

The surface of the infant planet developed shorelines, lands, and seas. Probably the internal heating and differentiation was a power-source for land movement and volcanism at the surface, which in turn led to lighter and heavier areas within the crust, the heavier subsiding to accommodate the bodies of water, and the lighter rising to make proto-continents. Ongoing accretion of matter falling into the waters from space may also have contributed to the new lands. These islands and rudimentary continents were havens of stability in an otherwise unstable, antagonistic world; a world of changeable waters. *Ps.27:5*: "For in the time of trouble he shall hide me in his pavilion: in the secret of his tabernacle shall he hide me; he shall set me up upon a rock." How stable and how inviting the first rock would have appeared when it rose to prominence out of never-ending water! Vast reservoirs of water, H_2O, are part of the Earth.

Surprisingly, one reservoir is both invisible and inaccessible! H_2O is bound into the crystal structure of some minerals, so quantities of it are locked into the solid rocks beneath our feet. Imprisoned oceans aside, sufficient free H_2O as solid (ice), liquid (water proper), and vapour occurs on Earth to drown it completely, should these waters become light enough to flow over the lands. (Water is lighter than rock, and will flow over it just as air flows over it, if there comes a general reduction in weights - such as would occur through reduced gravitational pull downward). Not only do the H_2O waters about us have the potential, under special circumstances, to drown the world, the water stored as ice in ice-caps temporarily sets vast quantities of this compound aside, so the sea-level rises and falls in timing with reduction and expansion of the ice-caps. Melting of the existing icecaps would produce sea-level rises of tens of meters. Geologic evidence all but proves such fluctuations in the level of the waters during past eras. Could it happen again, in our modern times?

Reassuring Mankind

Divine Revelation goes to lengths to reassure Mankind in this matter. In at least four separate places the scriptures mention a fixed shoreline. The world is not about to be ruined by water. Take as one example, *Jer.5:22*: "Fear ye not me? saith the Lord: will ye not tremble at my presence, which have placed the sand for the bound of the sea by a perpetual decree, that it cannot pass it: and though the waves thereof toss themselves, yet can they not prevail; though they roar, yet can they not pass over it?"

Someone may now point to instances of the seas crossing shorelines: tsunamis, storm surges, land subsidence. Phenomena such as these were understandably mystifying to pre-modern man. This is part of the reason the scriptures repeatedly emphasize that the shoreline is fixed: to reassure people that such phenomena are only local and temporary. Another suggestion may be made to the effect that the shorelines are gradually creeping. This creep could happen, say some, if man persists in various industries that increase the levels of certain atmospheric gases, thereby causing the temperature to rise and ice-caps to melt. Burning of fossil fuels is targeted as one of the culprits. We need have few concerns on this head:

1. The composition of the atmosphere has changed dramatically over the geologic past, but the effects of these changes upon the ice-caps are obscure. The mechanisms behind ice-ages, and the atmospheric effects of "greenhouse gases," are not clearly understood;
2. The levels of at least one of the implicated gases -CO_2- is at a dangerously, if not perilously, low level now. "Carbon . . . is being steadily removed as precipitated carbonates [limestone]

and organic matter buried with sediments. A rough calculation . . . indicates that CO_2 in air will fall to a level too low to support plant life within a few centuries, unless some other source of the gas is available.[2]" This crisis has now been averted by increased use of fossil fuels;

3. This in itself shows that the resources within the Earth were emplaced intelligently, implying they are intended to be utilized, albeit intelligently;

4. The scriptural language is void of any hint of a modern worldwide drowning event.

The Creator caused the "waters" of which the Earth consists to coalesce or gather together. He 'bears up the pillars thereof'." The same arm now lending all things form and stability, keeps the waters of the seas and oceans in their appointed places, and the same strong arm is a shield and a rock of safety to his people, even when disturbance and instability are on every side.

The Bible advises that the surface of the infant planet was watered by a mist (*Gen.2:6*), and the sun, moon, and stars as we recognize them were neither distinguishable from the viewpoint of an observer standing on its surface, nor did they function in concert with our planet to give our familiar days and nights, times and seasons. Was the mist a product of an atmospheric configuration that obscured, filtered, or dispersed the light from our familiar heavenly bodies? Or did the Earth pre-date the solar system, or originate in a location separate from it, being in the interim illumined by some light source(s) other than the sun?

---

2 Krauskopf, K.B., Introduction To Geochemistry, McGraw Hill, pages 617-618, 1967

Formation in present location is suggested by the Earth's compatibility with its sister-planets in terms of size and orbital path. Formation prior to or separate from parts of the solar system is suggested by the unique, almost foreign nature of the Earth's atmospheric composition, and by the uniqueness of the Earth-moon couple. The Earth, and the Earth-moon couple, could be unique anywhere. Their origin remains shrouded in mystery, as does the part played in their origin by the apparent set-aside, the "waters above the firmament," of which the mysterious comets are surely a remnant?

The land surface of the new world was then beginning to become land and rock as we know it. Various chemical processes and the impact of material falling onto the early Earth produced heat, which in turn led to the refinement of the rock-types and a virgin, rather desolate, landscape. The heating may have indirectly produced the ubiquitous mist, by motivating warmer, moist air to rise and encounter colder layers in what was then an unrefined atmosphere. Like some things new, the seas had not had time to arrive at a steady ongoing pattern of composition; various chemicals, perhaps leaching from recently-arrived space materials, found their way to some of them in quantity, so that in time metal-rich ores settled out almost like layers of sediment.

Modern industry exists because of the refineries and settling-tanks of those times. Diamonds and much gold are likewise treasures of the early Earth, or of times not long following. Rain, with the soils and landforms it helps create, displaced the mist early in history, presumably in time association with plants (see *Gen.2:4-6*). Rain is an ancient phenomenon, leaving imprints in certain once-soft sediments; were it not for the scriptures, it would not be known that the land was watered only by mist in the earliest times.

Another type of rain, that of hot, sometimes metal-rich materials from space, in combination with electrical activity in mists and waters, may have produced intriguing and useful results - perhaps even some free atmospheric oxygen, for which the Earth is remarkable.

Mist, warmth, light, atmosphere, and seas rich in active chemicals and compounds. Does this concur with the conditions attendant upon the coming into being of earliest simplest life?

No. The Spirit brings life not because there is hope, but in spite of there being no hope. Man cannot pass from death to life through any inherent virtues of his own.

Spontaneous Generation of Life

The Almighty is quite able to create life in the middle of a howling desert, in the most barren corner of the cosmos. He requires no assistance from mist, chemicals, or light. He designed life to function under conditions of moisture and light, so he placed the life into those conditions. Spontaneous generation of life has been conclusively and comprehensively disproved so often, it is now seriously pursued by only addicted atheists. And now, behold the Master-Hand revealed on the page of time through novel new achievements!

Gen.1:11

And God said, "Let the earth bring forth grass, the herb yielding seed, and the fruit tree yielding fruit after his kind, whose seed is in itself, upon the earth" and it was so.

Life! Life in abundance, life in profuse variety! It is fitting that the first living thing was a tree, for the origin of all earthly life was via a tree: a tree that functions in the same way as our earth-bound trees. The tree of life!

A tree has roots, to draw up hidden life. The tree of life has roots that draw on the spiritual River of Life (*Rev.22:2*).

A tree produces after its kind, always the same fruit. The tree of life produces after its kind - health, life!

A tree contains the potential of growth that is destined to appear on it, at its inception. The tree of life has the potential of all life forms, even from the beginning. Hence, all plants of every type existed, as soon as that part of the tree of life that was to give rise to plants, existed.

A tree grows by the older parts carrying the newer parts, and being channels of flowing life (sap) for the newer parts. The tree of life is a mechanism by which life passed via older species to newer species.

A tree grows by budding and shooting of new growth, in response to timing and environmental signals. The new growth, which buds and shoots, already existed as growth potential. New growth manifests at a predestined time in response to various signals from inside and outside the tree. The tree of life contains all the species within itself at the inception of the branch which those species are destined to become. (Although it yields but one fruit - life - yet in another sense it bears a variety of fruits, *Rev.22:2;* each branch yielding its own peculiar division of life.) New species manifest, or shoot forth, in response to pre-set timing and pre-arranged signals.

In a tree, the newer part of a branch is supported and supplied with life via the older parts, but the older parts do not give rise to the newer parts. In the tree of life, the newer species received life via the older, but the older did not give rise to the new.

The Kingdom of God is likened to a tree (see *Mark 4:31*). Jesus Christ is our Tree of Life. In him is health and life, all the virtue pertaining to "life and godliness" *2 Pet.1:3.* The Spirit is the only source of enduring, real fruitfulness. "I am the vine, ye are the branches . . . without me ye can do nothing" *John 15:5.* Note: Christ is the vine, his Spirit is life: but *ye are the branches.* Heaven is the source of life, and the commissioning of it; yet redeemed humanity, *something of earth,* is the channel, the carrier. The branches are people. In the creation of life, the branches were the species. The species did not give rise to the life, but they transmitted life. The branches transmit the pre-existent life, which comes from God. Life is all of God, yet its effectiveness on earth is dependent upon *an earthly agency.* It is from Heaven, pre-existent. It was dependent on earthly agency for visible manifestation. All Heaven, all Earth. Jesus Christ is all Heaven, all Earth (humanity). The creation speaks Jesus Christ.

Life forms pre-existed. Every plant (and animal) existed *before the foundation of the world.* "In the day that the Lord God made the earth and the heavens, and every plant of the field before it was in the earth, and every herb of the field before it grew" *Gen.2:4,5.* Vegetation existed before it was in the earth, before it grew. Yet it did not manifest or realize in our dimension without earthly agency, for at a particular time, on the third day, "the earth brought forth grass and herb yielding seed . . . ." Note, the earth "brought forth" vegetation on Day 3 - speaking of an ongoing process, put in motion at that time, *continuing through time.* The earth "brought forth" vegetation then, and went on bringing it forth, over time. The language is of an ongoing process. This was the tree of life mechanism, a translator with "roots" in the spiritual dimension and "branches" or physical fruits in our physical world. All life - even that of vegetation - is a supernatural phenomenon beyond man's reach. Yet the various life forms are real and visible to us. As with natural trees, the growth potential all exists as part of the tree at inception, yet is realized or physically manifest over time.

IV. IN TECHNICAL DETAIL, HOW WAS IT DONE?

The structure of all Earth-life proclaims the method by which the species originated in the simplest and strongest terms. Species were created and revealed in a way that is "plain...that he may run that readeth it" *Hab.2:2.* Even "wayfaring men, though fools," need not "err therein" *Isa.35:8.* A fool - a fool of God's making, need not "err therein." Mankind that is wise in its own eyes inevitably errs. But there is hope for foolishness - if it is "the foolishness of God, which is wiser than men." "Seest thou a man wise in his own understanding? There is more hope of a fool than of him" *Pro.26:12.* There is hope for fools, God's fools.

Cells

All living organisms, excluding viruses, which are not a fruit of the tree of life and are not truly living, are made up of a cell or cells. A cell comprises a nucleus and a cell body surrounding the nucleus. (In the very simplest life forms, there may be no nucleus as such, but nucleus material is dispersed within the cell, effectively functioning as though unified.) In the nucleus of each cell is a set of instructions, called genes. Every cell of any given individual has the same set of instructions in its nucleus. These encoded instructions, or genes, are so complex a set from any one-cell nucleus contains all the genetic information pertaining to that individual. The information stored in the microscopic nucleus of only one cell contains all the genetic information pertaining to the individual of which it is a part.

This genetic information (or instruction code, or "blueprint") will govern the individual's growth rate, size, colour, personal tastes, and so on *ad infinitum:* all his inheritable characteristics. In short, the gene-code is the essence of the organism. Surrounding the cell nucleus is the body of the cell. The cell body obeys and puts into effect the instructions of the genes in the nucleus. Thus a cell consists of an almost unbelievably sophisticated "blueprint" of encoded information, and the means of putting the information into effect. To put the genetic instructions into effect necessitates sophisticated mechanisms for communication within the cell and between cells. A cell is a gene code, with the means of putting the code into effect, which relies on the sending and receiving of signals. The gene code of each species is locked. As God's word assures us, species reproduce only "after their kind." Scientific technology is unable to unlock gene codes, and is therefore unable to make new species. The only evidence that one species evolves into another is a great body of words, and vain hope.

The Creator can unlock the codes, and he can set up a signalling system to not only unlock them, but "trip" them into a new code, and not only insert the new code, but transform individuals or fragments of individuals of one species into genetically complete new species. Thus there is no break in the continuum of life, once the first species of any particular division has been realized or manifested on the Earth. The entire division can be made or created, at a point in time, and a pre-set signalling system automatically brings every species to earthly reality over time, without any further effort on the part of the Creator. (There is little difference between the cells of similar species. Alter the gene-code, and the same cell could theoretically multiply into a grown individual of any number of similar species.)

Signals by Nature

Receiving of signals by nature is widely recognized. So much so, the scriptures take it for granted. Instances are legion. Hibernating animals of the northern regions of the globe are living proof of it. Some of these animals build their shelter walls of a thickness in direct proportion to the severity of the coming winter. Others will ignore the severest blizzards, yet go straight to shelter in clear weather. True winter sets in within hours. Not all such hidden signals need come from outside the created world. *"The locusts have no king, yet go they forth all of them by bands" Pro.30:27.* Signals such as those which call the locusts to swarm may well be from nature itself, built into the insect division. Further, some signals that have contacted the natural realm do not originate in the Creator at all! (The motivation behind the storm Christ stilled could not have come from God.) Communication into the natural worlds, either direct or indirect, is a long-standing, widely accepted concept. Above all, it is a scriptural concept.

"The voice of the Lord is upon the waters: the God of glory thundereth: the Lord is upon many waters.

The voice of the Lord is powerful; the voice of the Lord is full of majesty.

The voice of the Lord breaketh the cedars; yea, the Lord breaketh the cedars of Lebanon. He maketh them also to skip like a calf; Lebanon and Sirion like a young unicorn [rhinoceros].

The voice of the Lord divideth the flames of fire.

The voice of the Lord shaketh the wilderness; the Lord shaketh the wilderness of Kadesh.

The voice of the Lord maketh the hinds to calve, and discovereth the forests: and in his temple doth every one speak of his glory" *Ps.29:3-9.*

To make all vegetable life "before it grew" or "before it was in the earth" (*Gen.2:4, 5*) was a matter of making all the blueprints or gene- codes, and putting them in safe storage. (And a code does not require a physical filing cabinet.) As for the life - the life is the Spirit, so it exists at all times

- and once a cellular organism capable of transmuting in response to code-receiving has been set in motion or given life, all the division to which it belongs has been given life.

To speak to the earth so that it brought forth vegetation was a matter of internally re-ordering mineral to become vegetable cell(s), giving the cell(s) life, and setting up a communications system so the "master-computer-file" would automatically signal new gene-codes to "slave- files" in the nuclei of the vegetable cell(s). The cells that received the signals could well have been spores, seeds, or living, tiny fragments of plants, already on the earth. These then sprang up as new species, genetically complete from the outset. Thus all plant life existed before it was in the earth. It activated the moment the first living plant cell was made and the signalling system was activated. All plants of every form and variety were made and existed in completeness and perfection on the third day, even though many were not tangible, or observable, here on earth, at that time. The procedure could be simulated in a simple way using a modern computer.

Thus the species existed before they visibly grew. They were inherent in the tree of life. The life was carried through time, along the branches, passing like relay-batons from species to species.

Individuals of existing life forms may have given something of themselves, perhaps even their own life, to bring to birth and stability the new life forms. Yet it was all the work of the Spirit, and every species was a direct and instantaneous creation of the Divine. The life of the Spirit is manifested in the world by the workings of the Spirit. He makes the soil; he waters it with rain; he speaks, and his word is the seed, and his voice brings the dead to life. Nevertheless his agents are people, people who will give their lives, who will make themselves a "living sacrifice" (*Ro.12:1*), and through such he turns this barren world into a garden, and a garden into a paradise.

An Original Evolutionary Concept

The revelation of life forms through divinely appointed information technology? How do the fossils speak God's power and provision? A pre-darwinist evolutionary concept--- divine pre-ordination. *The Law of Progression from the General to the Particular.* The model, pre-dating Darwinism, relies on applied physiology – the science of the construction of living organisms. . Shown opposite is leading Victorian palaeontologist and anatomist Sir Richard Owen's Archetype. In information technology language, the archetype is species construction 'software', applied.

With minor exceptions and alterations these illustrations are from Reader and Gurche's outstanding and available 1986 publication *The Rise of Life (192 pp.)* William Collins Sons & co., London. Gurche restores Sir Richard Owen's original anatomical art work, whilst Reader gives the account:

Quote, "Owen first presented the *Law of Progression* at a meeting of the British Association for the Advancement of Science in 1846, illustrating it with what he described as the archetype of the vertebrate skeleton. ... Owen's archetype is remarkably similar to the simplest vertebrates subsequently found. .... In a series of drawings he showed how every bone in the skeletons of fish, reptiles, birds, mammals and man could have been adapted from the archetype. The successive development of the cranium, jaw and all four limbs is quite explicit; so too are the origins of eye, ear and nose. ... Based on the studies of fossils and comparative anatomy, it charted a perfectly believable course for the vertebrates' successive development, with the added benefit of discounting extinction – species did not die out, they were ... transformed.

Owen set down this answer to the question of how species originated ... . Species had an innate tendency to diverge from the ancestral form according to the dictates of a divine plan, he said, and the existence of the divine plan was proven in the very conception of the archetypal vertebrate:

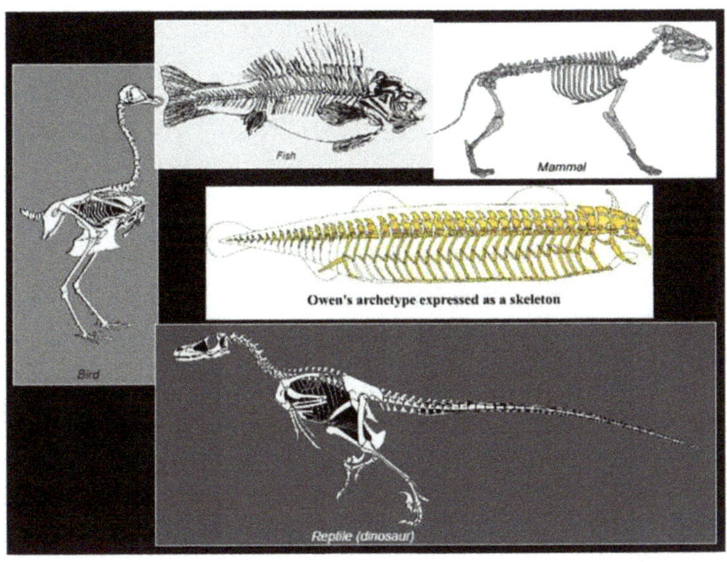

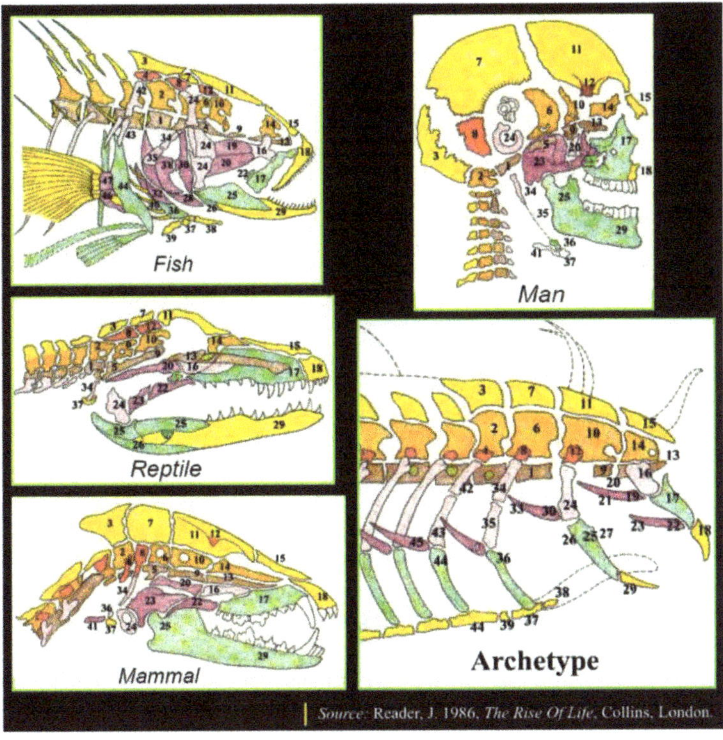

The Archetype related to Vertebrate Head Bones in Finer Detail.

'… the recognition of an ideal Exemplar for the vertebrated animals proves that the knowledge of such a being as Man must have existed before Man appeared. For the divine mind which planned the archetype also knew all its modifications.'" End Reader 1986 quote.

Owen long pre-dated DNA and modern information technology. Relying on the laws of anatomy, he nevertheless adduced with passable accuracy the basic skeleton of the yet to be discovered oldest vertebrates.

The Archetype is the physical expression of information - not the biologic ancestor. Owen, relying on the science of physiology, foreshadowed information driven transformers!

The Third Day

Gen.1:13

And the evening and the morning were the third day.

The third day was the great and loving provision of a stable earth, and plant life on it. There is good reason to believe the earth is at least four-and-a-half thousand million years old, and probably older, and simple, water-dwelling plants or even simpler organisms than known plants grew on it almost from its inception. That the great bulk of plant species, especially trees and grasses, did not arise until much later, is shown by the fossil record, and is a standing testimony to the honour of him who made "every plant of the field before it was in the earth, and every herb of the field before it grew," and who devised the mechanism that "let the earth bring forth grass," so that vegetation that had already been made, actuated and grew on the earth over time.

Gen.1:14-19

And God said, Let there be lights in the firmament of the heaven to divide the day from the night; and let them be for signs, and for seasons, and for days, and years, and let them be for lights in the firmament of the heaven to give light upon the earth: and it was so. And God made two great lights; the greater light to rule the day, and the lesser light to rule the night: he made the stars also. And God set them in the firmament of the heaven to give light upon the earth, and to rule over the day and over the night, and to divide the light from darkness: and God saw that it was good. And the evening and the morning were the fourth day.

At first impression, we may find ourselves thinking of the placing of lights in the heaven, combined with the onset of our familiar times and seasons, as almost anticlimactic, leading to an impression of the fourth day being a lesser brother to those preceding. This impression is in part an offspring of simplistic and superficial traditional theories. These simplistic theories gloss over and brush aside the extreme intricacy and depth of design of our planetary system. On the whole, the models proposed are of no more use in explaining the planets' origins than are spent and old individuals of spent and old species in explaining the origin of vibrant, genetically complete new species. The species are given infinite time and infinite chances and the planets are given infinite dust and infinite chances, and by enough talk, *voila* - the finished product!

The idea of a cloud of particles and a star leading to our planetary system has fewer bases in science than the postulation of a hippopotamus accidentally forming Michelangelo's *David* by falling into a tub of wet plaster. More hope of success in examining the remains of burnt flour mills for locomotive-sized bread loaves baked to perfection, than in studying the remains of fiery dust clouds for intricate planetary systems such as ours.

Planetary Systems

Planetary systems have been deduced from observations of outer space, but whether there are any like ours is uncertain. The planets of our solar system are no mere gas-spheres, neither are they embryonic stars, neither are copies of them prodigally scattered about like nuts on the ground.

The mainstream theories of origin of our system have been unable to accurately predict the composition of a single body within it. Since some of the outer planets, and many of the fifty or more "moons" of the planets, were not discovered until recent times, this is a near-perfect record of failure. Our planetary system now lies as shrouded in mystery as it once must have lain shrouded in various dusts and vapours.

This shrouding is partly a product of clouding of man's own vision, shortened and confined through our reticence to acknowledge or consult with our own Creator. We cannot bring ourselves to acknowledge his sovereignty, nor consult his words, but blindly stumble on toward ignorance, fear, and misery. And so, rather than acknowledge a superior Intelligence, some prefer to attribute the universe itself with intelligence, thereby joining hands with occultists and idolaters, and showing that heathenism is never far beneath the surface whenever we depart from truth.

For current purposes, the solar system may be regarded as a wheel. The planets swing around in near-circular orbits nearly in the same plane. This arrangement is the most energy-efficient and the most stable. It is that of a spinning disk, or wheel.

In terms of composition, the solar system consists of at least two wheels; for simplicity it may be envisaged as an inner wheel of stony spheres, of which the Earth is a member, and an outer wheel of gassy and rocky-icy spheres. In broadest terms of composition, it is a wheel within a wheel. The wheels rotate in the same direction. The Earth at this moment is rushing in a circle at approximately 28 km/sec, and almost certainly travelled at greater speed in the past.

An inner wheel of stone (heavier elements) and an outer wheel of gas and ice (lighter elements). Both spinning in the same direction; both - at least now - having a common centre, or hub. Wheels within wheels: a hub at the centre.

The hub at the centre - the sun - is a body of gas, or lighter elements.

Lighter elements, then heavy elements, then lighter elements. Wheels within wheels. Astronomers have found that the gases of the outer circle have a slightly different chemical "signature" to those of the inner body (sun), so even these two sets of compositionally similar bodies did not quite have a common origin.

Wheels within wheels. Light, heavy, light. Compositionally difficult to explain, without different sources for different parts. Different sources for different parts. Different sources for different wheels? Did the different wheels have a different origin?

Yet composition is not as great a barrier to common dust-cloud origin as the mechanics of the system. The mechanics of the system seem to rule out origin from a single spinning cloud, unless something with a hidden explanation happened afterward: namely, the sun slowed dramatically in its spin-rate. In terms of mass, 99.8 per cent - that is, effectively *all* the mass of the system - is the sun, the hub. In terms of angular momentum, or "spin," 99.5 per cent - that is effectively *all* the "spin" of the system - lies with the planets, the wheel(s). And the wheel(s) almost certainly spun faster in the past. So the wheels have the spin, but not the mass, and the "hub," the sun, has the mass, but not the spin that is in keeping with that mass - if all were initially part of the same body, and if the sun has not been slowed through a hidden process. A common origin of the sun and planets from a single rotating body of matter does not fit the mechanics of the system.

To cap it all, the sun, or "hub" is tilted 7 degrees to the plane of the "wheel(s)," the system.

A body of evidence begins to build, pointing to an origin from disparate sources.

What Effect Does an "Igniting" Star Have Upon the Space About It?

Physicists do not precisely know the answer to this question. The processes involved in the ignition phase may lead to some spectacular effects. Assume, however, that the inner, stony planets could have survived these effects - as some astronomers believe. Did the sun ignite before or after the stony planets formed? The sun's rays have an effect on space around it. At this moment the light from the celestial orb is pushing *outward* on the Earth with approximately 75,000 tons of pressure. We need not fear being pushed out of orbit by this hidden light-pressure. Compared to the force of gravity holding us in orbit, this light-pressure is a mere *touch.* The pressure of light is insignificant *on a body the size of the Earth.* However, on very light bodies, such as gas molecules, this pressure can have the effect of pushing them away. On slightly heavier particles, such as micro-meteorites, it has the effect of slowing them down, so they fall out of orbit into the nearest large body. Thus the sun has a continual clearing or sweeping effect on the solar system, and no sooner did it ignite than it should have begun to push any unsecured light elements away from itself.

Here again the idea of one single dust cloud with the bulk of mass at the centre encounters some difficulties. If the bulk of mass at the centre became the sun, and it ignited after the planets had formed, why is there comparatively little of the lighter gaseous elements bound up in the inner (stony) planets? Why was not more of the gas drawn toward the (then cold) sun, and incorporated in the planets that formed closest to the sun - the stony planets? Why is most of the lighter matter out away from the sun?

If the sun ignited before the planets formed, then the gases and vapours should have been pushed out to the position of the outer planets, as is in very broad terms the case. But then there should be no gases and vapours in the closer, stony planets, and the Earth for one should not have much water, or any atmosphere. The gases comprising the atmosphere would have been driven out to the outer gas and ice ring of planets, and thus be lost to the Earth. To explain this, some theorists actually suggest that the inner, stony ring of planets formed "dry," in an environment swept clear of lighter gases and vapours by the sun, and their existing gaseous and vaporous atmospheres were subsequently added to them by comets. Unless a higher, external Intelligence is invoked, such ideas surely border on desperation?

Solar System

The Outer Planets

Orbits are to scale relative to one another. Planet sizes are to scale relative to one another but not relative to the orbit sizes.

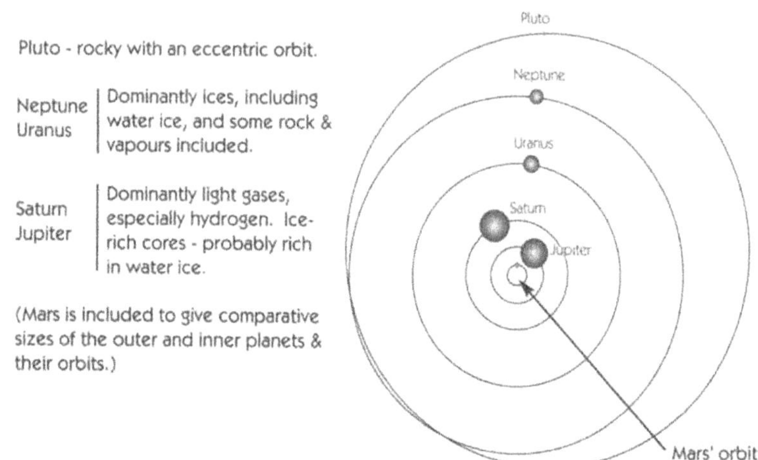

The Inner Planets

The orbits are to scale. Planets are to scale relative to other planets, not relative to the orbits. The sun, if shown to scale relative to the planets could not fit inside Mars' orbit.

The moon is 1/81 st Earth's mass.

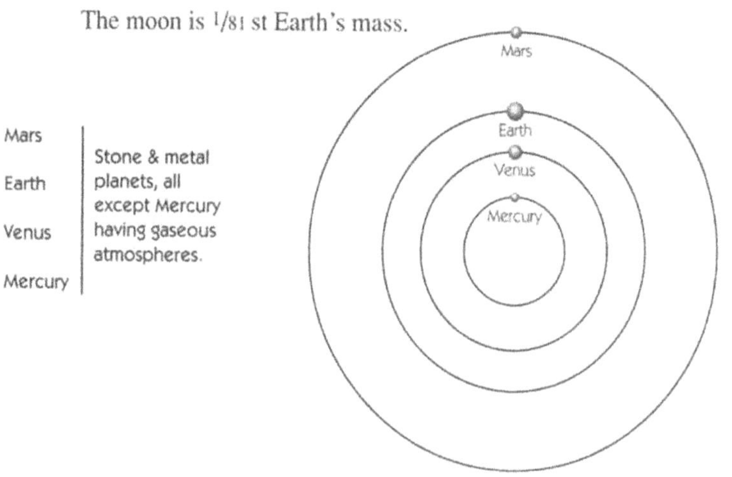

Is a sun in the centre of the initial wheel or wheels an asset or a liability? If ignited before the planets formed it should have driven away the gases and vapours now forming our atmosphere. If it ignited after the planets formed (assuming it did not destroy the closer ones in the ignition process), then why did some gas and icy/vaporous planets not form close to it? Its only asset at the centre of the system originally appears to be as a gravitational anchor for the planets.

V. WE HAVE YET TO ENCOUNTER TRUE DESPERATION

True desperation is revealed in theories that attempt to predict the composition and orbits of the various moons and secondary bodies within the planetary system. The differences in composition and character between the planets and some of their satellites or moons indicates some of these secondary orbiters come from a different source and a different place than the body to which they are now attached by gravitational attraction. Further, no satisfactory explanation for Pluto has been forthcoming from mainstream astronomy. (Pluto is not a moon - not now - but is a stony body orbiting the sun, out with the farthest gas/ice planets.)

Desperation enters with our own moon. Some have postulated an intelligent universe, and the idea of comets safely building our atmosphere seems to imply that comets can think: but conventional astronomy has to invent a space giant to account for the moon, a space giant that occasionally stands on Venus or some other suitable prominence, and adjusts our nearest neighbour according to requirement. Yet unless the evidence is pointing in a direction other than that which is obvious, the explanation has all the time lain before the eyes of scientists, in the rock strata, in the planets, in logic, and in the Bible.

Space Giants and Intelligent Ice-Blocks?

Conventional astronomy has found the moon a total conundrum. Because of existing models for formation of the planets, and because of the moon being old like the Earth, and chiefly because it is not now acceptable to own a superior Intelligence in published theories, the moon was traditionally paired up with the Earth from a time not long after the Earth's inception. The idea of its being intelligently introduced at the exact time when it was needed was largely ignored. The result is the theory of accretion of the moon from material left over from the Earth, subsequently discounted; the theory of separation from the Earth itself, subsequently discounted; and now, in desperation, the theory of a body striking the Earth at the exact correct angle, taking with it enough material to build the moon and not destroying the Earth in the process. All these are purported to have happened well back in history, not long after the Earth became established. The Earth and moon have been orbiting in association ever since. And here enters the space giant.

Tidal Layering and the Moon

Strange though it may seem, our moon is receding from us at a measured rate of 3-4 centimetres per annum. There is nothing personal in this -- it happens to all bodies in like mechanical relationship to the earth-moon.

The moon draws tides up towards itself. At the same time, the fast-spinning earth keeps dragging the waters around with itself. Each time a tidal bulge passes under the moon, a fraction of the earth's spin momentum is imparted to the moon via the gravitational link between the tidal bulge and the body causing the bulge.

So the moon is gaining momentum at the expense of the earth's spin. Theoretically this process continues until the two bodies synchronize --

earth's spin slows to keep exact time with the moon. By then, our satellite would be substantially farther removed from us.

The moon does not gain more speed through this process of momentum transfer. The impetus is imparted to our satellite as angular momentum. It may focus our thoughts to think of a tensionwrench. By increasing the length of the handle, the turning power of the wrench is increased. Angular momentum equals mass multiplied by velocity multiplied by distance. By increasing distance, momentum is increased.

Therefore, over time, our tides may have been diminishing. The lunar month would concurrently have been getting longer, and likewise our day, as the moon stepped back from a slowing earth.

The moon causes some of the tides on Earth. This has the effect of imperceptibly transferring a tiny fraction of the Earth's spin, to the moon's orbit. Remember, the Earth, with its tidal bulges, is rotating faster than the moon is orbiting. What follows may not seem logical, but on a couple such as the Earth and moon in stable orbit in a vacuum, this causes the moon to imperceptibly step back farther from the Earth, into a broader and therefore more powerful orbit. Over time, the moon slips away from the Earth, and the Earth slows its spin. Angular momentum must be conserved. Mathematicians and measurements agree. Therefore all the planets were presumably once spinning and moving faster, and were closer together, for most have or had tides of some sort.

Extrapolating backward in time from the present, going back one thousand million years, tides were a major problem. Going back three or four thousand million years, tides were a wall of water rushing around a frenetically spinning Earth . . . and the moon was in grave danger of falling into the Earth. It was too close. Hence, the space- giant to periodically adjust the moon. Or did flying iceblocks (comets) with an I.Q. do it?

Have done with astronomical fairy tales. The marrying together of the solar system over time, *after* the Earth was formed and established, is beginning to make sense. If the moon was not needed until well into the Earth's history, and placing it next to the Earth was an inconvenience and a pointless operation until that time, why not leave it somewhere else in the interim? Making a bolder leap: if an early and igniting sun was a difficulty to the early planets, could something cold but dispensable (comet material - mostly watery vapours and gases turned to ice) have been the initial central hub of the wheels? Were the wheels themselves then in the same plane, as now, or were the wheels separate from one another, and destined to be meshed into each other?

A moon being introduced when required, thus avoiding the necessity for re-adjustment of the Earth-moon couple, not only is logical but has strong support from geologic and astronomic studies. The question of possible meshing of rings of planets into one another, and of introduction of the sun, is not so clear. The questioner asks, 'how could it be done?'

We have thrown ourselves into the hands of mathematicians and accepted their verdict of the moon currently moving away from the Earth. We can do no more in the matter of the possibilities of introducing a sun and/or a ring of planets to a planetary system. Mathematics can decide whether or not it is possible. The verdict lies with calculation. And further advances in understanding may render such complicated procedures unnecessary, by clearly demonstrating that the sun and all the planets could have formed in the same plane originally. A common plane of origin, as in a spinning disk or spiral, would be beautifully simple. Nevertheless, until the spinning cloud can be explained without recourse to fairy tale, we must opt for a model without fairy tale.

Intelligent ice-blocks? No. Intelligent use of ice-blocks? Yes. A philosophy that puts its highest hope in dead matter or dead religious concoctions is a philosophy of ultimate defeat. A philosophy that honours the Creator of the heaven and earth is a philosophy of success. By giving honour to our Creator, we ultimately give honour to our fellow man, who is made in the image of God. We begin to rise, rather than fall.

The main hope of a mechanism for introducing planetary wheels into planetary wheels, and suns into the centres of such wheels, may lie with gyroscopes: balanced bodies, or balanced groupings of bodies, which by reason of their rapid and balanced rotation, retain their shape and stability. Indeed, the whole universe must be in some sort of complicated three-dimensional motion, for a group of bodies rushing through a vacuum and tied by gravitational links would be inherently unstable but for some spinning, stabilizing effect of the whole. All space flight relies on the gyroscopic effect. Rifle bullets and aerial bombs will not throw straight unless spinning. The Earth itself is a top. The solar system is even now giant wheels spinning in a frictionless vacuum, as a gyroscope wheel spins on frictionless bearings or on a fluid bath.

The Gyroscopic Effect

A spinning top is an illustration of the gyroscopic effect. A top that is not spinning rolls about at any angle. A spinning top tries to stand upright, and will remain upright when a non-spinning top will fall over. This is a product of the effect of inertia. Inertia tries to keep bodies moving (or not moving!) in the same way as they are already moving. A balanced body - such as a sphere, cylinder, disk, or wheel - once made to spin at speed, automatically tries to keep spinning without changing its alignment. The faster the spin, the more stable the alignment. Provided the spinning object is balanced and is in no danger of flying apart, the faster it spins the more stable it becomes.

Therefore, if the planets of our solar system were moving in orbits of diverse angles, or not moving with any speed, they would not be in any mechanical sense a single unit: place them in the same plane and rotate them rapidly with a strong central gravitational anchor, and they form a gyroscopic wheel in many ways amenable to being treated as a single unit - a wheel. Wheels, spinning in the vacuum of space.

The universe and the objects around us must be held in place by the most superlative mechanical design system ever devised. We are in the midst of a symphony of motion.

We are in the midst of a symphony, and in a sense, we began with a symphony. A strange and wonderful symphony. A few notes of which possibly reach the earth even now. After the symphony were a few piano recitals. Shall we hear these first, and then go back to the great composition?

The concept of a gyroscope, of self-sustaining, self-perpetuating circular motion, is first and foremost a biblical concept. Further, the idea of perpetually-spinning wheels within wheels is vaguely linked in a figure to the Earth itself, and, by extension, to the solar system (e.g., *Ez.1&10, Matt.5:34, 35*). Once these wheels within wheels, these spinning rings of planets, were set in motion, they were not left entirely unaltered. It is as though someone ran fingers over a piano, and lightly pushed each planet so its axis of spin tilted. This tilt, in the case of the Earth, gives us our summerwinter seasonal pattern.

The accompanying plucking of the piano strings propelled some moons from place to place within the wheel, and eventually gave us our own celestial near-neighbour. Such changes are consistent in general terms with a gyroscope. The overall pattern and balance of the wheel was not altered, but there was some slight re-arrangement of the position of some bodies within it, and all the planets of the wheel were tilted in some measure. This tuning and piano-playing has been attributed by some to chance, luck, intelligent ice-blocks, and educated asteroids.

All the planets are tilted in some measure, and many have foreign moons. If the mechanics allow it, could a strong gravitational tug by a body or bodies on a suitable trajectory outside the wheel have produced the observed effects? This seems much more satisfactory than chance events on a random firing-range. (The effect of the gyroscopic wheel pulls planets back into the plane of the wheel, thus maintaining the flat disk shape. Of itself, it has no influence on the alignment of the planets' axes. If the gyroscopic wheel-effect was sufficiently strong, a body moving at some distance outside the wheel might pull the planets strongly enough to re-arrange some moons and tilt the planetary axes, yet not pull the planets out of their plane of orbit?) Whatever the case, it seems more logical to play a tune on something so intricate, rather than pass it through a firing-range of random impacts.

The Bible speaks of wheels within wheels, and in a figure leaves a vague impression of a link between the Earth and such wonders of motion. But the Earth was not always here. It is part of a system that was built from something. If our perpetually-spinning planetary procession lying on a frictionless bed of nothing is a marvel to the mind, what of the mould in which it was cast? What factory produces these clockwork sculptures in star-dust?

Stars?

To a degree, the scriptures seem to implicate some or all of the following in the establishment of the Earth, and by extension, the planets. Water. A flood. The hidden processes of rain-drop formation. Stars. And, yes, music. Singing. Stars, singing, (e.g., see 2 *Pet.3:5; Ps.24:2; Job 38:4-30; Judges 5:1921.*)

Water. *2 Pet.3:5:* "By the word of God the heavens were of old, and the earth standing out of the water and in the water . . ."

Water. If the author of *Genesis* had attempted to explain all the phases and compositions of matter implicated in the history of the universe in a way understandable to all peoples . . . ? Obviously impractical. Such a course would be even more unworkable than attempting to explain that the sun does not itself rise and set, but only gives the impression of doing so. (Yet the fact of the sun's relative immobility combined with a spinning, circular Earth may be deduced from scripture. See *Job 38:12-14* and elsewhere.) *Water* as employed in *Genesis I* begins by taking in everything created, and then proceeds through a process of elimination to finally arrive at the water of our seas and rivers.

In doing so, it can be deduced to incorporate in its final composition all those substances in our seas and rivers: earthy materials or mineral matter; all atmosphere gases; and indeed the whole gamut of chemical compounds, gases, vapours, etc., which were associated with the formation of our planet. And, of necessity, the ices of these substances. Under no circumstances need it be taken as demanding pure H_2O. In some circumstances it need not include H_2O at all. In most if not all circumstances, when referring specifically to the formation of the Earth itself, it implies that H_2O was dominant.

When referring specifically to the waters "above" and "below," "the firmament of the heaven" - our sky - it implies a basic similarity or "syn-genesis" of the two waters. This implies that, in space, probably not far from the Earth, lies a great quantity of fluids, vapours, and some rocky materials, rich in H_2O but incorporating every major fluid substance of the Earth's crust and atmosphere. Or their ices. In the formation of the Earth, a wide variety of substances was involved, yet in some way H_2O-water and related compounds played a pivotal role. By extension, the same should be true of the other planets, especially those most like the Earth in composition.

This fundamental role of H_2O and related compounds in the formation of planets at first may seem far-fetched. To lay the foundation stones of the Earth in *water?* Is this practicable? The centres of the stony planets are iron and other metals, or rock - hot, hard, and assuredly without water. The outer planets are hydrogen gas like the sun and . . . ice!

Ices of water. Ices of CO_2. Ices of methane. Ammonia. Nitrogen. Sulphur dioxide. Ices and vapours of the Earth's atmosphere and its relatives and derivatives. Some stony matter is incorporated, in varying amounts. Even the two gas giants, Jupiter and Saturn, are thought to have at their core ice. (The centres of these gas giants must be hot; the ice will be kept from vaporizing by extreme pressures.) There is no ice at the centre of the stony planets because rock is heavier than water, and forced it out. Topographic features produced by sudden escape of water-like fluids may still be seen on the surface of Mars. The planets were built on water. "For He hath founded it upon the seas, and established it upon the floods" *Ps.24:2.*

Floods! The Earth was founded upon floods! Not a flood, but floods; streams of differing source and composition. Streams amendable to sorting and differentiation by passage through gravitational fields or by the winnowing effects of radiation "winds" from stars. Streams that were floods, that suddenly and spectacularly rose, then as mysteriously died away. H_2O water played some hidden, pivotal role in planetary formation from those floods.

Whence These Full and Rushing Streams?

To manufacture all the elements of the Earth requires star-furnaces. The alchemists of old searched for a method of converting common elements to rare elements. We now know they needed a large star; or better, a cluster of stars. Had they the proper equipment, they could have changed common soot into diamond, but soot is carbon, and diamond is carbon of crystal form. Soot and diamond are the same element. The components of water are different elements to silver, and the components of air are different elements to gold, and it is dramatic changes such as could transform elements into silver and gold, for which some alchemists were searching.

In the far corners of space, astronomers have detected radiation sources even now transmitting at multiplied British billions times the power of our sun. Some of these could be the long-departed, dying remnants of the furnaces that converted light elements to heavy elements for our planets. The conflagrations called upon to crack and fuse atoms may have consumed parts or even all of an existing galaxy. There are more than a thousand million stars in our galaxy, of which the sun is but one average member, and our galaxy is but one average galaxy amongst a British billion other galaxies. The numbers become meaningless.

Furnaces such as these do not eject rivers, but floods, floods that are oceans, maelstroms of stardust hurtling through emptiness perhaps at some fraction of the speed of light itself.

At some stage the floods, or streams of floods, must have been turned, and circled upon themselves. In time the whirling eddies accreted into bodies of semi-solid, then solid matter, or balls of gas and vapour, depending upon the composition of the flood-stream, and perhaps upon the agents of accretion involved. These processes of accretion, or "gathering together" (*Gen.1:9*), are as clouded in mystery as the early Earth was clouded in dust and vapours; as clouded as a cloud itself, hidden as the mystery of a cloud, as the mystery of rain-formation in a cloud.

"Who hath divided a watercourse for the overflowing of waters, or a way for the lightning of thunder? . . . Hast thou entered into the treasures of the snow? Or hast thou seen the treasures of the hail? . . . Hath the rain a father? Or who hath begotten the drops of dew?" *Job 38:22, 25&28.*

The formation of rain, hail, and snow is an enduring mystery, only dimly perceived by man. The initial formation of the droplets and ice- crystals, as well as their subsequent growth prior to falling, is only partly understood. Every raindrop is believed to have at its centre a tiny speck. The drop grows around that speck. Raindrops are therefore agents of accretion and growth through accretion. All attempts at triggering rain have failed. Jeremiah knew why. There is something implicated in the formation and/or accretion of raindrops and hailstones in clouds which cannot be replicated by human technology. For this reason he asks, "Are there any among the vanities of the Gentiles that can cause rain? Or can the heavens give showers? Art not thou he, 0 Lord our God? Therefore we will wait upon thee: for thou hast made all these things" *Jer.14:22.*

The formative Earth stood "out of the water and in the water" *2 Pet.3:5.* It was "established upon the floods" *Ps.24:2.* And in some obscure way, perhaps reminiscent of the accretion and growth of raindrops, hail, and snow, water itself was a catalyst in bringing particles together. Whether or not water, H_2O, was the sole and only agent in this process of accretion or gathering together, is not clear. One thing we know: neither H_2O nor related natural compounds of themselves are causing new planets to grow now, in the vicinity of Earth nor in any laboratory. Special conditions existed to facilitate the process. These conditions were such as cannot be fully replicated artificially. As is the case for rain, something beyond the everyday was involved.

Something beyond the everyday? Something that would cause water and perhaps other compounds to act as catalysts, shepherds gathering together dispersed components into a unified body?

Something out of the everyday? Force-fields? Pulsing energy waves? Sound blasts? Magnetism? Extrasensory signals? Stars that "sing"? Although the text of *Job 38:7* is alluding first and foremost to angels - spirit-beings of great power and beauty - it also has a physical signification. It alludes to morning stars, or a cluster of stars peculiarly involved in the formation of the planets; and these stars "sang together." Note, they not only "sang," they "sang together." They "sang together" in a symphony of star-sound.

The Earth's nursery was guided and guarded by stars - morning stars. Something of the emissions and activities of these stars worked in unison to cause the Earth to be "gathered together." As it accreted, it stood "out of the water and in the water." At some stage, it reached a level of development at which great bodies of water broke out onto its surface; gambolling seas, frolicking oceans. "Or who shut up the sea with doors, when it brake forth, as if it had issued out of the womb?" *Job 38:8.* At this early, formative stage the seas themselves were enveloped in darkness - not because of a want of universal light, but because of heavy clouding (*Job 38:9*). Then morning broke over the infant planet and the new world was perceived to have circular motion - circular motion in the sense of a rotating man-made imprinting device (*Job 38:14*). What was the cause of this spin?

It seems possible for star-furnaces to exude a flood of star-dust. It does not appear inconceivable that various streams within this racing flood coalesced into planets. The flood could conceivably have turned in circles and this imparted its momentum to what are now spinning rings of planets. Stars and related objects, strategically positioned, were part of these processes. But why do the planets spin on their own axes? No sooner did they exist than it seems they began to spin. Some currently spin at different rates to others, perhaps as a result of later events in their histories; in general, their spin is in the same sense of the clock, and it is not inconceivable that back in time, near the beginning, they all spun the same way and at a much faster rate. (It is this spin that gives the Earth its stable day-night pattern.) What set them spinning?

Some theories have them spinning as a product of initial eddying in the parent streams. This encounters the difficulty of adding to a ball whilst the ball is trying to spin the material back off itself. Others resort to explaining it with intelligent asteroids. These hit the planets in a pattern to set them in motion. A few have suggested that the impact of light and similar radiation may have a mysterious rotary effect upon objects in space. Perhaps some truth is to be found in all these notions, even in the last. Perhaps some hint of an answer lies in those two great and enduring mysteries, electricity and magnetism, both of which are bound up in the existence of light.

The Parting of Light

Job 38:24 asks the cryptic question, "By what way is the light parted, which scattereth the east wind upon the earth?" Heat entering the Earth's atmosphere causes air-circulation, and the sun's light brings heat: is this all the meaning intended here? Does light of itself cause air-circulation? How is light "parted"?

Light is one variety of electromagnetic radiation. Electricity and magnetism are inseparably bound into the existence of all matter, and especially light. A starter-motor relies on electric current passing through a wire loop in the presence of a magnet. The wire loop begins to spin. Was the primeval Earth designed as the electrically-conducting spinner in a starter-motor? Did light and related radiation have some part to play in setting up a magnetic field in the ions and particles about the early Earth, and/or in triggering strong flows of electric current through the Earth itself? Could an unperceived effect of light or similar radiation be the engine behind the stupendous winds sweeping most planets other than Earth at this moment? This is conjecture.

Whatever the motivation, the early Earth began to spin. Like the other planets, it would naturally have begun to spin with its axis standing upright. The planets should have all had the same posture, flights of spinning tops hurtling around a gravitational anchor at the centre. Was there one or more than one ring of these spinning tops? Was the anchor at the centre or centres another huge planet, a proto-sun, or the sun?

Let us give reign to our imagination, and leave it to the mechanics and mathematicians to pass a verdict. Assume for sake of argument that amongst the cluster of "morning stars" were a pair that formed as twins, from a body of gas shaped like a bone with equal bulges at the ends. At that time they were not shining, being a little younger than the main cluster. They were balanced by the processes of spin and various gravitational attractions, one embryo-star in fact edging slightly away from the other over time. Also associated with the early star cluster were spinning rings of formative planets, the offspring of a space flood, and streams of matter from a "star furnace." As these streams raced through space they had become curved, as do the spiral arms of nebulae; and as providence would have it, finally rolled into flat disk(s) of formative planets, with a quantity of material telescoping into the centre of the disk(s). This was not without the assistance of strategically placed stars or other celestial objects.

Whether purely as a product of this space-flood, or partly as a product of materials already present on site, the twin-star/dog bone was in the centre of the now-spinning flood, and aligned perpendicular to the spinning "wheels" - like the axle of a wheel, but with a future star at either end. Whether or not the planets all had a common centre from the outset, or were in two or more wheels or rings each with their own central hub or anchor, we leave to technical advisors. Perhaps the stony planets, and our Earth, were in one ring near the middle of the dog- bone axle, with a huge ice-sphere forming the central anchor, whilst the gas/ice planets were somewhere else along the axle, with a ball of gas or even perhaps one of the embryo-stars at their centre.

The upshot of the arrangement, for our intents and purposes, was a fast-spinning, compact gyroscopic wheel with a dispensable ice-rich body at the centre, with a balanced future star out on both ends of a long axle running through the centre of the wheel. Thus in the place now occupied by our sun was a giant ice-rich body (similar to the comets in makeup), and the wheel was initially held in place by the counterbalancing supports of two large bodies at roughly equal distance along its axis. Once the wheel was spinning and balanced, the two support-bodies could be moved in some measure without destroying the shape of the wheel. How far they could be moved we leave to gyroscopic theory. This model obviously has difficulties, and should only be taken as thought stimulation; but consider now the virtues of models along lines such as this.

-- If one of the twin "dog-bone" stars could be edged away from the wheel(s), whilst the other was edged in, then the sun has a twin, as do the great majority of stars the size of the sun. A body the size of the sun is our closest star. It is now in association with two other objects, but nevertheless is a candidate for co-formation with our own sun. (It is one of the Pointers, southern hemisphere.)

Is this possible? (-the following is mostly entertainment value)

1) A whirling spiral of matter, remnant of a nova, or a "star furnace".

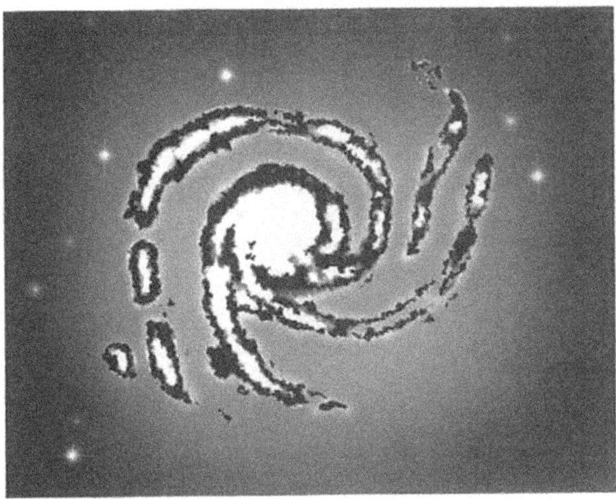

2) A group of "space floods" from the whirling nebula race towards a formative twin star, or a "dog-bone star". (This dog-bone would be spinning end-over-end in such a way as to keep the ends apart).

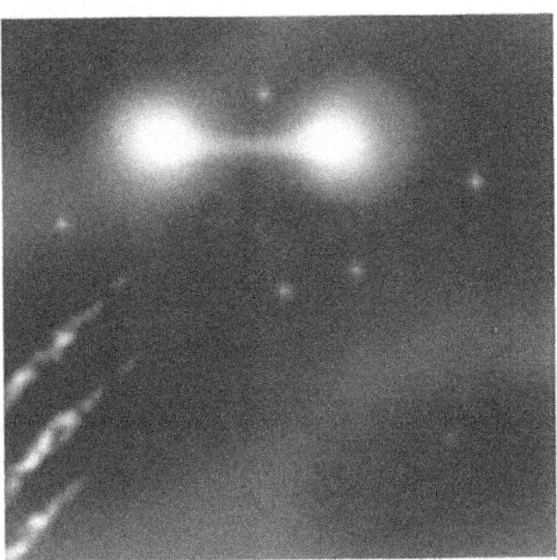

3) Two (or perhaps more) are captured by the unformed stars.

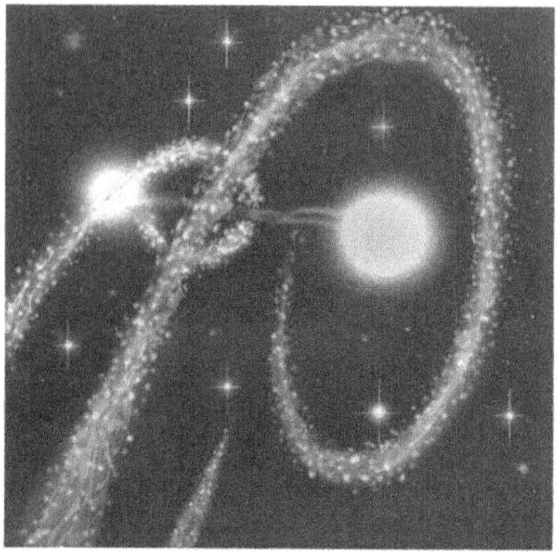

4) In time, they become spinning discs of formative planets around the "dog-bone" (The smaller disc in the middle is kept stable by equal gravitational forces from the ends of the "dog-bone", and a large icy "hub" at its centre).

5) Over time, the dog-bone grows longer, thinner, and spins less and less, as mutual tidal stresses in the two ends produce a braking and separating effect. At some time the ends "ignite". One moves away: the other is our sun. The sun and the discs gradually move into the same plane, assisted by gravitational anchors - perhaps large bodies of ice? The icy centre of the smaller disc is drawn slightly towards the approaching sun.

Disintegrating, it flings future comets out across the sunny side of the disc, so most do not collide with the planets.

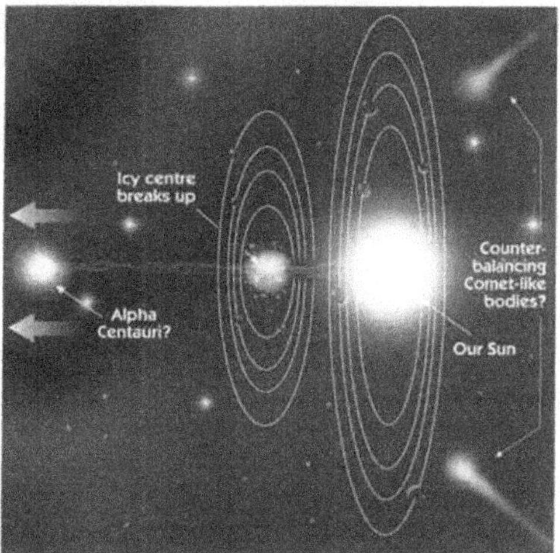

6) The comets, Pluto, the axial tilts, and various moons were a product of the perturbations associated with this "docking".

- By separate formation of the sun, and perhaps of the various planetary-types, we eliminate the difficulty of the strikingly different composition of the various components of the solar system.

- We likewise eliminate the difficulty of a slow-spinning centre in a fast-spinning wheel.

- We can also introduce the planets to the shining orb after it has become stable - postignition.

- We open up a field of investigation in which the various permutations and combinations may be systematically tested, until possibility becomes a feature of origin models.

The Introduction of the Sun

For the purpose of illustration, then, let us assume the sun was introduced, along the lines of fitting spinning wheels over spinning wheels, and spinning wheels over hubs. Let us also assume it was slipped in along the "axle" of the wheel, whilst another body slipped away from the other end of the "axle," a process balanced through the effects of spin and strategically placed bodies acting as gravitational anchors.

Initially the Earth was cool. Very quickly it warmed. Between chemical reactions of newly-met substances and radioactively-decaying elements fully charged, for a long period of time the Earth was probably more in need of ice to cool it than a sun to warm it. As for light, the difficulty in those times in an expanding universe may have been in finding a dark place rather than in finding light. Other than as a gravitational anchor, the sun as we know it would have served little purpose. (There is one item of information to consider here which points half-heartedly to a sun always *in situ.* Theoretically, once ignited, a star such as our sun burns at two-thirds to three-quarters of its capacity for the first quarter of its life. This is deduced from physics theory. If this output can be reduced even further, then a sun that neither clears the sky of diffusing particles, nor provides clear days, nights, and seasons, could have been in place from the outset.)

To return to our wheels-and-axle model: As the Earth gradually changes from requiring cooling of its surface to requiring heating at the surface, and as the surrounding light-sources move further away, the sun compensates by moving closer. (The same effect, we learned, could have been achieved by a sun *in situ,* but gradually increasing in output from almost nothing. This does not appear to fit the history of such bodies.) So the sun moves in to compensate for gradual diminution of other heat and light. If it were bringing the outer ring(s) of gas/ice planets with it, it would have had time to clear their inner space of gas and debris, leaving a clear area for the stony ring inside the vaporous balls.

By a docking action best described as a *coup de magnificence,* it locks into central, or hub position, the disks of planets also coming into the same plane, the axis of the fiery orb nevertheless being inclined to that plane. *En route,* it partly vaporizes the icy comet material it is bound to replace, absorbing the remainder upon arrival, if the central ice-sphere has not already flung itself into the far distance, to return to its place of origin from time to time as comets. The perturbations and dislocations associated with this precision meshing gave useful results.

A large body moving in the vicinity of the disks perturbed the planets sufficiently to give the Earth axial tilt. Thus it began to exhibit seasonal variation once the sun came into proximity to it. Some planets gained new moons, and new materials were impacted onto some planets' surfaces, courtesy of the disintegrating, somewhat rocky ice-ball originally at the centre, or perhaps through other secondary events. Pluto, the lonely stone outrider, may have been propelled into its long circuit through disturbances accompanying events such as these; and various orphans, such as the asteroids, may likewise be the offspring of these momentous changes. Asteroids are thought to be the dispersed remnants of stone and metal mini-planets, and since some have chemical similarities to elements in the sun, the suspicion arises that they are remnants that were not swept away by or drawn into that body, before the main disk of stone/metal planets was meshed in. Most of the asteroids would therefore be the heavy, gas-stripped remnants of the innermost part of the "flood" from which the gas/ice planets formed.

Substantial quantities of this material could have fallen into the formative sun, and some could have been seared by the sun as it "ignited." Surviving remnants, distant from the new sun, formed into several miniature planets. These in turn fragmented into the orphan asteroids, most of which now wander like deprived waifs in a belt between Mars and Jupiter. Some of their components show a similar "signature" to some elements in the sun, and some have components that have been flash melted.

Of all the planetary alterations and re-adjustments, those nearest the incoming sun were the most intense and held the most significance for our Earth. For at this *juncto,* our own moon glides onto the page of history, most likely being at least partially sourced from the lighter outer portion of overheated and highly perturbed Mercury. Some traumatic event has left this closest neighbour of the sun with an oversize iron core, and the missing stone fits well as the moon. Something dramatic happened to Mercury, and something produced our own unique moon. Proof or otherwise of a link between the two events would not alter the fact that both happened. But let us step back a moment, to survey progress. One way or another, we have a steadily increasing sun, finally becoming the sun more or less as we know it today.

As the sun increased, or came closer, it steadily swept away the shrouding, light-diffusing gases and particles from space about the planets. This in turn "turned on" or "made the stars" "in the firmament of the heaven."

Those stars which then existed, at least, for it should be remembered that many of the now-visible stars are in fact younger than our sun, so many stars were not simply "unveiled" on day four; they were made from scattered materials on day four. An incoming or a steadily increasing sun therefore harmonizes with the biblical notion of the stars not appearing until sometime after the Earth had been established.

The sun itself, of necessity, was also in effect initially absent, and then veiled, and since production of the moon was very likely to have been associated with the sun's full inception or arrival, neither sun nor moon was "made" until the stars were "made." And since day and night, times and seasons imply a sun and a moon in proximity to the Earth, these also were coeval with the stars. Furthermore, putting the solar system together from disparate sources in an intelligent pattern begins to explain its complexities.

It may be able to explain more yet.

Designing a Planetary System

Consider yourself in the position of the designer of a planetary system.

In pursuit of your plan for life, and a suitable planet for it, you have calculated the need for a satellite or moon of a certain size and mass, needed from a specific time onward in history. This time will be relatively late in geologic history. Your moon will not be required until immediately preceding the advent of complex organisms. This means that for at the very least four-fifths of the history of the planet, the moon is not needed. Placing it into orbit around the Earth from the earliest times would slow the Earth's spin and necessitate various major orbital re-adjustments from time to time. Yet the best time to form the moon is back in time, when the planets are younger. You have a moon, but you do not need it in its final location as yet. What do you do with it?

You store it somewhere. Where do you store it?

You logically store it at or near its place of origin, and in a place from which its final "owner" can "collect" it.

What is the moon's place of origin?

Our nearest neighbour has been built to size and weight. It is exceptional among the stony planets for being large for its mass. It is built from rock, with very little heavy metallic core. Having little heavy metal content, it has less weight for size than those stony planets with large metal cores. This is no accident, for the moon as seen from Earth is the same size as the sun, and since the sun and the moon are man and woman in a type (see *Gen.37:9, 10; Ps.19:5; Rev.12:1*), their equal size is a standing testimony to the biblical teaching that male and female ultimately weigh the same in spiritual balances, even though their roles are quite distinct.

The moon, being mostly rock, is of similar composition to the rock mantle overlaying the metal cores of the stony planets. Mercury, the body currently closest to the sun, is missing a quantity of its mantle. Whether this was the source of the moon, or whether another planet even closer to the centre of the solar system was divided up for the purpose, the end result is the same. The moon almost certainly came from near the centre of our planetary wheel, at a time when the sun was increasing or moving in. The heat and disturbance logically had the effect of making nearby bodies ready to shed parts of themselves.

You have made the moon to specifications. You need now to store it and transport it to its final site, at the desired time. It seems probable you will bring something with it, or arrange for it to gain it during arrival - an atmosphere. This atmosphere will gradually fret away under the force of the sun's radiation and the Earth's superior gravitational attraction, and will thus become a standing supply of essential re- supply compounds for the

Earth's atmosphere. As the newly-revealed trees and the complex forms of life draw essential compounds out of the atmosphere and waters, and tie them into the Earth as limestone, fossil fuels, and so on, you will re-supply these compounds by a steady stream from the newly-positioned moon.

The element most heavily drawn upon will be carbon, so you arrange for the moon to be coated in a rich supply of CO_2 - either bringing it with itself from its storage site, or gaining it *en route* or soon after arrival. This could be achieved by encasing it in a sizeable dry-ice-rich comet. This supply will fully deplete at a time allowing CO_2 levels in the Earth's atmosphere to deplete to crisis levels - just as industry begins to re-supply this compound by burning the fossil fuels. (Life on Earth had just a few centuries remaining when man began to re-supply the atmosphere with this vital compound.)

You have manufactured a suitable body of rock, shaped it, begun to prepare its surface to make it an excellent all-over reflector, and stored it for the duration. Where did you store it?

There are sights to be seen in the heavens that relegate the brightest diamond to nothing more than *rock,* and the most lustrous pearls to *oyster concretions.* Just before dawn breaks, the morning star on rare occasions gives forth a light of beauty ever to remain in the observer's memory; and certain atmospheric conditions can sometimes grace the moon with a softly-coloured aura to which words fail to do justice. The morning star and the moon. The two objects in the heavens of incomparable grace and beauty. Christ is likened to the morning star (*Rev.22:16*), and in a distant figure, woman is the moon, and therefore the moon in some way speaks of the elect, the church, the bride of Christ. Would it not be fitting if the morning star and the moon were once together? Christ and his church, together since time was young?

The planetary sequence outward from the centre of the solar system is: Mercury, at or near the probable source of the moon; Venus (the morning star); Earth. Of all the planets, these three have their orbits closest each other's, and are the most logical "stairway" out which the moon could have travelled. Tie the moon as loosely as is feasible to one of these, and allow the next planet out from it to swerve in toward it, or perhaps utilize a propelling impact on the moon at the propitious moment - and, transfer! It could be done, although mathematicians tell us it would be a sophisticated procedure, not attributable to chance.

Assume the moon was projected outward from the region of Mercury and the sun early in history.

Assume it resided with Venus for much of Earth's early existence, only being captured by our planet relatively late in geologic time. What evidence exists of prolonged association between Venus (the morning star, next closest the sun to us) and the moon? Venus is only a little smaller than the Earth, and therefore able to control a moon-sized satellite. As we have learned, it is a step on the stairway between the moon's probable origin and its destiny. Prolonged association with a body the size of the moon should have greatly reduced Venus's spin rate. Venus has almost zero rate of spin. The moon causes tides and some movement and heating effects within the Earth itself. It should have had some effect on the history of Venus.

Geologic Record of Earth, compared to the history of Venus

The earth seems to have 'come alive' in some fundamental way, a mere 550 million years ago.

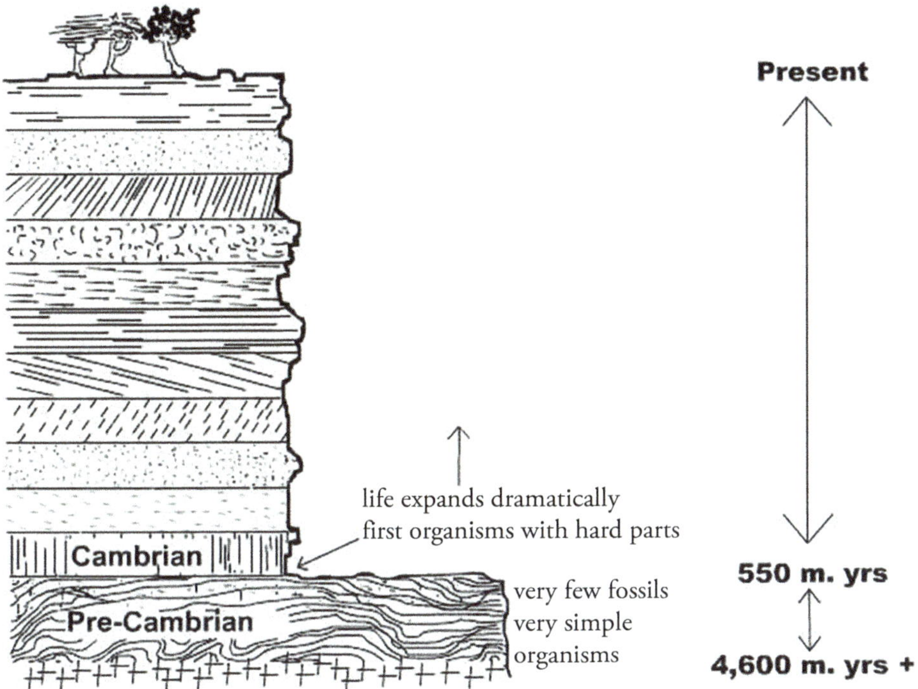

The history of Venus, if anything, is the reverse.

"The age of the surface of Venus can be worked out from the number of craters that have formed on it over time. We know the rate of impacts from our study of the craters on the dated surfaces on the Moon. Based on this, the surface of Venus appears to be relatively young. This is a very strange finding. On Earth we are missing only the first ten percent of our history in the rock record, but on Venus, there is no record of what happened in the first 85 per cent of its history. There are no old surfaces covered with craters, such as we see on Mars, Mercury or the Moon. The present surface of Venus is somewhere between three and five hundred million years old. What is curious is that not much seems to have happened there since. The 950 impact craters that were produced on Venus over that period of time are mostly uneroded. Five hundred million years ago, the Cambrian Period on the Earth was marked by the appearance of the first hard- shelled animals. Quite a lot has happened here since then. Venus has had a very different history. A few hundred million years ago, it covered its surface with a great splurge of lava. Apparently exhausted by this great outpouring, geologic activity on Venus hasn't managed to produce more than a trickle of lava since then."[3]

At a time potentially concurrent with a pivotal change in the Earth's geologic history, Venus's crust and interior appears to have gone dead. Apart from a few impact craters, and some fitful volcanism, nothing has happened to Venus's rocks for a long time - whilst the history of the Earth is the reverse. This could also be reflected by magnetic activity. The "morning star" currently has no magnetic field.

The nearby Earth, of only approximately one-fifth more mass, has magnetism. This magnetism is yet another essential of the modern world, and could well be a product of tidal stresses and movements generated in our metallic core. Finally, Venus is shrouded in a thick atmosphere of CO_2. Whether any of this could have come with the moon - perhaps as dry ice (frozen CO_2) - is problematical; the fact is, the Earth has used up approximately six hundred times its current atmospheric and oceanic reserves of this compound, and its nearest neighbour is coated in it; and this nearest neighbour logically harboured the moon.

You, as engineer of the planetary system, have acted in a logical pattern. You made the moon at a time propitious for such actions; you have kept it at a suitable site; you introduced it precisely when it was required and not a moment before. And so this inspiration of poets and lovers alike makes

---

3 Taylor S.R., pages 132-133, 1998

her stately progress across the sky in a manner at once graceful, deeply significant for all complex life, and essential to life.

The Arrival of the Moon

When did she arrive? (Or should it be, when did we collect her?)

If the Earth had no large moon for a period of time, then acquired one, the event would be reflected in the rock strata in no unequivocal fashion. The record of it would appear in the geologic strata as a trumpet-blast, as the change between a horse-drawn cart and an automobile, even the invention of the wheel itself. It would stand out universally; it would be in the language of every geologic text; it would be all but a household word. Since the Earth was made by an intelligent, logical creator, it should also not long precede the advent of complex animal life - which depends upon a moon, but before which, no moon was required.

The scriptures inform us that before the moon was "set in the firmament of the heaven," the only life that existed was "made;" that is, it was simple life. After the various lights were set in the firmament, (Day Four), complex life was *created* (Day Five). The advance in complexity of life implicated in the word *create* is profound. Thus, simple organisms, perhaps best described as "organized seaweed," did exist before the fifth day, before the moon's advent. The structure of those ancient pseudo- animals was simple. They possessed few, if any, internal organs; they did not have skeletons or shells; they did not require strongly aerated waters, regular strong turbulence, or the host of other factors partly or wholly tied up with the moon.

The trumpet-blast in the rocks is the signal event of all geologic time, almost a household concept. It is the only feature in rock-strata which is universally and unequivocally agreed upon as a sign of a single, contemporaneous event world-wide. It not only created great turbulence in all but the deepest or most protected waters, but for perhaps tens of millions of years kept most of the world's sediments from finding permanent rest, whilst mountains rose and were cut off, and strata were tilted and folded. From this point in the geologic column upward, strata and world history were profoundly changed in some way.

In the system of strata immediately above it, underwater deposits prevail almost to the exclusion of land deposits; and these water-laid strata contain abundant fossils of complex life. This is the so- called Pre-Cambrian/ Cambrian Unconformity, an indicator of a worldwide event. It lies at the base of what could perhaps be paraphrased as "The Strata of Ancient Life," or Palaeozoic - of which the Cambrian System is the lowermost strata-grouping. From this point - the bottom of the Cambrian - the familiar geologic column with its shadow of a tree of life within it progresses upward as though it has really only just begun.

Although a relative few outcrops do not display an unconformity at this level, geology from its early times has recognized the Pre-Cambrian/ Cambrian interface as coincident with a subtle and deep- seated change in the environment in which rock strata were deposited, and some have conjectured moon-capture as a possible cause. The event was no more than six hundred million years past - relatively recent!

It goes without saying there were tides and some engines of atmospheric/ oceanic movement prior to our moon's timely *debut,* but the new arrival injected new meaning into these processes, and indeed brought something new to the whole Earth.

Thus from all these evidences - we have but touched on a few, and merely dabbled in the edge of an ocean - we may reasonably surmise the Fourth Day to have been at very least of a thousand million years duration, and to comprise such works as expand the mind. The advent of the moon we can clearly and logically follow. The sweeping away of interplanetary vapours to reveal the early stars seems logical; the threading together of families of planets appears necessary but difficult to conceive; whilst in the case of the sun, some *coup de magnificence* must have been achieved to account for existing features. Whether the fiery celestial orb itself was moved, or whether it was added to - a procedure almost as intricate as moving - or whether theorists have overlooked something, and a star like our sun can grow slowly from a small, quiet beginning - momentous events have shaped our Earth and its fellow-travellers. These events are part of a skilfully-woven tapestry, a tapestry in which the background is space, and the needle and thread are megatons of rock, seas and oceans of compact vapours, and balls of fire a man could not traverse if he walked for a lifetime.

Could we now pause, step back to review progress, and plot the course ahead?

Are we deducing the possibility of remarkable intelligence and design in the celestial spheres? Are we uncovering an irresistible logic and pattern, such as a Being of intelligence would use? Do we sense that we are not alone?

Have we embarked upon a pathway of success in deciphering the worlds and their histories? Blind chance stumbles, and starves beside a banquet; we know nothing of the heavens, and make a feast of a few bones?

If we have enjoyed some small success, what to lose by going farther? Having perhaps come to an improved position by employing a Bible and a few basic facts, why not venture on the Bible and a laboratory, and see what transpires?

One consideration is reassuring; in terms of the origins of the solar system, it will be difficult to become more mystified than end-of- twentieth century mainstream science.

We will venture: bring out the chemical analyses, the moon rocks, the factual data - hard-won and expensive - and test the theory. The danger, the fine human effort, the sacrifice of the manned lunar program has more reward to reap. The holy Word of God was taken to the moon and spoken to Earth from the moon, and this will redound even more to the glory of God. "The stones cry out" *Luke 19:40.*

VI. BRING OUT THE MOON ROCKS

And make way for the King! (See *Luke 19:36- 40)*

Those astronauts who ventured to the moon and ventured to honour the God who made the heavens and the Earth brought back the key to the moon's origin and enabled a giant leap in mankind's understanding of the worlds he lives amongst. They also brought back, written in stone, truth in confirmation of the Truth.

Now, unless evidence is not evidence, every person of this Earth can look up at our graceful planetary companion and know without any doubt that the great God cares for them, personally, which they may verify with their own eyes, in the heavens on one hand and in the Bible on the other. A giant step for mankind: mankind technologically and mankind personally.

The first moon landing of itself was probably sufficient to provide, in time, a revolutionary and reassuring view of our solar system. In time, scientific thought will inevitably tend toward this same conclusion, unless evidence is not evidence. This rocket program did good service for humanity, and the word of God will not return void. "Them that honour me, I will honour" *1 Sam.2:30.*

The suspicion arises that if mainstream scientific thought had presented some of those astronauts with the results of the analyses of the material they sampled, they would have deciphered the history of the moon long ago. Some of them at least were not straight jacketed by a tradition of blind chance creating the heavens and the Earth. The type of people who brought back the luckiest flight of all, Apollo 13, could perhaps have tracked the wanderings of the moon with all dispatch. Howbeit, we shall attempt to do so herewith, and although it is never wise policy to be overly definite in some things, the case is strong. Gambling - the moral and economic mistake - is best eschewed; notwithstanding, if there is not a winner with a good prospect to back here, there never will. And with the name Mercury on the favoured entrant, can we lose?

To details and to rock analyses.

Important Facts

Even before men went to the moon, several significant facts were known.

Our near-neighbour and nightly companion was known to be low in density, as though depleted in heavy minerals such as iron. The rock analyses confirmed this depletion in heavy elements. Rest assured, if there was any hint of heavy and precious metals on the moon, the whole world would know. A few gold nuggets would go some way toward defraying the cost of travel. No heavy ores have been found, not even silver, despite the silvery sheen of much of the surface.

Contrast this depletion in heavy elements with the topmost layer of the Earth, "whose stones are iron, and out of whose hills thou mayest dig brass" *Deut.8:9.* On the surface of the Earth are entire hills of iron, especially on the older or Pre-Cambrian parts of the surface. And roughly one quarter of the Earth is metal core.

This factor of metal depletion, already suspected, was confirmed through the rock sampling and analyses.

This depletion of heavy metals in the moon, coupled with the anomaly of enrichment in metals on the *surface* - note: *surface* of the Earth - the last place to expect something heavy, if it could have sunk deeper; this depletion on the one hand and enrichment on the other is a factor to be considered in any model of Earth/moon origins.

Speculation as to the consistent, effective reflective properties of the lunar surface led to an assumption that the brighter areas at least were made up of whitish-coloured, pearly-lustred mineral, confirmed by human inspection as feldspar, gem-quality specimens being labelled moonstone long before mineralogists were certain it featured large on the planet from which its name derives. Another cause behind the overall reflective consistency is the fragmenting effect of impacts, producing innumerable reflecting facets. No meteorite ever fell onto the moon by accident, without purpose. Whether or not the meteorite hammering has fulfilled yet another hidden purpose by releasing gaseous elements from mineral grains for subsequent gravitational fretting away to the Earth, we leave to chemistry and mechanics - and likewise conjecture on a past lunar atmosphere. Suggestions of buried ice - unproved as yet but strongly indicated - automatically lead on to suggestions of more than ice alone in the past.

Our neighbour was designed to specifications.

Someone put the gold on the Earth's surface - surface - and left it out of the moon.

Someone arranged for the moon's surface to be given the properties of an overall reflector.

And other provisions besides.

The depletion in metals coupled with an essentially stone makeup confirmed the suspicion that the silvery crescent that evolves to a golden orb can only be explained under existing knowledge if it was originally part of the stone component of a pre-existing planet. During removal, heating and at least partial melting of both bodies must have occurred. The queen of the night sky has been "double-baked." In contrast, most of the Earth has been "single-baked," at least in the broad sense. Analytical comparisons of the rocks effectively prove it to be so.

The moon is not a *primary* body. Its source almost certainly lies in another planet. It is a *secondary* product.

A planet was divided or at least depleted to provide our night-light. "*I will divide Shechem, and mete out . . . Succoth.*" *Ps.60:6.*

Which planet?

Perhaps *a disintegrated* planet? Parts of it may be impurities in the sun, a part of it may be Pluto. It may perhaps no longer exist, and its remnants other than those providing our monthly recycling reflectant disk - may have effectively disappeared.

Perhaps the *Earth?*

The near-spherical mineral and metal aggregation upon which we live shows no obvious evidence of depletion, but until all possibilities are eliminated, since some chemical similarities exist between the two, Earth origin is a candidate.

Perhaps one of the *other planets?* Check:

- **Mars**: Relatively small, possibly depleted. Rocks appear somewhat different to the moon's. Rock material, believed (on the basis of gas inclusions typical of Mars' atmosphere) to be thrown to the Earth from that planet as meteors, chemically distinct from moon rock. Delete.

- **Venus**: Not obviously depleted. Surface rock of different appearance to the moon. (No detailed analyses yet available.) Unlikely.

- **Mercury**: Depleted. Originally of the order of twice current size, estimate being based on the size of its disproportionately large metal core. This would make it of the order of the current size of Mars, with a rock-volume sufficient to make several of our moons. No material currently available for analysis.

Mercury is the front-runner with an unknown, lost planet and the Earth trailing. Venus is trailing in the far distance.

Unknown, lost planets and Venus will presumably stay in the race until probes and analyses declare the winner.

But unless the powers of reason as employed herewith are benighted, the Earth is about to retire, badly injured. Unless evidence is not evidence, the moon will glide onto the stage of Earth history at or near the Pre-Cambrian/Cambrian Unconformity, to close with gentle grandeur the Fourth Day. That this is so seems to be the only existing logical meaning of the moon rock analyses. The honour men gave their one and only Creator during the venture of retrieving them will be repaid with increase.

The Stones Cry Out!

Whether the powers of reason employed herein are benighted or no; we shall take a risk, and aim for the moon. If some error in fact or in logic deceptively creeps in, we shall call on layman's ignorance by way of an apology, and be the first to admit that the reasoning employed herein is via a complete fool, who at the end can only confess, "Alas, Master! It was only borrowed" *2 Kings 6:5.*

In broadest terms, at least four categories of lunar origin theories have enjoyed support from time to time.

An early and obvious idea saw the solar system with all its varied components coalescing more-or- less concurrently in its present, finished state. This straightforward idea has much in its favour, but in relation to the case in hand encounters major hurdles. Two of these we have already studied. The moon is not a planet as other planets: it is a secondary planet, made from an existing stony body of some sort. Further, two bodies, spinning and rotating about each other in a vacuum, and held together by gravity, if elastic at all so as to suffer tidal stresses, slow and separate, before ultimately falling together. So requires the law of conservation of momentum. We are losing the moon, and we are slowing down.

(The imaginary dog bone proto-stars previously suggested as possible supports of a formative spinning disk, being composed of fluids, were destined to slow and separate in some measure.)

Without external intervention, the co-existence of the Earth and moon throughout geologic time in anything like the present configuration appears mechanically impossible. And as previously suggested, storage elsewhere and introduction would surely be tidier than periodic re- adjustment?

In its favour, this model does accommodate an old moon, found by radiometric dating to be of comparable age to the Earth. The model may confidently be dismissed.

Another one-time favourite spun the requisite materials off the early Earth. The Pacific Ocean basin was suggested as one possible site of origin. This idea engenders warm, family-oriented feelings, but unfortunately neither the mechanics nor the chemistry will open their hearth to give it a place around the fire. The mechanics are readily seen to be no better than for the first model, and indeed are worse: whilst the chemistry is so seemingly perverse as to point partly to syn-genesis, whilst concurrently ruling it out!

Chemically speaking, the only way the moon could originate from the Earth is by profoundly altering the requisite quantity of rock through heating and various other processes. Yet the two bodies have similarities that point unmistakably to a common source - syn-genesis! Some of the analysts may perhaps have fleeting moments during which they wish the astronauts would take the samples back to the moon!

At the end of twentieth century, the favourite is the impact model. This invites anything but placid thoughts of family affairs. This model features a precipitate, violent encounter. It combines elements of the above two theories, and calls on a third planetary body perhaps larger than Mars to strike the place we call home, fragment, and for the orbiting fragments to come together. This when all was young, in a formative solar system in which planets formed in some sort of mad billiards game with blind chance behind the cue.

Already the old mechanical problem of conservation of momentum rears its head, and the suspicion is further raised that the model only has credence because a computer program sufficiently large to comprehensively analyse all the mechanical factors was not in existence when time caught up with the inescapable scientific urge to have a model!

Scientists propose models and theories out of habit, because it is expected of them. Seldom do the actual people involved unanimously support it, and probably fewer still believe it. Proposing theories is necessary to advance. An idea is put forward, so that it can be discussed. Unfortunately, the communications media and sometimes other *scientists* - from other fields of science - take the theories seriously. Even if the mechanics of an impact origin are possible, it is patently obvious they are not possible by chance. Meanwhile, this theory is flatly self- contradictory, unless reason itself has recently taken up quarters on the obscure side of the body lunar. Ah! Those moon rocks!

Oxygen Isotopes

In order to understand why the impact theory is flawed, we shall visit oxygen isotopes.

Isotopes translate as slight variations in the mass of the individual atoms of a given element, brought about by presence or absence of somewhat irrelevant parts of the atoms. For our purposes, isotopes mean slight differences in weight amongst atoms of an element. Oxygen is somewhat unusual in having several stable isotopes; they do not change into each other or radioactively decay. Because they are stable, the ratio of the total number of oxygen atoms of one isotope (weight) to those of another isotope (weight) from the same "manufacture batch" remains constant over time. The total number of each isotope within the "batch" remains the same.

Although individual isotope ratios will vary from time to time and place to place within the "batch," because the total number of each and every stable isotope remains the same overall, a mathematical relationship exists between the measured ratios within that "batch." So, these isotopes have the potential to tell us whether or not the solar system came together from the same "batch" of newly "manufactured" materials, or whether disparate sources were called upon.

Oxygen is the major mineral-forming element of rocks. (That is why so little free oxygen is in the atmospheres of the planets - it very actively bonds into compounds.) This essential and active element comprises roughly half the stone of the Earth and the moon. And the mathematical relationship between its isotope ratios indicates whether or not these rocks drew upon the same or a different "batch" of parent oxygen. Above all other compositional similarities - and other similarities exist - it is the discovery of similar isotope "signatures" in moon samples and in comparable stone from the crust of the Earth that is currently pointed to as indicating some sort of syn-genesis of the two planets.

The first question the enquirer may perhaps now ask is why the two bodies would not have drawn on the same "batch" of oxygen, anyway, especially if all materialized from the same whirling cloud of elements. Why shouldn't the oxygen have all been the same?

All was not mixed and random in the primordial "cloud" - as the solar system itself declares! Mars and many of the meteorites have oxygen isotope ratios foreign to each other and foreign to those of the Earth and moon.

Which model of solar system origin could perhaps explain this? Was it a common cloud of elements culminating in blind chance playing a frenetic game of billiards? Perhaps. The cloud could have been sourced from different sources of manufacture, which were imperfectly blended. On the other hand, the biblical reference to floods implies distinct streams of fluid-like materials perhaps issuing from disparate sources.

Moon and near-surface rocks of the Earth possess some common ancestry, oxygen isotopes proclaiming so the most loudly.

What Are the Implications for the Impact Theory?

An impactor the size of Mars hits the Earth, and the moon ensues. According to the theory, most of the moon coalesces from fragmented remains of the impactor, with some Earth material included.

So most of the moon was originally Mars (so to speak); and Mars, we have not long been advised, the real Mars, has different oxygen isotope ratios to the Earth/moon. So Mars (so to speak) would have supplied different isotope ratios than those of the Earth, and the moon should therefore have different ratios to those of the Earth, since it was mostly made from Mars.

How can introduction of a foreign body explain the presence of the same isotope ratios, if one batch of isotopes is extracted from what is basically the remnants of the foreign body?

It seems the only way this theory could work would be for the impactor to largely become the Earth, as well as produce the moon, so that the isotopes would be the same in both. Oxygen in rock cannot magically run all around the Earth's crust from an impact site.

Unless . . . unless . . . fragmented material from the impactor not only made the moon, but also rained back down around the globe, thus seeding the whole surface layer (crust) of the Earth with the same material as comprises the moon! And this could perhaps explain why heavy, metallic material lies not only in the centre of our ball of rock and mineral, but also on its surface; the heavy elements on our surface were contributed from the inner parts of another planet!

At last we begin to see light - but no mathematical model or program will ever allow all these events - not as an *Earth* impact. It is manifestly unworkable for Earth to have collided with Mars to arrive at the modern arrangement. Move over, Michelangelo, here comes Mars! The existing impact model itself demands that the rock mantle of the Earth melted as a consequence of the impact, scarcely conducive to a firm substrate for receipt of the imminently arriving, metals-enriched remnants of the impactor. And what conceivable process could sort the space-bound splashfragments so that the ones somewhat depleted in some elements, such as iron, stayed aloft to convene as the future timekeeper of the spawning of the corals, whilst the remainder fell in some remarkable pattern to contribute to our continents and our economy? As a practical proposition, the Earth-impact theory is unworkable, as its proposers perhaps suspected. It served its purpose as a useful focus of research. Shall we therefore move on?

Are There Any Existing Models Comparable with Introduction?

Introduction from elsewhere in the solar system appears to answer the questions. Mercury, aptly named, is well in front in the race to be the source.

And here lies the pivotal factor, and the significance of the moon rocks.

Mercury, almost assuredly, is what it is today because a large portion of its stony mantle was lost.

Part of the missing rock could have formed into a mini-planet - now our moon. Other parts may have been thrown toward Earth.

Models of the early Earth encounter grave difficulties in accounting for our unique system of continental land masses, and for the enrichment of various rare, valuable, and often heavy elements within these masses.

Some even turn to a rain of meteorites onto the early Earth to account for our surface chemistry.

And astronomers think a part of Mercury may have become a cloud of potential meteorites in our path.

So, part of Mercury may have travelled here directly, whilst part may have taken a more circuitous route, as a part of a small planet, now the focus not only of howling dogs, but much speculation.

When she finally was introduced, the momentous event triggered the Pre-Cambrian/Cambrian Unconformity.

The corollary of the Pre-Cambrian/Cambrian event saw Venus pour out her soul in a planet-wide sea of basalt lava, presumably triggered by the upward pull of a system of massive ice bodies passing in close on their joyful errand of fetching the bride. What a train! What a party upon arrival! Probably only an astronaut could know exactly the refinement of the procedures in docking fastmoving dry-ice buffers onto a planet, and then hurtling effectively a giant comet into Earth orbit. Entry as a component of an ice-body addresses the mechanical problems of the introduction theory. Either through correctional impacts with other ice, or through rapid dispensing of the bulk of the attendant ice itself at mechanically auspicious points in orbit, introduction becomes a mechanical possibility.

The moon rocks speak the same language as the Word. Guarantor of the Word is the Author of it. None have ever fully trusted him and been disappointed.

Update: "Thus, the Earth and the Moon have identical ε^{50}Ti values within ± .04 ε-unit. For comparison, bulk meteorites have ε^{50}Ti values that span 6 ε -units (Fig.1). The isotopic homogeneity between Earth and the Moon for a highly refractory element such as titanium has important implications..."[4]

Explanatory note: "...bulk meteorites have ε^{50}Ti values that span 6 ε -units." Titanium isotopes in meteorites analysed here on Earth range widely -- 6 ε -units. Zhang *et al* indicate not via their text but via their Figure 1 that there are in fact two classes of meteorite which are exceptional. These are Aubrites and EH Chondrites. Aubrites and EH Chondrites have near-identical ε^{50}Ti values to Earth and Moon, almost within ± .04 ε-unit. Their titanium is isotopically very close to the mathematical trend of Earth and Moon! Zhang *et al*'s Fig.1 shows Earth, Moon, Aubrites and EH Chondrites essentially falling on the same mathematical fractionation line. Meteorites as a whole display a wide range of titanium isotopes but these two specific classes are exceptional. Their composition "may mean that they were originally formed near the center of the solar nebula that created

4 Zhang J., *et al*, "The proto-Earth as a significant source of lunar material," Nature Geoscience, pages 240-241. Published on-line 25 March 2012

the solar system, possibly within the orbit of Mercury.[5]" They probably originated in or near Mercury!

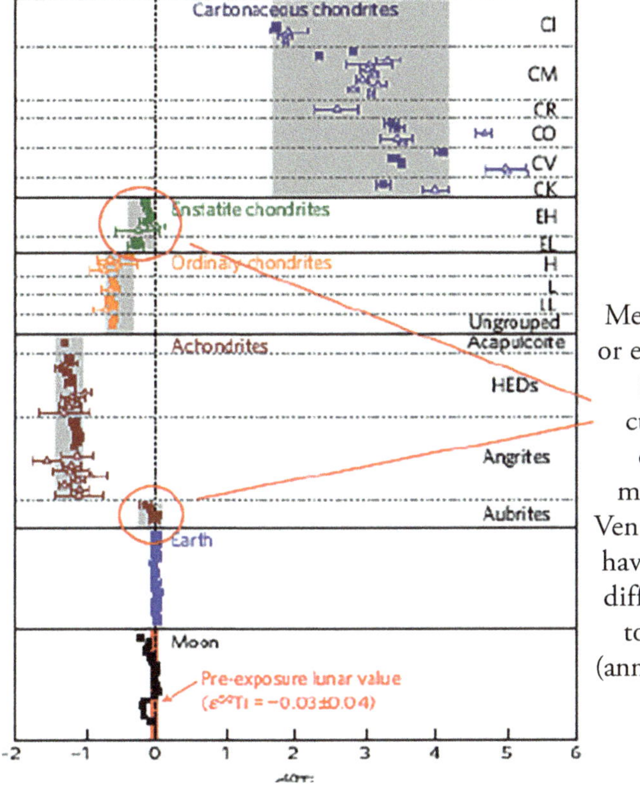

Meteorites which possibly, or even probably originated in Mercury. There is currently no consensus of opinion regarding meteorites sourced from Venus. Meteorites known to have come from Mars have different titanium isotopes to the earth and moon. (annotation by PB Heywood)

Figure 1 | Titanium nucleosynthetic heterogeneity, ε50Ti = [(50Ti/47Ti) sample/(50Ti/47Ti)rutile-1] x10^4, for carbonaceous, enstatite, ordinary chrondrites, and achondrites. Used by permission.

Recent moon rock analyses confirm that at least part of the moon and part of the Earth have a common source. The source may have been Mercury. Of course, a number of permutations and combinations could be invoked to explain these isotopes. None of these permutations allow a giant Earth

[5] Wikipedia, The Free Encyclopedia, s.v. "Enstatite chondrite," https:// en.wikipedia.org/wiki/Enstatite_chondrite, accessed May 2018

impact -- not a shred of evidence of giant impact has been found on Earth -- but they do allow giant impact, almost certainly involving Mercury. Other small planets or planetoids, perhaps originating even closer to the centre of the system, may have been impactors, or been impacted.

It may be useful to keep in mind that under certain circumstances, colliding planets may partly vaporize, and then re-form into a planet - with hybrid chemistry! Furthermore, modelling suggests that the material ejected from giant impact could be hybridized material. And if an impactor originated in the inner solar system, near Mercury, it would probably have major chemical similarities to Mercury, whilst not being identical.

So even if a space ship landed on Mercury today and measured isotopes, little has been achieved. The existing surface is almost certainly not original. Perhaps half the original rock of Mercury is missing! Lumps of rock with broad but undeniable similarities to the (remote sensed) surface of Mercury fall to Earth. Their isotopes (which cannot be remote sensed) clearly suggest that they came from the same source as the surface layers of Earth and Moon. Given these forensics, what would a jury declare?

"Although the formation of the moon was thought to be a solved mystery, its validity seems to be in question. Whether or not researchers decide to take the challenge to determine how the moon was created once and for all is still up in the air."[6] The moon, unofficially solved even before *Apollo* arrived on it, triggers repetitive noise from bushland, in the night. It's up in the air. This much has recently been established.

It is perhaps fitting to terminate our investigation of the Fourth Day with some thoughts of its purpose. Such herculean labour must have a motivation. The product of that effort will have its own symbolism, and

[6] Jessica Lear, Science Recorder, Published online Feb. 2013

a symmetry that can instruct us and lead our thoughts toward a deeper meaning.

A Planetary Family

The sun, moon, and stars are a type of the family (e.g., see *Gen.37:9, 10*). For this reason the size of the moon as viewed from the Earth is the same as the sun. Many a child has conjectured that the moon is the sun, come back at night with its fire extinguished. This is not without its element of truth. After all, the moon is the sun; it is the reflected light of the sun. Yet both are equal if weighed in balances - the balances which measure *spiritual value.* The sun is easily the strongest thing in our visual dimension. "There is nothing hid from the heat thereof" Ps.19:6. So, a man fulfils his destiny by exercising what strength has been given him, especially in the searching out and destruction of danger, crime, and evil, the upholding of virtue, protection of females and children, and nurturing of righteousness. This especially applies to his own children (if he has been given children) or to those who have been specifically entrusted to his oversight.

There are unequivocal biblical guidelines as to how he should act in this regard, so that "he that reads may run," (e.g., *Eph.5:22-33, & 6:4*). In a type, the man is Christ, giving his life for the church and supplying its needs. The man imparts leadership and strength. The sun is primarily strong. The moon is primarily gentle. The woman imparts compassion. The moon's beauty is bound up in discretion, in modesty, in a peculiarly unassuming grace that conquers. The sun and moon are clear and guiding types of the male-female couple. By extension they show how society functions. They show how a successful family-based unit functions. They speak of Christ, "the Sun of Righteousness," and his bride, whose light and grace is his light and grace. There is no life without the moon, even though the sun is the source of it.

Are the sun and moon ever unfaithful to each other? When mankind obeys the figure and example in the heavens above him, the world prospers. Society becomes full of life and vitality. When he forsakes the heavenly principle, society dies, and the Earth becomes cold and dead.

Gen.1:20

And God said, "Let the waters bring forth abundantly the moving creature that hath life . . ."

Hitherto such life as existed had been of the simplest construction, little more than modified mineral; not active, moving, breathing life in the common sense of the term. To external appearances, the world up to this time was dead. For the great part of its existence, the Earth was without obvious, vital life. This vital life was the purpose of the Earth's existence.

Over endless eons, a seeming eternity, the purposes of God were hidden. Time ground on like a slow millstone, until time itself seemed to become meaningless, an ever-present haze. The Earth slept. "All things continue as they were from the beginning of the creation" *2 Pet.3:4.* Evidences of the Spirit's active role seemed a thing of the forgotten past. Yet even when all seemed dead, the divine purposes were at work. The secret of the Lord was hidden "with them that fear him" *Ps.25:14.* At a point in time, the proper point in time, in the fullness of time, a seemingly dying world vitalized. The languid oceans became turbulent, charged with nutrients and oxygen. The interior of the Earth began to feel new forces and re-activated within itself. The atmosphere renewed its circulation, and new vapours were added to it. The waters "*brought forth abundantly the moving creature...*"

The purpose of the created world is life. In the fullness of time it will bring forth life, life such as has never been seen before. "*For the earth shall be filled with the knowledge of the glory of the Lord, as the waters cover the sea*" *Hab.2:14.*

Complex life was brought forth from waters. This is a testimony to the honour of him who is able to convert unstable, unformed raw materials into stability and functional complexity. The employment of waters in this enterprise at first may appear inappropriate. Firm flesh, rigid skeleton, and mechanical complexity are not features we immediately associate with fluidity. The scriptures inform us that just as plant life is based on modified mineral, (earth), complex animal life is based on modified fluid chemical substances; all complex life gives the appearance of *coming from water. "Let the* waters *bring forth abundantly the moving creature that hath life.* " All advanced life - all advanced life - gives a very clear sign of being brought forth from water. This is shown by the staged development in the womb.

For many years the world's institutions of higher education taught that an individual's growth reflected his ancient ancestry. This was because we go through a "fish" and an "amphibian" stage in the womb. This fish/amphibian (or aquatic) phase was pointed to as evidence of fish and amphibians in our distant ancestry. All the time these educators believed they were speaking of evolution, they were in reality attesting to the truth of *Genesis.* "*Let the waters bring forth . . . the moving creature . . .*" We certainly all begin our lives in water in the womb, and the meaning goes deeper than this. The full depth of the meaning of *Gen.1:20* is still in the process of being plumbed. Expect some surprises!

VII. THE ORIGIN OF SPECIES

We shall leave geology for the moment to investigate the theory of darwinistic, or common descent, evolution. And first it is necessary to understand the meaning of the term, “species”.

Are all human beings the same species? An Alsatian and a dachshund? A horse and a donkey? A mosquito and an elephant?

The species definition.

The term, “species”, comes from the same root as the word, “special”. In the minds of early biologists such as Linnaeus (1707 - 1778), it conveyed meanings such as, fundamental, specially created, self- contained. Others have tried to broaden this meaning to accommodate Darwinism. However, it is apparent that if one species could grade into another, species would not be species and biology would collapse into disorder.

This definition assumes prolonged observation out in the natural world, without any interference whatsoever by Man. Species are an *observed* phenomenon. **If any two organisms can together produce offspring, which in turn can produce offspring, which continue over time to produce offspring, then they are the same species**. Rephrasing:

Any pair of organisms that can reproduce viable offspring are the same species. This definition may also be taken to cover organisms that can reproduce asexually, if their offspring are automatically assumed to be the same species as the parent. If people wish to claim that asexual reproduction can lead to new species, then they must invent a definition to meet the circumstances!

(Of course, if people wish to prove common descent evolution, they can do so by saying they witnessed one species giving rise to another. This is easy to claim for organisms which have not yet been accurately classified into species. There was a time when people regularly proved that dust turned into lice, decayed beef turned into maggots, and grain even turned into mice. The microscope chased away the proof. The species definition above was not invented by the author of this book: it is the standard definition, employed by geologists and biologists the world over. If evolution is occurring today, then it will produce new species which meet the definition.)

Are all humans the same species? Alsatians and dachshunds? Horses and donkeys? Mosquitoes and elephants? Indeed, horses and donkeys can be crossed to produce mules, but a mule cannot reproduce offspring. Likewise, lions and tigers have been crossed in zoos, but they remain separate species.

If all that was available were the bones of a miniature poodle and of a wolfhound, and you had never seen either animal, or any living dogs at all, might you be forgiven for thinking that they were a different species? Might you doubt whether they could together produce offspring? And if you found the bones of a small horse beside those of a donkey, might you be forgiven for entertaining the thought that they could have been the same species? (And, even more confusing - what if you discovered the bones of a donkey, a mule, and a horse? Could you not be forgiven for imagining that here was a link between the donkey and the horse?)

This problem, known as the species problem, is very real. Unless the fossils can be brought back to life, there is no way of being certain whether the organisms could have reproduced together. Geologists admit to this difficulty, and even write books upon the subject.

Classification of fossils into species is to some extent an artificial classification. It must be. Of course, with some fossils there is sufficient difference in the skeleton or shell to leave no question - but between extinct organisms of similar structure, there is no certain way of telling which is one species and which is another.

Species Origin

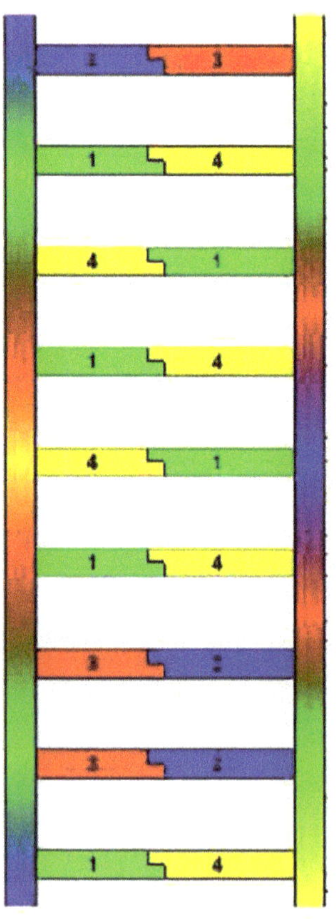

As the atom is the fundamental building block of matter, so the cell is the building block of every living thing. We all begin as one cell, and we grow through multiplication of this cell.

Essentially a cell is an interactive instruction code (DNA) surrounded by chemical substances that put the instructions into effect.

Conceptualised, flattened fragment of DNA

DNA is an acronym for Deoxyribonucleic Acid -- an information programmable molecule found within living cells. Its sophistication as an information store and transmitter, governing the biologic organism of which it is part, staggers belief. Each species has its own specially coded DNA.

In simplest terms it stores information utilizing a code based on 4 (a conventional computer uses a code based on 2).

Excluding mankind, the essential difference between every living organism, from the simplest to the most complex, is nothing more and nothing less than the information programmed into it. The information governs the form the organism will take as it grows -- whether it grows to be a mite or an elephant. Man's physical body is in a sense also a product of information. For instance, it seems likely that humans could function with the internal organs of other animals -- if only we could re-programme our automatic immune systems to "read" the foreign flesh as "human". In other words, by signalling the correct intelligence, one species could theoretically be changed to another -- but not immediately change in outward appearance -the visible change appearing in its offspring!

Update: Species origin has to do with information being transmitted to a living cell. The information devices of cells are now thought to be "quantum programmed." DNA is being researched for applications in this superior information technology. Should quantum information technology take the stage, the lesser actors will be sidelined. The strongest computer in existence today would be rendered obsolete by a fully operative quantum computer. There are compelling reasons to attribute quantum signalling capacities to the natural worlds.

How did new species arise?

The answer to this question must meet the following requirements:

- Explain adaptation of new species to environment
- Explain how new species can arise without being the genetic offspring of an old species

- Explain how species are functional units built from discrete packages of information (The platypus, for example, is obviously the outcome of a selective process acting on a finite number of discrete packages of information; those discrete packages of information being available to birds, mammals, and reptiles.)

What clues have we been given?

Although our understanding of matter, and of the information devices in living organisms, is limited, we do know that a very sophisticated information capability exists in every cell.

The purpose and function of some parts of the DNA molecule remain unknown. The mechanism of the autoimmune system is likewise dimly perceived. It is becoming less dimly perceived, and no awards are being handed out for deducing that it involves information operated "switches." When we come to the transfer of information between a cell and its external environment, DNA, which is a major player in information transmission, is no better understood than is the immune system. We do know that the two-way passage of information between the various components of an organism and its information command involves the movement of molecules whose properties and physical shape are central to the information transfer process.

Let us now visualize the living cell as a sophisticated information device in some ways analogous to a computer. Assume that there is a central control in this "computer," which in effect designates the "species" or "model" of the "computer." Assume that this "computer" has been designed to transform into a new "model" when the environment surrounding the "computer" requires it to do so. Assume there are regular power signals originating outside the "computer," which if read intelligently by the "computer" will enable its transformation into a new model.

As a species modifies in response to environmental conditions, the parts of its DNA that are coded with information relevant to those environmental conditions receive information feedback. A species, as we know, does change in response to its living conditions. Its DNA must therefore also change, not fundamentally, but superficially. Areas within the DNA coded with information relevant to the living conditions receive information in the form of various attendant molecules and other modifications. (This collection of information by species is central to a new discipline within genetics, called, epigenetics.) These superficial modifications to the DNA form a type of "transformation agents." Assume DNA has been designed so that, when all the transformation agents are in place, a suitable power signal from outside the "computer" will result in transformation. A new "model" or "species" arises. It is the product of:

- The design of living organisms so that environmental pressure causes DNA sites which need to be changed to be re-programmed through interaction with these sites of various molecules and chemical agents, which, when in place, act as transformation agents, only if:

- A signal or sequence of signals from outside the organism interacts with those molecules and with the DNA to effect fundamental and directed change. As we have learned previously, these empowering signals are a product of the Earth, sun, moon, and other celestial objects, and presumably the Earth's magnetic field and the sun's radiation (including as it does, radio, visible light, and so on), are implicated.

Because of our very incomplete understanding of matter, electricity, and chemistry, we cannot at this stage specify the exact events involved in remodelling DNA. When we hear of technicians using the molecules that exist within living cells as superior diodes, of the computer-like features of DNA, of the possibility of employing biology in information processing, suspicions are aroused. It should be possible to change chemical bonds and re-locate atoms within living organisms utilizing some sort of light/radio/electromagnetic trigger, provided the chemical setting is suitable and the molecule has been designed for it. Intuitively it is possible to design a computer so that its central information command will reprogram in response to information feedback from the environment around it, synchronized with a sequence of power signals from without.

How Did Life Itself Begin?

We have learned that information technology is foundational to living things. All life forms may be regarded as information acting on inert chemicals to form into a body, which is vivified - living. Vivification - the imparting of life - may have more to do with information technology than we would at first imagine. It goes without saying that creation of life, even the simplest plant, will never be achieved by man. Yet we go tantalizingly close to doing so, and a combination of recent discoveries and the Bible shows why.

If we read the first chapter of *Genesis*, we see water and earth as an integral part of the creation of all life. Water and earth are spoken to, and they bring forth the living creatures. Initially, we think of earth as contrasting with water - almost an opposite - which presumably is an aspect of the intended meaning. However, if a common meaning of earth is applied - clay or clay-like - water is by definition included. Water is commonly bound up in the molecular structure of clay and other minerals. Thus, water could be playing a part in both instances. The part it plays includes intelligence transfer.

"Water: It's the foundation of life on Earth."

"It now seems that the effects of water on living organisms transcend mere [classical] chemistry: they are intimately linked to the most basic processes in the cosmos. Put bluntly, you owe your existence to quantum effects in water . . . All the bonds affecting water molecules are ultimately caused by quantum effects, but hydrogen bonds are the result of one of the strangest quantum phenomena: so-called zero- point vibrations . . . Just take some water and swap the hydrogen for atoms of its heavier isotope deuterium.

You end up with a liquid that is chemically identical, yet poisonous to all but the most primitive organisms.

The only difference is in the zero-point energy . . . they are finding an astonishingly delicate interplay of proteins and water molecules, orchestrated by those all-important hydrogen bonds. Once struck by photons of light, the shape of the protein changed, breaking some of the hydrogen bonds This triggered a chain of events in which fragments of some water molecules . . . interacted to move protons through the protein. it is no accident that chains of amino acids trap water molecules as they fold up to form a protein. water molecules report the DNA sequence to the protein while it is still some distance away then as the protein gets closer, the water molecules are ejected from the site until it binds to the DNA... the water molecules relay messages to the protein they can even warn the approaching protein about potential problems with the DNA before it arrives "[7]

Was water perhaps in harmony with clay minerals, the medium through which the vivifying "spark" was passed to the cell? Was this "spark" analogous with or comparable to an enabling "message," a "message" at once powerful and intelligent, which set the "computer" and all the information devices going in the cell?

Again, the essential of the species is information. Ultimately it will be mathematically based information, and it gives visible outcomes.

Gen.1:20

And God said, "Let the waters bring forth abundantly the moving creature that hath life, and fowl that may fly above the earth in the open firmament of heaven. "

---

7 Robert Matthews, *New Scientist,* pages 32-36, 8 April 2006

If *Gen.1:20* was the only verse in the Bible, it would be sufficient of itself to silence all the gainsayers and reduce the whole world to awed silence before the great God.

All complex animal life came forth from the waters under a strong action translated *create* (v.*21*). Complex animal life includes land animals and birds. Land animals and birds all have a water-based genesis (as shown in the womb) and have an over-shadowing component of earth (they have earth- related flesh). Now, see in *Gen.1:20* a distinction. "Fowl that may fly" embraces any creature that may fly, and takes in insects, flying reptiles, bats, and birds in the strict sense. "Fowl that may fly" therefore takes in two major divisions of life: flying water (insects), and flying water-based but earth-modified (birds, bats, *etc*.). In fact, the scriptures qualify themselves by attesting that birds, bats and reptiles - "fowl of the air" - are indeed earth formed, (even though water-based). Compare *Gen.1:20* and *Gen.2:19.*

Our text is informing us that all complex animal life is water-based; those divisions that live on land are water-based but earth-over formed; and in the difficult case of the flying divisions, which both live mostly on land, one division is water-based only and the other division is water- based but earth-over formed. Give God the glory. To accommodate further this distinction between insects and birds etc., see another distinction. Insects - those watery "fowl that may fly" - in terms of timing of origin are primarily associated with the creatures of the seas and oceans, and pre-date the earthy-fleshed "fowl of the air." The "fowl of the air" - birds, bats and flying reptiles - are associated with the land animals, and post-date the insects. *Gen.1:20* accommodates these two associations. An equal concurrent alternative in the original language gives the phrase "and fowl that may fly" the exchangeable meaning, "let fowl fly." This exchange phrase gives the whole verse two equal meanings: it becomes two verses.

One: "And God said, 'Let the waters bring forth abundantly the moving creature that hath life, and fowl that may fly above the earth in the open firmament of heaven.'" This verse refers especially to insects.

Two: "And God said, Let the waters bring forth abundantly the moving creature that hath life, and let fowl fly above the earth in the open firmament of heaven." Referring especially to birds, bats, and flying reptiles, which by inference from *Genesis 2:19,* "And out of the ground the Lord God formed every beast of the field, and every fowl of the air" were associated with the land animals.

Thus the scriptures cover in a few words that for which man requires a small textbook, and does not lead the reader down unwanted side- tracks. The insects were created directly with a waterbased origin on the fifth day. The birds, bats, and flying reptiles were likewise created on the fifth day, but awaited modification involving an earthy component and were not manifest until the sixth day.

How can creatures be "created" on the fifth day, and be "formed out of the ground" on the sixth day? In a way analogous to the manufacture of "every plant of the field before it was in the earth, and every herb of the field before it grew" *Gen.2:5.* The processes were necessarily more complex and sophisticated for animals, but the precedent had been set with the plants, and simply carried over to the higher forms. Genetic codes or "blueprints" were made/created, stored, and automatically signalled to living cells on the Earth at pre-arranged times. Some modification to an existing print or pattern led to the land animals being created with a watery origin, and over formed "out of the ground." This is precisely the nature of complex animal life. It is essentially water-based, but land creatures have modifications fitting them for their terrestrial habitat. They are all made on variations to a common code. Man is also made in this way, but the variations in the common code in his case are so extreme as to invoke the use of that strong word, *create,* signifying a life-division in its own right.

The greatest unsolved difficulty with code-signalling lies with the events surrounding transformation of living material from an older species into the new, genetically perfect individuals of a new species. The signalling we can visualize, for cells are made for the purpose of sending and receiving signals, and nature abounds in extrasensory signals. What happens at the moment the new gene-code is projected into a cell? The cell then becomes the cell of a foreign species, and so is automatically attacked by the immune system of the host animal. Does another set of signals give the foreign cell the status of a native or natural cell? Does an animal transform safely and naturally under the influence of such masking signals? Does an individual of an old species fall asleep and arise as the genetically complete father/mother of a new?

"The idea of teleportation was once considered impossible. Yet today physicists regularly teleport single photons over distances of 600 metres, and can also teleport whole caesium and beryllium atoms. More precisely, they can teleport the quantum information contained within a photon or atom onto a distant photon or atom. Within a decade, the first molecule may be teleported in this way, and within a few decades researchers could teleport more complex organic molecules and perhaps even the first virus or strand of DNA. To achieve this, physicists exploit an exotic property called quantum entanglement. If two particles are brought together in such a way that their quantum wave functions vibrate in unison, then they form a bond like an invisible umbilical cord that connects them even if they are separated by vast distances. If you later disturb one particle, then the information you impart onto it is transmitted instantaneously to its partner -- so the entangled partner forms a ready-and-waiting template for whatever information is to be teleported."[8]

---

[8] Kaku, M., *New Scientist*, pages 36-37, 15 April 2008

Are there any large scale quantum effects in nature that might be candidates for interaction with DNA and other programmable molecules inside living organisms?

Can pursuit of this question lead us towards the mechanism of species transformations?

Adam was only one, and by a process analogous to anaesthesia and tissue culture, God took the female component of him and "builded Woman." He was then able to reproduce, and such was his genetic complexity that he is to be looked upon as effectively all peoples and all nations of all time. All the internal organs of similar species could theoretically be interchanged, if the hosts would accept them. Is this the procedure divine ingenuity employed? Masking of an individual's immune detection system whilst it was transformed to a new species? In this way there is no break in the continuum of life, and no need to decide whether the egg came first, or the chicken. The chicken already existed, and life was passed to it via a dinosaur. The dinosaur's life was passed to it via simpler forms, and the simpler form's life was breathed into it by the Spirit and sustained by the Spirit.

Each and every species was realized on Earth, or manifested, as a direct product of the Word of God, as a direct creation of God, according to a pre-determined plan and purpose. As the scriptures show, this was through a process of gene-code storage and pre-arranged signalling. Individuals of new species arose instantaneously and in genetic fullness. Hence, all complex life was created on the fifth day, the aquatic and insect components were manifested on the fifth day and during the day following, and the land-animals and birds were modified and then revealed on the sixth day. All are water related, and land animals are earth-modified. This is the testimony of the Bible.

Unconformity

The interface between the oldest 'basement' rocks (the Pre-Cambrian) and those strata overlying these older rocks (the lowermost of these being the Cambrian). This is the only feature of the geologic column easily recognizable world-wide as a product of a single event. Radiometric dating suggests 540-550 million years past as the time of this pivotal change. Life exploded dramatically at this point in time, as did the rate at which continents moved and rock accumulated. It is the sudden change in the nature of rock strata and in their fossil content that make this a universally recognizable feature of the earth. An unconformity in the sense of a discrepancy between the angles of tilt of the strata does not always occur.

This is precisely as we may read in the rocks. That remarkable pattern, the shadow of the tree of life, expands its way upward from the Pre-Cambrian/Cambrian Unconformity, one of its branches yielding plant life in increasing sophistication, and the others bearing increasingly complex aquatic, insect, and then land-dwelling organisms. The species appear abruptly, without any forewarning or evolutionary transition. Nowhere is this better illustrated than at the Unconformity itself, where fossils of a kaleidoscope of diverse phyla appear to materialize as though from the revitalized *waters* themselves. Despite this apparent materialization from sterile matter - whether water or earth - a continuum can nevertheless be traced, as though life was passed on from one life form to another. This pattern, or shadow, fits perfectly the function of that biblical translator, the tree of life, and fits in turn the growth-sequence of trees, which pass life through their branches so that already-existing life can bud and shoot forth in profusion at pre- arranged signals.

As for the Darwinistic evolutionary hypothesis: David once called himself a *dead dog* and a *flea* (*1 Sam.24:14*), and this may be the nearest to reputable backing the theory will ever receive. When we hear of "the fig tree bearing olives or a grapevine, figs" *Jam.3:12,* we may pay attention to such imaginations.

Gen.1:21, 22

And God created great whales, and every living creature that moveth, which the waters brought forth abundantly, after their kind, and every winged fowl after his kind: and God saw that it was good. And God blessed them, saying, "Be fruitful, and multiply, and fill the waters in the seas, and let fowl multiply in the earth."

Here we have the creation (without pre-existing pattern) of all complex life, with special reference to the great whales as signal evidences of creative genius. No sooner was advanced life created than the aquatic arm began to manifest, as the fossils show, in teeming abundance in both number and variety. The other watery (but only partly aquatic) arm manifested on the fifth day - the insects - is not neglected, for the multiplication of fowl is noted in v.*22*. That special notice should be made of the lowly insects may seem unusual, until we study both the fossil record and the world around us. Insects easily outweigh by mass all other land-dwelling life, and are much older and more prolific than any other flying organisms.

Note the use of *let:* "let fowl multiply." An ongoing process not restricted to the fifth day.

Gen.1:23

And the evening and the morning were the fifth day.

The creation of life without existing blueprint or pattern coupled with manifestation of the seacreatures and first winged organisms make the fifth day an illustrious achievement. We see many living species; the fossil record tells of thousands more of which we know almost nothing. The fifth day witnessed the *debut* of advanced aquatic life, and takes in events from the time of the moon's introduction through to the land animals, a mere few hundred million years of time, but a veritable eon in terms of illustrious achievement.

Gen.1:24-27

And God said, "Let the earth bring forth the living creature after his kind, cattle, and creeping thing, and beast of the earth after his kind": and it was so. And God made the beast of the earth after his kind, and cattle after their kind, and every thing that creepeth upon the earth after his kind: and God saw that it was good. And God said, Let us make man in our image, after our likeness: and let them have dominion over the fish of the sea, and over the fowl of the air, and over the cattle, and over all the earth, and over every creeping thing that creepeth upon the earth. So God created man in his own image, in the image of God created he him; male and female created he them.

Biologists find the task of drawing a precise dividing-line between simple plant life and simple animal life impossible; and so it is with water-dwelling and land-dwelling forms. Some bacteria are half-plant, half animal; the amphibians and some insects likewise have one foot in one category and one in another. These technical sticking points are more than adequately covered by the scriptures; simple species by implication are lumped with the plants under the action-word *made,* whilst all life forms higher than these fall within the gambit of the action word *created.* The only life form to be *created,* (in the strict sense of the word) on Day Six was man. The lesser creatures were all *created* on Day Five, and those destined to go on *terra firma* were made of earth, or over-formed of earth, on Day Six. Discern the extreme technical detail of word usage in *Genesis.*

Animals with life cycles in water and on land are covered by the biblical account, being children of both Days Five and Six. See how creatures of all different sizes, gaits, and habitats are included: "cattle (larger, moving as sheep or ox) creeping thing (smaller, moving slowly or low to the ground) and beast of the earth (not covered by the former two; especially cat and dog, and similar animals)." Precisely which of the "creeping things" first appeared on Day Five and which on Day Six, is the study of a lifetime, and whilst sidestepped by the scriptures, is accurately covered by the terms employed. The template was made on Day Five, created by a novel, unprecedented act of genius. The basic template was merely altered superficially on Day Six: formed (meaning formed-over), made of earth, of what had already been created of water. A touch-alteration of an existing masterpiece.

As the shadow of the tree of life in the rock-strata shows, all land- animals derive from the same group of branches as underwater life. (They do not derive from underwater life, but from the same branches as underwater life: and the branches are *a process, a translator, a realiser of supernatural realities.*) The scriptures and the strata speak the same language, the language of a template. A template of all advanced life created without pre-existing pattern on the fifth day: manifestation or realization of this life over time: major modification enabling manifestation of land-creatures on Day Six. Insects created on Day Five and not subsequently over-formed of earth; earthy flying creatures likewise were created on this day but subsequently earth-modified and revealed on Day Six.

All these events analogous to a tree, in which existing but hidden growth-patterns are revealed over time, and older growth supports and aids new growth, but does not produce it. The new growth comes from a hidden source within the tree itself, and ultimately from a "mother- source" beyond the tree, which is tapped and translated by the tree. Life is passed along the branch (that is, via existing species) but is not a product of the branch. The new growth breaks out in response to timing and signals.

The rock-shadow of this tree is uncannily similar to a natural tree. Some branches truncate and die, but in general they progress smoothly upward into dense foliage. One branch reaches a little above all the others, and has on it a strange and remarkable flower, or product. (The tree bears different products on different branches, although all its fruits are *health* and *life.)* This branch - or should we say this shadow of a branch - grew taller than all the others, and yielded one fruit only. Not only was the branch taller, and its flowering unique, something was grafted into or added to the flower at its inception, so that the life form produced was a product of an earthly tree and a heavenly, an eternal, insert. As though the tree was drawing life from the throne of God, and one branch reached as high as the throne of God, and *a divine connection,* or *a divine aspect* was imparted to its highest tip. Its highest flower was *created in the image of God.*

Note; it was *created.* This was the great accomplishment of the sixth day. Created without peer, without precedent, without parallel in the natural worlds. An animal, yet an octave higher than the highest of the animals, as animals themselves are higher than the plants. The first man - spoken of as "them," for he is to be thought of as all peoples, nations, and tongues, which in reality he was - this first man was a force to be reckoned with. He - that is, they - was/were the uncontested crown of the animal world, and so high above it to be the king of it. His height and physique we can only imagine; his genetic totality meant he had no mutated or damaged genetic material in his body, which was so complete part of it could safely be removed to make the female, and the same could likewise have been done to their children to give them marriage partners.

No animal on earth could but obey him, and no condition on earth could occasion him (them) pain or sorrow. Having complete purity, he spoke with God face-to-face, and being made in the image of his eternal Creator, he could not age, sicken, or die. Happy man! Happy world, with an overseer and a husbandman of this calibre at the helm! The crowning glory of the created worlds, the god (at that time) of this world, capable of bringing all natural things to unity and perfection, entrusted with the happy and joyous task of spreading paradise worldwide. This was the first man as the world first saw him, and did him homage.

Man's Physical Makeup

Was man's physical life passed on to him via lower animals? Did his physical body - as distinct from his ability to commune and converse with the supernatural - come via the animals, as the Tree of Life mode of origins suggests? Did the Master Hand take a fragment or a cell from a lower creature, change its code, and nurture it to "form man of the dust of the ground" (*Gen.2:7*)? Our physical makeup suggests as much, for our physical bodies are made up of cells which function in the same way as the cells of animals. If the Creator did utilize pre-existing materials in our genesis, this in no way detracts from the achievement. The question is of small consequence. Whether a living cell from another animal was used, or an existing blueprint was amended, and our bodies were begun from innate materials: we were *created.* This is deeply significant. We were created. A basic division must exist between the bodies of animals and the body of the highest animal. This physical division has not yet been discerned.

The mystery of heredity - the transmission from parents to offspring of inherited features - was first solved by a semi-amateur, Mendel (1822-1884). He solved the mystery by applying simple mathematics (demonstrated by his famous pea breeding experiments). This inevitably led to the conclusion that mathematical codes - information technology - are somehow involved in heredity. Mathematically coded information must be involved. Mendel assumed species to be special, and the principles of heredity demanded that species are, as Mendel assumed, special, reproductive, "islands unto themselves" - they reproduce only after their kind. The codes would become hazy and diluted if species could grade into each other.

Though many are suggesting that the human body is amenable to the same genetic manipulation as lower life, the language of *Genesis* points to some hidden difference. The human body will be found to be significantly less amenable to manipulation than many currently envisage. Add to this hidden cellular difference an integrated intellect/ personality or soul, and a spirit with *divine potential,* and man is a unique being indeed. His life is in some basic way different to the life of animals. All animals breathe, but of man it is specifically said, "*God . . . breathed into his nostrils the breath of life*" *Gen.2:7,* as though his life is in some way special. As for the presence within man of an essential being or spirit: when we hear of animals holding religious meetings, and find them thinking on matters of eternal destiny and higher existence, then we will know there is no difference between us all, and "*the hidden man of the heart,*" the spirit within man, does not exist.

Man contacts the supernatural via his spirit. The voice of conscience is often acting as a contact with our spirit. The hidden source of discernment, the voice of inner guidance, the ability to rise above circumstances to great heights or conversely to fall to abysmal depths - these are evidences of a spirit within us. This hidden "inner man" makes man unique in the physical worlds. It is a sign of divine potential, of creation "in the image of God." It sets man apart from the lesser creation. Yet even his body will be proved to be unique. Common logic combined with the Bible tells us he will never be able to reproduce himself other than by the sexual reproduction method. Whether or not technology has a hand in it, the conception of every child will always be such that a father and mother exist somewhere, with the moral obligation to love and care for the child. This has always been and always will be.

By a similar extension of logic, God would not put into man's hands the ability to inadvertently destroy himself. Lust, anger, greed - these are the things that destroy man and his world. Technology itself is morally neutral. We have nothing to fear from the technologies which led to genetic engineering and cloning, consumption of fossil fuels, industrial chemicals, nuclear energy, and such like. Man was created, and created in the image of God. Cloning techniques have yet to prove successful with the bulk of animals, leave alone an animal that was created as a separate division of life with inbuilt divine potential. Man will never reproduce divine potential except in the way appointed to him - sexual reproduction.

He has been susceptible to abusing this method, ever since Adam opened the door to evil. Nothing is new in that regard. The technology of genetic engineering, and indeed all technology, will be found to be morally neutral. Since reproduction of children without a natural mother and father is not morally neutral, here is yet more proof of its impossibility. And so with other technologies which have been causes of concern.

The intelligent use of resources around us is not destined to lead to our inadvertent destruction. These resources were placed here for a reason. The intention is intelligent, responsible use of them. They will be sufficient for their purpose. Intelligent Providence did not place tools and resources in our hands to destroy our future or ourselves by their use. Technology and use of nature is not wrong of itself. Man has become wrong of himself, and instead of bringing paradise to the world has brought ruin. We need fear nothing from technology, or from scientific advance. We should fear everything from self, from pride, from lust, from blind ignorance. The first man inhabited paradise, and was a paradise. The paradise he inhabited is here no more. It cannot return. There is a higher Paradise, a state where once again self, and lust, and sorrow are foreign; this Paradise is to be looked for elsewhere, although a foretaste of it can be experienced in this dimension - not through abandoning technology, and trying to return to paradise on this earth, but by returning to our first ancestors' pure fellowship with purity, personified. We should look forward, and look higher, and not look back.

We were created to have dominion on the earth, and to utilize it. We cannot annul this, nor return to primary innocence, nor return to Eden.

Gen. 1:28-31

And God blessed them, and God said unto them, "Be fruitful, and multiply, and replenish the earth, and subdue it: and have dominion over the fish of the sea, and over the fowl of the air, and over every living thing that moveth upon the earth." And God said, Behold, I have given you every herb bearing seed, which is upon the face of all the earth, and every tree, in the which is the fruit of a tree yielding seed; to you it shall be for meat. And to every beast of the earth, and to every fowl of the air, and to everything that creepeth upon the earth, wherein there is life, I have given every green herb for meat: and it was so. And God saw everything that he had made, and, behold, it was very good. And the evening and the morning were the sixth day.

Geologists inform us the sixth day was one of the least in terms of time of all the days of creative activity. Notwithstanding its comparative brevity, its import far outweighs all the preceding creative acts. Observe that v.*28* begins with a blessing: "And God blessed them [Adam: man]." God is on our side. Every human being has been personally blessed by the God who is love. The Almighty takes no more (indeed, far less) joy in seeing his children fail, than a human father takes joy in seeing his offspring fail. "*Have I any pleasure at all that the wicked should die? Saith the Lord God: and not that he should return from his ways, and live?" Ez.18:23. "For I have no pleasure in the death of him that dieth, saith the Lord God: wherefore turn yourselves, and live ye." Ez.18:32.*

When God blessed, he blessed *"them"* (v.*28*) - - all peoples, every person who has or will ever live. Adam was in reality all peoples, so much so that "he" is termed "them," even though at the outset even his wife, Eve, had not been separated from his body. Adam was one individual, whilst he was all peoples. And so, all peoples were blessed by the God who is love and who is the perfect father. They were instructed to "be fruitful, and multiply, and replenish [complete, consummate] the earth."

Up to this point the Earth and the creatures within it had been described as "very good" (v.*31*) . If mankind had fulfilled his initial calling instead of exercising his inherent free will wrongly, the Earth may have soon advanced from "very good" to "better yet," and from "better yet" to *consummate* and *complete* (replenished). We know from *Romans 8:20* that "the creature [creation] was made subject to vanity [seeming empty pointlessness], not willingly [not of its own choosing], but by reason of Him [God] who hath subjected the same in hope [in the end, something better will come of it]." One instance of this "vanity," or seeming futility to which the universe is subject, is the principle of ever-increasing randomness or decay. Another is the death of animals.

From our text, it appears that at least one of these "vanities" was meant to be addressed by Adam. The wording is not definitive, but *Genesis 1:29&30* seems to imply that the paradise into which Adam was placed and which he was intended to extend all over the earth did not involve the death of animals for food or their use for menial tasks. Both man and the animals are pointed toward plants rather than flesh for food (meat). "*I have given you . . . and every beast of the earth . . . every green herb . . . the fruit of a tree . . . for meat [food]*" *Gen.1:29, 30.* By no means should this be taken as a pointer toward virtue in vegetarianism or as a discouragement of the utilization of animals of every type in scientific experiment and technology. The Almighty packed the earth with carcasses, for our benefit. (Our vehicles are powered by some of them, and we build with others.)

The death of an animal is of no eternal consequence - a mere "vanity." The entire and total reason for existence of plants and animals is as an aid to man. Their death has no higher significance. Nevertheless, "the lion shall eat straw like the ox," and "the wolf shall dwell with the lamb" *Isa.11:6, 7.* In some way, peace in the animal kingdom was linked to paradise on earth. Man, a creative being like his Maker, must needs have some sphere of activity, of ownership, of oversight, an outlet for his energies and talents: the earth was his to oversee, to improve, to re-create, to complete: and care of the animals, birds, fish and all living creatures fell to him. He was then quite adequate to the task. "*And God blessed them . . . and . . . everything that was made . . . was very good.*"

Gen.2:1-3

Thus the heavens and the earth were finished, and all the host of them. And on the seventh day God ended his work which he had made; and he rested on the seventh day from all his work which he had made. And God blessed the seventh day, and sanctified it: because that in it he had rested from all his work which God created and made.

"Thus the heavens and the earth were finished, and all the host of them" Gen.2:1. In six days God brought into being all material objects, or the raw materials of which they were to be formed. So multiple, so diverse were the products of this activity, they are termed a host (v.*1*). This multiplied diversity, this *host,* was brought into being through a diversity of operations and processes. Some things, as we know, were *created* - created *ex nihilo,* out of nothing, and created *ex nihilo* coming from no existing blueprint, pattern, or precedent. Others were *made, made* or *formed* of already created materials, modified from existing patterns, improved, advanced, revised to suit new requirements. Some the earth brought forth, others were of a watery base, and yet others were a combination of both.

A *host* of variety was brought into existence through multiple operations and processes. So it says, *"God . . . rested from all his work which he created and made [equally: created to make]" Gen.2:3.* God created and made: he *created to make* - created the matter, or created the base, from which he subsequently made or formed the final product. Multiple, diverse processes, leading to multiple, diverse products. A variety of processes and events leading to a variety of products. Integrated creative activity over time!

But now, with the close of the sixth day, the final creative module or evening, the task is finished. "Thus the heavens and the earth were finished, and all the host of them." From this point in time no new matter and no new species were required to make the worlds complete.

The Seventh Day Rest

"*And on the seventh day God ended his work which he had made; and he rested on the seventh day from all his work which he had made*" *Gen.2:2*. On the six days, God worked. On the seventh, "*He rested.*"

Since we know that "*the Creator of the ends of the earth fainteth not, neither is weary*" *Isa.40:28,* and "*He that keepeth Israel shall neither slumber nor sleep*" *Ps.121:4,* then how can God rest? If one cannot grow weary, how is rest possible?

The Creator rested and found sweet refreshment in the company of his creation, especially in humankind. For humanity was initially without fault and without blemish, and spoke with his Creator face-to-face as man to man. As the apostle Paul says of his friend Philemon; "Yea, brother, let me have joy of thee in the Lord: refresh my bowels [inner affections/ feelings] in the Lord" *Philem. 20.* In the spiritual dimension there is no sleep, but there is rest and refreshment in the communion of kindred spirits. This communion, this fellowship, was the seventh day rest. The Creator fellowshipped with his creation.

Compare and contrast the six days of work with the seventh day.

Modules of creative achievement defined each of the six days. "The evening and the morning [of work] were the day."

The seventh day did not consist of any such time-measurable modules. So the seventh day was timeless.

It was, it *is,* eternity.

There is no reference to evening, morning, or any time-related framework. Rather, the seventh day is introduced as though having no pedigree or origin in time - pre-existent, eternal, beyond definition. As such it speaks as of one who was a type of Christ in his priestly office: "Without [earthly] father, without mother, without descent, having neither beginning of days, nor end of life; but made like unto the Son of God; abideth . . . continually" *Heb.7:3.* Like the one who was a figure or type of Christ, the seventh day is without earthly pedigree, outside earthly time, beyond physical definition. The seventh day is Jesus Christ, "The Lord of the Sabbath, the Lord . . . Sabaoth" *Mark 2:28; Jam.5:4.*

We have to do with eternity.

The six days are work successfully completed.

The seventh day is the eternal celebration of that success. The six days are the achievement.

The seventh day is the celebration of that achievement.

The six days are the winning of the victory. The seventh day is celebration of the victory.

The six days occur in time.

The seventh day is timeless: it completes, consummates, and encapsulates the six. In fact the seventh day "swallows up" the six in victory: the victory of the resurrected Christ and all those who are "more than conquerors" in Him. For the day of resurrection is an extension of the seventh day into the eighth, the first day of the week, swallowing up all in victory; and Jesus Christ becomes all in all. "In the end of the Sabbath, as it began to dawn toward the first day of the week . . . the angel of the Lord descended from heaven, and came and rolled back the stone . . . and sat upon it. His countenance was like lightning . . . and for fear of him the keepers [soldiers] did shake, and became as dead men. And the angel answered and said unto the women, Fear not ye: for I know that ye seek Jesus, which was crucified. He is not here: for His is risen, as he said" *Matt.28:1-6.*

He is risen with power on the first day of the week and that power is available to be used on the days of the week, which in effect are all now graced with the victory of the seventh day. "For the law of the Spirit of life in Christ Jesus hath made me free from the law of sin and death. For what the law could not do, in that it was weak through the flesh, God sending his own Son in the likeness of sinful flesh, and for sin, condemned sin in the flesh: that the righteousness of the law might be fulfilled in us, who walk not after the flesh, but after the Spirit . . ." *Ro.8:2- 4.*

The six days are the works of God in the lives of his people - graced with resurrection power. "But if the Spirit of him that raised up Jesus from the dead dwell in you, he that raised up Christ from the dead shall also quicken your mortal bodies by his Spirit that dwelleth in you" *Ro.8:11.* The six days are the salvation of God; the seventh is the everlasting fruit and reward of salvation, witnessed by a new heaven and a new earth. *Ro.8:30:* "Moreover, whom he did predestinate, them he also called [as Christ called his disciples]: and whom he called, them he also justified [made just in the eyes of absolute Justice]: and whom he justified, them he also glorified [gave supernatural glory to]."

"What shall we say to these things? If God be for us, who can be against us?" *Ro.8:31.* "Nay, in all these things we are more than conquerors through him that loved us" *Ro.8:37.* "Be not deceived: neither fornicators, nor idolators, nor adulterers, nor effeminate, nor abusers of themselves with mankind, nor thieves, nor covetous, nor drunkards, nor revilers, nor extortioners, shall inherit the kingdom of God. And such were some of you: but ye are washed, but ye are sanctified [made *sanct* or set apart], but ye are justified in the name of the Lord Jesus, and by the Spirit of our God" *1 Co.6:9-11.* The six days are forerunners or types of the Day of Grace: the era of salvation. The seventh is the eternal enjoyment of salvation in its fullness - a perfect, complete new world. Complete victory! Victory in the face of every obstacle!

The seventh day is the *blowing of the silver trumpets of redemption* (*Num.10:7-10; Lev.25:8-10,* etc.). These trumpets are the money with which each adult is bought back from death, an equal sum for each individual *Ex.30:11-16.*

The seventh day is *shouting Lev.9:24; Josh.6:1-5; Ezra 3:10, 11; Mark 11:8-10.*

The seventh day is *music;* more than music, a *symphony;* a symphony such as this world cannot make *2 Chron.5:12-14; Ezra 3:10, 11; Rev.14:2,* etc. "Praise him," it exhorts, "with the sound of the trumpet." Again, "praise him with the psaltery and harp." Not the psaltery and harp alone, but, "praise him with the timbrel and dance." The timbrel and dance, moreover, "praise him with stringed instruments and organs." More than stringed instruments and organs "praise him upon the loud cymbals." Over and above loud cymbals, "praise him upon the high sounding cymbals." *Ps. 150* Yes, "let everything that hath breath praise the Lord." Everything and every person. He is worthy.

The seventh day is *dancing - 2 Sam.6:14,15; Ps.150:4; Luke 15:25.*

The seventh day is *strong drink,* but not the strong drink of this world *Num.28:7; Deut.14:26; Eph.5:18.*

The seventh day is the inescapable *commandment of joy for the people of God Deut.12:18; 14:26; 26:11.* The extinction of all regrets.

The seventh day is *the tabernacle of God with men. Rev.21:3, 4.* The Tabernacle standing upon silver redemption *Ex.38:27,* its cunning workmanship of blue, scarlet, and purple on fine linen *Ex.26:31.*

The fine linen speaks of Christ's flesh: the blue is his divinity; the scarlet, his humanity; the purple, being a blending of blue and scarlet, speaks of his accessibility; whilst his eternal, matchlessly superlative nature is a thread of pure metallic gold, woven throughout.

The seventh day is Christ in multiple splendour. "Thou art fairer than the children of men: grace is poured into thy lips: therefore God hath blessed thee forever." *Ps.45:2.* "He shall spare the poor and needy, and shall save the souls of the needy. He shall redeem their soul from deceit and violence; and precious shall their blood be in his sight. And he shall live, and to him shall be given of the gold of Sheba . . ." *Ps.72:13-15.*

The seventh day is the *sound of multiple golden bells* and *the fragrance of aromatic ointment* heralding acceptance of the sacrifice *Ex.28:33- 35; Ex.30:22-32.* It is "the precious ointment upon the head, that ran down upon the beard, even Aaron's beard: that went down to the skirts of his garments . . ." *Ps.133.*

The seventh day is the awarding of wreaths, crowns, diadems, exquisite jewellery, exalted offices. *Dan.12:2, 3; Ro.2:1-16; 2 Tim.4:7, 8; Rev.2:7, 11, 17, 26* etc.

The seventh day is *the family gathered about the table, and none missing. Luke 13:28, 29; 16:22, 23; Matt.8:11.*

The seventh day is the eternal marriage banquet of the Lamb. The six days are preparation for the banquet. Then, the beginning becomes the ending, the six days become the seventh, death is swallowed up in victory, and Jesus Christ is all in all.

VIII. "THE GREAT I AM"

Gen.2:4

These are the generations of the heavens and of the earth when they were created, in the day that the Lord God made the earth and the heavens . . .

Amidst the multiple facets of *Genesis 2:4&5,* one shines illustriously. A glance at the Bible reveals that the narrative up to *Gen.2:4* employs only the word *God* in naming The Great I AM. At *Gen.2:4* there is a pivotal change. The Creator will from now onward be known by a higher name, a fuller name, a more illustrious name. A name that speaks salvation and victory to those who believe; confusion and defeat to the rebellious; and terror to the Devil. A name above all names. *The* name above all names. *Jesus Christ is Lord.* The *Lord God* (*Gen.2:4*). A cosmic principle, the cosmic principle, the paramount *fact:* Jesus Christ is Lord.

The God who created all things, the God of creation, is also the Lord of all things created. There is not one iota, one speck of Creation, outside his power, outside his authority, outside his powers of intervention. Not only is he God, "he is Lord of all" *Acts 10:36:* and as such, nothing is outside or beyond his powers. He is Lord - Lord in its fullest meaning. . . . "A sparrow shall not fall on the ground without your Father. The very hairs of your head are all numbered." *Matt.10:29, 30.* "Fear ye not therefore . . ." *Matt.10:31.* Jesus Christ is Lord, Lord in the complete meaning of that term, the only one who is Lord in the completeness of that term. Nothing escapes him. Nothing defeats him.

He is absolute ruler, now. The devils tremble. The powers of darkness are shaken, and give way.

The unbelieving and the religiously blinded do not understand. But to those who believe, who "have received the Spirit of adoption, whereby we cry, 'Abba - Father!'" To these, this is their sword, their shield, their rock of defence, their strong tower, their joy, their assurance, their victory. Jesus Christ is Lord! Know this in truth, in the heart, and know victory. Are we surrounded by sin, and susceptible to it? Jesus Christ is Lord, and has the power over it if we look to him by faith. Are we the target of poverty or sickness? Jesus Christ is Lord in that circumstance. Are our outward circumstances contrary to us? Has difficulty locked us in? Jesus Christ is Lord! Trust his words.

"Yea, though I walk through the valley of the shadow of death, I will fear no evil: for thou art with me . . ." *Ps.23:4.* I may not feel you with me: but I know you to be Lord, Lord without question, without equal, Master victorious over all the powers of sin and darkness. Nothing can happen but what you permit: and if you permit it, it is done in perfect love, and together we can meet it.

To know Jesus Christ as Lord is "to withstand in the evil day, and having done all, to stand" *Eph.5:13.* It is the "hope we have as an anchor of the soul, both sure and steadfast . . ." *Heb.6:19.* It led David in the midst of apparent disasters to proclaim, "My heart is fixed; I will sing and give praise . . . I will praise thee, 0 Lord, among the people . . ." *Ps.108:1, 3.* It led Job, ruined, his children all killed as though by the hand of God himself, dying in misery, to assert, "though he slay me, yet will I trust him." *Job 13:15,* and furthermore to testify, "I know that my redeemer liveth, and that he shall stand at the latter day upon the earth." *Job 19:25.*

Perhaps no better illustration of it is found than in the criminal crucified beside Christ. Beside him he saw a man totally destitute, so marred by the sins and diseases of the whole world as to be unrecognizable, yet this man he addressed as both Lord and God, and made him the King of all (*Luke 23:39-43*). Which all goes to prove that the lordship of Christ is first and foremost spiritually discerned; even though it has physical outworkings and will one day become a physically obvious fact, it is now something which is made real to us by the Spirit of God. Divine love reveals it to us.

The reason why the world around us - and indeed, we, ourselves - are not perfect, despite the total overlordship of God, springs from delegation of authority. Just as a parent/guardian may delegate some powers to a child whilst retaining ultimate control, so Man was delegated certain powers, although God remained "the Lord God." Just as a child, given certain powers, may perhaps abuse them to his own hurt, so man abused his freedoms to his own hurt, In man's case, this led to the setting up of lesser "lords" and lesser "gods," who have some power with those who worship them, but ultimately will be overthrown and shown to be altogether false by the Lord of Lords, when he consummates this Age.

The believer knows "that an idol is nothing in the world [it no longer has power over him], and that there is none other God but one. For though there be those that are called gods, whether in heaven or in earth - as there be gods many, and lords many - but to us there is but one God . . . and one Lord Jesus Christ, by whom are all things, and we by him." *1 Co.8:4-6.* Jesus Christ is Lord! He has created all things, and he is "the Lord God." *Gen.2:4.*

In terms of ultimate authority (and authority is a state of being, not a feeling), "his name, through faith in his name, hath made this man strong . . ."*Acts 3:16.* Through faith, the name of the Lord is as if Jesus were present in person.

An additional, technical aspect to the change from *God* to *Lord God* may be deduced. Since, from the beginning of *Gen.2:4,* God is now the Lord

God, the Lord of all, it follows that all has now been created. Everything now exists. Nothing new of a physical nature remains to be created. It follows from this name change that the step-by-step account of creation is now complete. That which follows *Gen.2:4* can only be a commentary, an expansion, a deeper revelation of that which has already been done up to this point. The methods employed by the Creator will now be elucidated. The purpose and deeper meaning of his works will now be brought to light. *Gen.2:4&5* itself is a multi-faceted gem of enlightenment in this regard, a textbook, telescoped into a handful of words. It shows us the methods the Creator employed, and opens the door to a scientific understanding of the preceding narrative.

Gen.2:4, 5

These are the generations of the heavens and of the earth when they were created, in the day that the Lord God made the earth and the heavens, and every plant of the field before it was in the earth, and every herb of the field before it grew: for the Lord God had not caused it to rain upon the earth, and there was not a man to till the ground.

This marathon sentence means exactly what it says. It is an awe- inspiring dissertation of hard, down-to-earth fact. This compact, complex statement is the key that turns the lock. It is the horse on which the scientifically factual side of the creation account rides. It is the pith, and the essence, the principle, by which creation can be explained rationally.

The meaning of this sentence runs deep. First, it is clearly and obviously asserting that all vegetation was made before it obviously grew in the earth. The *pre-existence of all plant species.* The species were made and created in a definite order, but they were manifested on Earth at the time when they were needed! They were manifested to suit a purpose. The timing of their manifestation receives little attention from the Bible, being left to man to discover from fossils.

How does our text inform us of *manifestation to suit a purpose?* By asserting that, although they had already been made, the plants did not grow and were not in the earth, partly because there was as yet no rain to water them and no man to till the ground.

Although not obvious at first glance, the text goes deeper than asserting pre-existence of vegetation. It implies *pre-existence of all species.* It is properly understood along the lines of: "This is the nub of the matter of the 'comings into beings' of the stars, the sun, the Earth, space, the landscape, plants, animals, man, everything. 'Comings into beings.' not 'coming into being' - many different 'comings,' many different 'beings.' 'These (plural) are the generations (plural) of the heavens and the earth (meaning all things)'. A whole variety of processes leading to a whole variety of products. More than one process, enacted at more than one time, leading to any one finished product.

Part of this 'comings into beings' process is the creation of all things, in fullness and completeness, at a point in time - the day of creation. A secondary but integrated part of these 'comings into beings' is manifestation at the appropriate moment. The plants are a prime illustration of this secondary aspect of 'comings into beings.' Integrated creative accomplishment involving a variety of processes over time!"

Genesis presents a scientific model, highly sophisticated. Four main divisions of life were made or created, these divisions being, in chronological order: plants, aquatic animals, land animals, man. Every species of each division came into existence on the day that division was made or created. Individual species are then evidenced in the earth, over time, according to a definite purpose.

We have barely scratched the surface, either of the biblical text or the model of creation which may be derived from it. *Genesis* embodies an extremely advanced, technically detailed, self-harmonious, integrated creation model, about which volumes are destined to be written. The technical depth is unfathomable.

Gen.2:6

But there went up a mist from the earth, and watered the whole face of the ground.

The astonishing technical accuracy of this document again becomes signally obvious. It is almost certain that our planet coalesced as multiplied small particles, and that this process was facilitated in some way by the presence of water or water-like compounds. As the particles came together, pressure and increasing heat drove the moisture outward and upward into the formative atmosphere, where it encountered cold air and perhaps various ices, thereby producing a persistent and ubiquitous primordial mist.

In course of time came the rain and displaced the mists - not by a chance progression of nature, for some special input was required to trigger rain. "God . . . caused it to rain." *Gen.2:5.* The formation of raindrops remains a partial mystery to this day.

Gen.2:7

And the Lord God formed man of the dust of the ground, and breathed into his nostrils the breath of life; and man became a living soul.

This illustrates the integrated, multifarious processes involved in *Genesis.* To this point in the narrative we know of man created in the image of God, as though he could have been a completely spiritual, or angel-like being (*Gen.1:27,28*). And so he is. But we are now advised of a more pedestrian aspect of his origins - "formed . . . of the dust of the ground" *Gen.2:7.* He is spiritual, eternal: he is simultaneously earthy, of the earth. He is a spirit; he has a soul, or personality/intellect; he lives in a physical body. His spirit is eternal: it is the essence of man, and can exist without the body. Yet man is not man without a body, a body in many ways similar to those of animals; and he can develop his personality/intellect so as to become a complete and mature three-fold being with his body as one component. He is "created . . . in the image of God."

Gen.1:27. He is "formed . . . of the dust of the ground." *Gen.2:7.* He is a "living soul . . . the breath of life . . . [was] breathed into his nostrils." *Gen.2:7.* Not only so, but he was one individual - Adam - whilst he was all mankind, including the female half - Eve. Thus it is apparent that the *Genesis* text is an account of integrated, multi-faceted processes and procedures. These processes and procedures call for sophisticated species handling/storage and advanced genetic engineering.

Gen.2:8

And the Lord God planted a garden eastward in Eden; and there he put the man whom he had formed.

Man was *created;* he was also *formed.* His genetic blueprint was created; his spirit is a part or a potential of God himself; but his physical flesh has been formed of earth. He is God but he is not God: he is animal but he is not animal. He is both, and he has great potential. Of no other animal is it said, "God took him, and put him into the garden [his ecological niche]." *Gen.2:8,* as though mankind existed, perhaps fellowshipping with his Maker in some sort of subconscious, womb- like existence, before his physical body was formed and he was lovingly placed on the earth. See the multiple, integrated processes called for by *Genesis.*

Eden is here mentioned for the first time. Eden is a specific geographic region. It was known to peoples of ancient times. On the balance of probabilities it most probably lies somewhere in the region of the head of the Persian Gulf. This part of the world has undergone some topographic alteration over time, but many Bible scholars find sufficient points in common with the given description to place it in this general locality. (The Ethiopia of v.*13* is equally Cush, believed to be an ancient land of the Mesopotamian region; the river Hiddekel is the Tigris (v.*14*); the Mesopotamian region with its changeable topography about the head of the Persian Gulf therefore is a likely candidate for the site of Eden. The gold and precious stones of v.*12* are presumably a feature of the ancient past, of little or no assistance now in pinpointing its exact location.) Eden is a specific geographic region, albeit of a location not amenable to exact pinpointing. As such it is a type or a figure of the whole habitable world of that time.

Man was intended to replenish or consummate the entire habitable Earth, meaning that the whole Earth was to become, in a sense, Eden. The entire surface of the habitable globe was intended for man, as a garden of peace and paradise without exception. Although Eden itself must have been an idyllic environment, embellished with all features of desirability and beauty, yet the bulk of the middle latitudes of the Earth of that time were not far behind it!

Some unknown, benign influences set apart the environment in which earliest man found himself. The geologic record of the times of man's *debut* and of the times immediately preceding it suggests abundance of water; clear, flowing streams; absence of hot, dry deserts; and a flora and fauna at once so diverse, so robust, it seems to belong in a world different to ours.

Eden, whilst unquestionably a specific location, speaks in some measure of the world at large of those times. It is to be regarded as the centre, or the centrepiece, of the habitable Earth.

Gen.2:9

And out of the ground made the Lord God to grow every tree that is pleasant to the sight, and good for food; the tree of life also in the midst of the garden, and the tree of knowledge of good and evil.

It becomes more apparent that the Garden of Eden was in some way the habitable Earth in microcosm - a figurative shadow of the whole globe. The Lord God made to grow trees pleasant to the sight and good for food in a whole variety of localities around the globe, not in one site only. Eden may have been peculiarly well endowed, but not to the exclusion of the remainder of the habitable Earth. And since the trees of life and of knowledge were central and essential to all of Creation, the presence of these trees in the midst of the garden implies that the garden was in a sense the whole world or the centrepiece of the world.

Without the tree of life, there is no life. Without the tree of knowledge, there is no long-distance communication. Both these trees are supernatural, yet they are trees that exist and produce observable effects in the physical worlds.

The tree of knowledge is perhaps the easier of the two to understand. When a whole group of people begin, inexplicably, to follow the same superstition, worship the same idol, subscribe to the same fashionable notion, the tree of knowledge is in operation. We are all "plugged in" to the same communications network (or tree). We have all eaten the fruit of it. So when "the spirit of the age" seems to infect a whole body of people at the same time, it is evidence of a hidden but common line of communication.

This communications network potentially taps into both good and evil. It was the unwarranted accessing of this network (or tree) that introduced all our problems in the first instance. Not that the tree itself is evil, or anything other than perfect. The transmission of depictions of moral degradation by electronic media outlets does not make electronic communications wrong in itself.

Mankind is currently "plugged in" to some branches of the tree of knowledge of good and evil.

The tree of life is likewise a tree that functions supernaturally, yet produces tangible results in the physical world.

The Tree of Life!

Geologists have deduced that every phylum of complex life or its simple, early representatives originated during a frenzy or "explosion" of life-generating activity of no more than possibly ten million years' duration. This generative activity immediately followed the generation of a feature of the geologic column known as the Pre-Cambrian/ Cambrian Unconformity (the only evidence in the rocks of a simultaneous world-wide land-levelling event caused by water - surely triggered by the introduction of the moon at the close of Day Four?) Future compression of the time-span of this concentrated creative activity to ten thousand years . . . or ten years . . . cannot be ruled out.

All divisions of complex animal life - some albeit very primitive in their earliest expression - suddenly leaped into existence, and from thence proceeded to expand upward, like a tree. Plant life, although not "exploding" at the same time as the animal divisions, nevertheless followed a similar, tree-like, upward expansion. Thus all life has been introduced to the Earth as though by a tree - periods of abrupt species generation, or budding of new branches, followed by periods of steady growth, and some die-off, during which species follow species in some sort of succession, as though forming branches.

This is the language of *Genesis* - periods of creation followed by manifestation of those newly created species over time. From the point of "explosion," there is a pattern of upwardly advancing, expanding life, in which more complex forms appear to derive from their simpler predecessors. This pattern is not unlike a tree. The advancing species form the branches, each segment of branch appearing to derive from the segment underlying it.

According to *Genesis,* all species of each major division of life were made or created on a particular day, but were not manifested, or triggered into action, until it suited the higher purpose. In like manner, a tree contains within itself all the variety of growth which it is ultimately going to display - in completeness and in perfection - although that growth - leaves, flowers, fruits, etc. - may not yet be openly manifest. And when new growth arises, it superficially appears to have arisen from the growth immediately preceding it, just as some species superficially appear to have evolved from those underneath them in the rocks.

The analogy to the biblical Tree of Life is uncanny - a divinely appointed vehicle or conduit of life, with its roots in the supernatural "river of life," and its effects or practical results in the natural Earth. And unlike our trees, which can only produce one variety of fruit, this emissary from heaven gives rise to a spectrum of products, so that each budding new branch, at its initial inception, contains within itself all the life forms which are to form that branch (see *Rev.22:2*).

What is the mechanism by which pre-existent species are stored, or carried, through time, then propelled into action at a pre-arranged, appropriate moment? If the tree analogy is correct, do the preceding parts of the branches - earlier species - act in some way as conduits or carriers of the new life, as a branch acts as a carrier of the life-giving sap? Like a tree budding in its season, are the new species triggered into action by signals from within and, perhaps, without, the tree? Do surrounding environmental conditions play a part? Is the breaking forth of new species governed by signals?

Signals!

All organisms, including our own physical bodies, are a collection of chemicals obeying signals. The cells constituting all living things are simply a set of instructors - genes - surrounded by a set of servants! All that is required for any organism to exist (man excluded) is the instructors (genes), the servants (the living body of the cell surrounding the genes), and an environment in which the cell can live and replicate. Thus it is possible to hold a 90-ton whale on the tip of one's finger and not even know it is there.

Time, and a suitable nurturing environment, will transform the tiny living cell into a marine giant. But we can go a step further. We do not need an actual whale cell, now, to have one in the future if we can trip the genetic locking mechanism in another living cell and change it to a whale cell at a future time.

All we require to create a whale is a master-computer, programmed with the genetic code of the whale, a living cell situated where it can replicate and grow into a whale, and a signalling mechanism between the master-computer and the cell. And if the gene-code in the cell is designed so that it can unlock and "clock" into another code at receipt of pre-arranged signals, the cell that is waiting in the ground or in the waters could conceivably be part of an existing organism. So if we have the genetic code in the master-computer, pre-programmed to be signalled to receptor cell(s) at the appropriate moment, and arrangements have already been made - perhaps through other pre- arranged signals - for reproduction of that cell into a mature individual, then we have our whale. It exists, in perfection. It may not be visible to the eye, but it certainly exists.

This model does not entail one species giving birth to another, but hypothesizes that materials in the Earth, including living cells associated with living organisms, were re -organized by having their internal ordering instructions changed, thus leading to individuals of new species. As for the signals: the ability of elements of the natural world to receive and obey extra-sensory signals is a long-standing, accepted biblical concept; and all living cells are constantly receiving and responding to various signals.

The mechanisms by which signals could have been employed in the transformation of life forms are currently beyond our technology; nevertheless, it does not seem outside the realms of possibility to instruct select individuals of one life form to accept the presence within themselves of cells of another species. These foreign cells are instructed to function as a part of the existing organism, so that the organism continues to live and function whilst it is transforming. Such transformations would have been abrupt in terms of geologic time. The new creatures would have manifested in full genetic diversity, being in fact created new. If the Creator so chose, he could have begun each new life form as a single pair (as with mankind) or any number of individuals spread over the world.

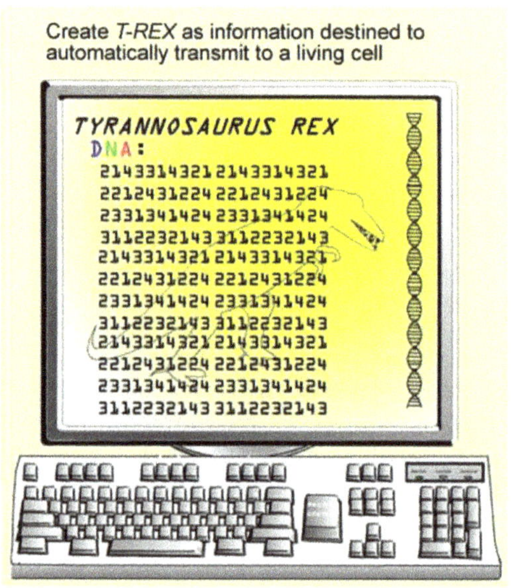

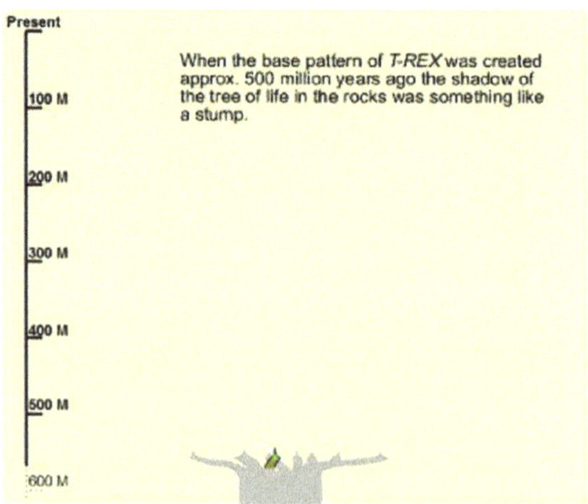

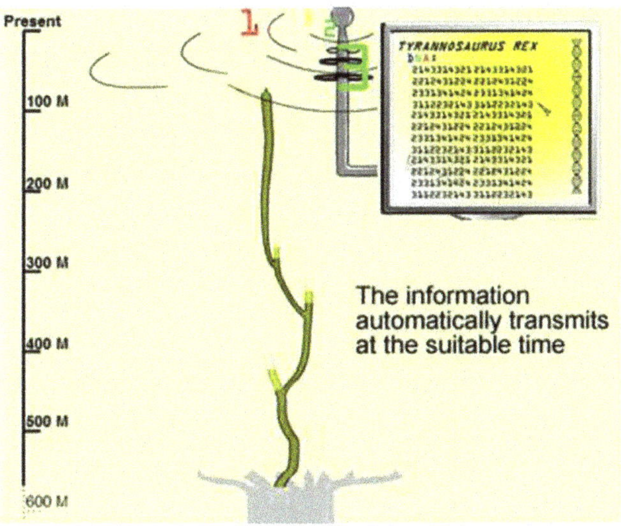

The species which carried the life that was passed to the new species may have gone on living, or if its purpose was fulfilled, have died out.

This model explains the geologic record. A set of blueprints are made and encoded ready to be broadcast at a predestined moment. Materials and/or organisms capable of receiving the encoded signals are placed in the ground or the waters. Every species destined to evidence as a part of that branch then exists, in perfection. No more creative work in relation to that branch is then required by the Creator, although there is certainly no obstacle to extra modifications being made further along the branches by the Master Craftsman.

If cells from existing life forms did in fact transmute into new life forms, then the analogy to life-sap passing along tree branches is perfect. The idea of signals leading to new growth also matches against natural trees.

Information Technology

Update: The pre-ordained revelation of living things was accomplished through information technology. The Earth was "founded . . . by wisdom," and the heavens were "established . . . by understanding." *(Pro.3:19).* The procedure for building complex structures by wisdom and understanding follows different lines to that of building them with a wheelbarrow and trowel.

We may postulate information pre-programming, as an aspect of the "wisdom and understanding" by which the universe, including the species, was revealed. We raise the possibility of at least three mechanisms through which this may have been achieved:

- Information storage and transmission, principally involving the solar system

- Environmental change

- Information capacity inherent in the design of DNA itself Could these work in concert?

What precisely is the role of each?

Did these roles change throughout geologic history? Are these the only mechanisms involved?

How did they work in concert to bring about the transformation of one species to another?

Is there an ingenious capability to self-extend built into DNA? Imagine a DNA strand to be a long aggregation of cogs, or gearboxes. Microbes do not require as many gearboxes as elephants. Assume DNA - of which we know so little - has "buttons," which environmental change can "push." By pushing the button, the DNA is activated to the building of a new category of gearbox. The manufacture of basic patterns of gearboxes is inherent in the molecule, whilst individual and specific new species information came from outside. When the world stood in need of trees, preordained environmental conditions caused the "tree gearbox" buttons to be pushed, and the way in which living organisms are designed led to vast new gearbox availability in some plants.

The same or subsequent environmental changes triggered the laying down of potential "flying" and "tree-climbing" gearboxes in some animals. Trees appeared, and in time animals began to climb trees and to fly. Environmental pressure alone could not cause an organism to develop treegripping claws and wings. However, if DNA was designed so that an environmental signal would cause it to lay down wing and climbing-claw building capacity, and quantum (i.e., atom- altering) signalling in combination with environmental circumstances gave specific "building instructions," could the climbing and flying organisms begin to be revealed?

If the pre-programmed realization of the species was achieved through quantum signalling, with environmental conditions as triggers, research should reveal the mechanisms. Research has barely dipped its toe in this pond. If any one thing can be concluded from science's understanding of quantum information processes and living cells, it is that evolutionary teachings to date must have been drawn from the ethereal ether; there hasn't been an oversupply of facts! One line of approach could be to exhaustively analyse the DNA of an ancient life form, and compare it with that of a recent species. The coelacanth is a possible candidate.

Coelacanths were fishes prominent during the Devonian Period. This gives them a probable age of the order of 350 to 400 million years. Other living organisms have a longer history, but perhaps have not been as thoroughly analysed for genetic information? The living representative(s) of the coelacanths closely resemble other members of their family, although they are currently classified as different species to any of those so far described from Devonian fossil remains. It seems reasonable to regard coelacanths as truly ancient organisms. Work on these "living fossils" is underway. A layman's reading of the "drop in the bucket" of information currently available would not contradict, and perhaps would support, the following.

- The information devices of ancient fishes were modern; that is, they were of the same functional design throughout time.

- The DNA of the coelacanth is of the same order of complexity as that of fishes that appeared more than 100 million years later. This could support the idea that DNA could have carried latent information within itself?

- The DNA of fish is markedly different from that of land animals. As *Genesis* tells us, land animals were "formed of earth" on Day 6, a novel and semi-unique input of land- dwelling capacity, the impartation processes of which we may or may not be able to fully comprehend.

Thus the information currently available points to information storage and transmission mechanisms being basically the same throughout geologic history. It could allow for DNA to have been a pre- programmed "storehouse" of some information, with environment as a "trip" or "trigger." When environmental conditions called for new species, latent modifications that had lain dormant in the DNA itself, combined with external quantum information-signalling, brought about the transformations.

Probable evidence of such "latent modifications" has been unearthed by scientists studying genes involved in limb development (Hox genes). Researchers have "found that the genetic capability seen in tetrapods to build limbs is present in . . . primitive fish."[9] The discovery that fish possess genes associated with tetrapod limb development long before the appearance of tetrapods indicates that advanced genetic information was latent in early species.

Would a cell with reprogrammed DNA be recognized and attacked by the autoimmune system? As we learned previously, the functioning of the immune system is an enigma. Notwithstanding our ignorance in this area, we have strong circumstantial evidence that modified cells can exist in organisms without being recognized as foreign. Cancer is a striking example of a mutated, or different, cell, escaping detection by the immune system.

Assume now that environmental pressures have caused a strain or race within a species to become isolated, and a cell or cells within an individual of this separated race has been reprogrammed for a new species. This

---

9 University of Chicago Medical Center, "New Genetic Data Overturn Long-held Theory Of Limb Development", ScienceDaily, www.sciencedaily.com/releases/2007/05/070523132701.htm, accessed 8 April 2018

reprogrammed cell will contain all the genetic information required by the new species; but how will the new species be born and reared?

In any unfolding species sequence, individuals of one species were physically similar to the next. It is theoretically possible for an animal of one species to conceive, give birth to, and rear an individual of another species, provided it has been programmed to do so. The two species can theoretically be made conformable through re-programming. Thus, one species does not give birth to another, since it has already (in a real sense) become the other.

Because of re-programming, the mother saw its offspring to be its own, and treated it as such. Mothers' milk, if necessary, was rendered acceptable through immune system re-programming. Foods and lifestyles were similar. Impartation of the complete new species code into the DNA may have taken place when only one or two cells required it - perhaps in the mother and father (?) before conception, or soon after conception. Many aspects of living things remain conjectural.

Something keeps species reproductively isolated. For example, even if a horse and donkey can be successfully crossed to produce a mule, something prevents the mule - and all such hybrids - from going on to produce offspring so as to generate a new species. There is, in nature, a "species lock." We have conjectured that this "lock" or "bar" is an aspect of the workings of the autoimmune and reproductive systems, and involves information technology and biochemistry. The "lock" must be simple. How was the "combination" of this "lock" tripped, to allow species transformation?

The Direction of Recent Research

"Researchers at the John Innes Center have made a discovery, reported this evening (24 July) in *Nature,* that explains how an organism can create a biological memory of some variable condition, such as quality of nutrition or temperature. The discovery explains the mechanism of this memory - a sort of biological switch - and how it can also be inherited by offspring."[10]

"Epigenetic changes to DNA have intrigued and puzzled researchers. They are physical changes to DNA that don't involve the base sequence, but rather act on top of the sequence, and ultimately shape gene expression. What are these epigenetic molecules? How do they affect organisms? Learn about epigenetics."[11]

Comment: This developing field of epigenetics suggests the possibility (as predicted by creationtheory.com, shortly after the turn of the millennium) that DNA is designed to pick up environmental information as time passes. Presumably, it is also designed so that, once a critical amount of additional information (our transformation agents) is appended, the scene is set so that species transformation can occur. The transformation agents are acted upon so that their characteristics became a permanent aspect of the DNA. The events involved in transformation remain obscure, but presumably environmental pressure for change plays a triggering role, whilst some sort of quantum signalling must happen at the critical instant. This transformation will be a product of the heavens - especially, the sun-Earth-moon system. It may well involve light and the magnetic field. Yet it will simultaneously be a product of Earth-bound species, themselves, which are in a state of readiness to transform.

Details and speculations aside, the biblically-based model fits the observed facts. It reinforces the fundamental truth of species reproducing after their kind, and only after their kind. It gives the correct order in time of the appearance of the main divisions of life. (Plants; aquatic and

---

[10] Biotechnology and Biological Sciences Research Council, "Epigenetic 'memory' key to nature versus nurture," ScienceDaily, http ://www. sciencedaily.com/releases/2011/07/110724135553.html, 25 July 2011

[11] H. Chial, & J. Akst, "Spotlight on Epigenetics", Scitable by *Nature Education,* http://www.nature.com/scitable/spotlight/ epigenetics-26097411, accessed 26 May 2012

watery animals including insects; birds and land animals; man.) It implies sudden proliferation at various points throughout geologic time, of fully-developed, genetically mature life forms according to an intelligent plan, but not necessarily in the same order as the life forms were actually made or created. It explains the unheralded, awesome explosion of species.

It ends the confusion over the origin of the species.

It also explains why the tree of life was the source of the garden, and why the garden was in a sense the centrepiece and source of the whole world. Before Adam lost his perfection, he could physically access this tree. It is a real tree, although obviously not a tree as we know common trees. Even now it exists, a feature of Paradise, accessible to angels, which, like Adam at first, are perfect in the complete sense of the word.

As for the tree of life, so for the tree of knowledge of good and evil: Adam in his perfection could clearly see its products and processes (fruits). But the tree of knowledge is with us yet as an integral part of the biosphere, whereas the tree of life is no longer accessible as a real tree in our physical realm. We can catch a glimpse of the way in which life was made, we can deduce the impartation of superior messages (knowledge) in the biosphere about us, but we cannot ourselves make life.

The River in Eden

Gen.2:10-14

And a river went out of Eden to water the garden; and from thence it was parted, and became into four heads. The name of the first is Pison: that is it which compasseth the whole land of Havilah, where there is gold; and the gold of that land is good: there is bdellium and onyx stone. And the name of the second river is Gihon; the same is it that compasseth the whole land of Ethiopia.

And the name of the third river is Hiddekel: that is it which goeth toward the east of Assyria. And the fourth river is Euphrates.

If the reader is a little bemused by this description, he/she is not the first. Why does a source-river run out of Eden, to water a garden that was in Eden?

How does a water stream "become into four heads"?

Where and what are the rivers Pison and Gihon - unknown to modern topographers - and why the seemingly anecdotal reference to gold and to precious stones of obscure compositions? (The gemtypes cannot be positively identified by modern linguists. Bdellium could in fact be an aromatic gum.)

The Tigris (Hiddekel) and Euphrates are identified, but how can they be associated with Ethiopia, a land outside their drainage basin? And if the alternative for Ethiopia - Cush - is intended, why is Ethiopia mentioned? Is the intention here to give Eden a specific location, yet concurrently make it something larger?

The river went out of Eden. It is in giving that we receive, and in giving ourselves, we find true security. The river is health; the river is life. "If any man thirst, let him come unto me, and drink. He that believeth on me, as the scripture hath said, Out of his belly shall flow rivers of living water." *John 7:37, 38.* The river became (in some profoundly meaningful way) four riverheads. The number of the Earth is four. This river went out to water the four corners of the world. Ethiopia and farther.

"*Go ye into all the world, and preach the gospel to every creature*" *Mark 16:15.* In that land there was gold and precious stones. The graces, the gifts, the fruitfulness also of the Spirit. "*And these signs shall follow them that believe;*

in my name shall they cast out devils; they shall speak with new tongues . . . they shall lay hands on the sick, and they shall recover." Mark 16:17, 18.

Eden was paradise on Earth. It was intended to overspread the Earth. It was a place where Heaven had come down to touch this Earth (see *Rev. 22*).

Eden also speaks of the chosen nation Israel, which was to be a blessing to the whole globe. It therefore speaks further of the spiritual Israel - the church, the body of Christ's genuine followers. And it goes deeper than this. Eden testifies of Jesus Christ the giver of the water of life; of God the author of the river of life; of the incomparable riches the Spirit confers upon his people. Eden is the everlasting gospel, the spread of peace, the source of joyfulness. It is what the earth could have been and what the new earth will be. Before the final day comes, the gospel will be preached in the four corners of the earth.

Eden was originally a specific geographic location. At the same time, it speaks in a type, or a shadow, of what the whole Earth was intended to become. Yet it speaks even more forcefully of what the individual human life has the potential to become, and which, by the workings of divine Creativity, it will become in the process of time. Fruitfulness, usefulness, supply, peace, safety, harmony, beauty. Heaven on Earth and Earth on the way to becoming Heaven.

IX. ONE OF THE MYSTERIES OF EXISTENCE

Gen.2:15

And the Lord God took the man, and put him into the Garden of Eden to dress it and to keep it.

Mankind, Adam, was "created . . . in the image of God" *Gen.1:27,* and his Creator personally "breathed into his nostrils the breath of life [animating power/igniting spark]" *Gen.1:27.* Yet he was "formed . . . of the dust of the ground" *Gen.2.7.* He was a direct product of Heaven, "made . . . a little lower than the angels" *Ps.8:5.* Concurrently he was "formed of the dust of the ground," a product of the tree of life in its role of realizing/evidencing Earth-bound life from its supernatural source. Thus, the tree of life, the translator that gave us all the animals, the plants, and ourselves, is another aspect of God himself at work. This is illustrated in Christ himself. Jesus Christ is God, yet, "a body hast thou prepared me" *Heb.10:5.*

A body, an earthy body, formed of dust, formed after the same manner as the bodies of animals, under the tree of life mechanism. Thus, Jesus Christ, our tree of life, in a sense the tree of life, is the author of life whilst being a product of that authorship himself. Such is the intimate and intricate nature of the Man-God relationship, the oneness of divine and human existence. God is man and man is God. (But God is not a [fallen] man that he should lie.) Such is the nature of man's essential existence, God was able to take him . . . "and put him into the garden" *Gen.2:15.*

This seems to imply that Adam, like Christ, had essential existence before he was given a physical body. Alongside the lesser animals, he was a product of the tree of life. Yet, unlike the lesser animals, he has within him tree of life potential himself, as though the tree of life begins and ends in God, a totality, a circle, and man is part of this circle, close to God in terms of his essential being.

Gen.2:16,17.

And the Lord God commanded the man, saying, Of every tree of the garden thou mayest freely eat: but of the tree of the knowledge of good and evil, thou shalt not eat of it: for in the day that thou eatest thereof thou shalt surely die.

"Surely die," or, "dying thou shalt die"; an ongoing, increasing, multifaceted progression. Compare with the testimony of Christ: "I am come that ye might have life" - "that living, ye might live."

Just as the tree of life has coursing through it the life force, so the tree of knowledge has in its "veins" a coursing medium of communications capability. All long-distance communication is via trees - transport and communications networks. The existence of life necessitates a tree of life. The transmission of information necessitates a tree of knowledge. Since this network (or tree) accesses every corner of everything, it is a medium through which an innocent person could encounter the possibility of evil - and lose his/her innocence. (We have already deduced that the possibility of evil must exist by definition as a feature of the supernatural - but not as a feature of the perfect God.) Thus the cosmic communications network, the tree of knowledge, potentially accesses evil as well as good, making it "the tree of the knowledge of good and evil."

To illustrate this communications concept: we know God is altogether faultless - he is "perfection perfection." We likewise hear of a Devil, reputed to be in a sense an antithesis of virtue - "vile vile." Going on hints from scripture, it seems reasonable to deduce that the possibility of evil that we have deduced as being an inescapable feature of the supernatural cosmic Everything is personified in this Devil. The possibility of evil somehow concentrates in this supernatural entity - once "the anointed cherub" (*Ez.28:12-17*), the uncontested prince of the angels, but now totally debased through personal pride.

Imagine for a moment the scenario should "perfection perfection" encounter "vile vile" face-to-face in exactly the same way two opposite chemical reagents would encounter one another. Therefore, we deduce it does not happen this way in the supernatural realm. In the supernatural, two antitheses encounter one another, and even transmit messages to one another (*Job 1:7*) without annihilation of the weaker. Therefore there must be a neutral communications medium. A tree of knowledge of both good and evil.

This communications medium itself is faultless.

Eden as our first parents experienced it was analogous to a sealed room or enclosure in which everything was perfect. Outside this room exists the possibility of imperfection or evil. There is no imperfection, no possibility of evil, inside the room - unless it is given access by the perfect beings within the enclosure. The room is therefore, in a sense, Heaven - where no imperfection finds a place, where evil has no power. Inside this enclosure is an essential, faultless communications terminal.

This terminal is an integral part of the enclosure. The terminal is not wrong - it is perfect. The communications tree is not wrong - it is both faultless and essential. The perfect beings within the enclosure have no compulsion and no need to access this network. They have been specifically warned not to do so. They cannot access it without intentionally disregarding the express command of their Creator, with whom they speak verbally, face-to-face each day. Thus, Eden was altogether faultless, paradise, Heaven on Earth, and the tree of knowledge of good and evil was basic to this utopia.

It is surely a source of wonder that the act of merely touching the fruit of this tree would give the knowledge of the possibility of evil entry into paradise (*Gen.3:3*). Concepts such as these surely stretch the mind. The fruit was attractive to the eye and the imagination (*Gen.3:6*). The merest touch - the faintest enlightenment in the matter of the possibility of moral concepts, of virtue and vice - would prove fatal to pure innocence. Going further, and consuming the fruit, would digest or absorb into our intellect these cosmic facts of moral virtue and vice, and all that this entrains.

Once digested into our intellect or soul, the new knowledge would inevitably be absorbed in some measure into our spirits, thoroughly alarming our hitherto dormant consciences *en route.* Entering in upon our spirits and taking hold there, this *knowledge of evil,* this *separation from perfection,* would fix itself like an inoperable malignancy, passing itself on inexorably from generation to generation.

Surely these concepts tax the mind.

It seems this fruit awoke man's conscience, so from then onward he knew good and evil, he experienced good and evil, and he possessed in some measure communication ability with powers of good and evil. In some mysterious way, this had the effect of making the Devil the "god of this world." The one-time "anointed cherub," now utterly debased but nevertheless capable of seducing, stunning beauty (*Ez.28:12-17*) would thereby be handed the "title-deeds" to this earth.

In place of man giving the commands, man's enemy would be able to take at least partial control. Destruction and death - death universal, death ubiquitous, death in all its forms, in all its facets - would fix itself upon us.

Death, inexorable and ever-increasing, is marching down through history in time with a growing cohort - disease, deprivation, misery. Surely these causes and effects are not easily comprehended, but the results cannot be denied.

The knowledge of evil was bound to erase innocence; without innocence there could be no perfection and no paradise; without perfection there could be only death. But as yet Adam has not eaten of this tree.

The Help Meet

Gen.2:18

And the Lord God said, "It is not good that the man should be alone; I will make him a help meet for him."

One way to assist our understanding of the word *meet* is to consider the thrust of its meaning in other usages. Hence, *meeting*: to come together by mutual consent at an appropriate time and place. *Meet* implies something altogether appropriate. A *match;* a point-for-point *match.* Wellington *met* Napoleon at Waterloo. Item for item, manoeuvre for manoeuvre, by divine providence, he was equal; he was successfully equal, on every point. *Meet* means something that is *just right* - almost supernaturally *right.*

All marriages that are supernaturally appointed bring together two people who are *just right.* They are *a meeting* - a meeting of helps who are helps indeed.

Observe that the Almighty did not need to create woman. He had already done so. She was created in Adam. The word *make* is employed in describing the bodily advent of the female.

This verse, located, as it is, near the beginning of the scriptures, discounts the notion of virtue in celibacy for celibacy's sake. "It is not good that the man should be alone." Celibacy only has virtue if it is directly appointed for a person by the will of God at work in his life. Thus even St. Paul did not desire it, but he embraced it because his Lord willed it for him personally.

Gen.2:19

And out of the ground the Lord God formed every beast of the field, and every fowl of the air. .

All complex life was created on the fifth day, on a water base. "And God said; Let the waters bring forth abundantly the moving creature that hath life, and fowl that may fly . . ." *Gen.1:20.* "And God created great whales, and every living creature that moveth, which the waters brought forth . . ." *Gen.1:21.* As we have already learned, this explains one of the mysteries of biology, why it is that all complex life appears to go through a fish and amphibian stage in the womb. We were created on a water base.

All the sets of branches of the fossil (shadow) tree of life had budded and shot by the end of Day Five. With the exception of Man, no more creation, in the full meaning of the term, was to take place. All land animals, including those capable of flight, were *created* on Day Five. They were *formed* (of earth) on Day Six. That is, the shadow tree of life branches were modified; pre-existent blueprints were adapted; complex life was given land-dwelling capability.

Why?

Gen.2:19, 20

And out of the ground the Lord God formed every beast of the field, and every fowl of the air; and brought them unto Adam to see what he would call them: and whatsoever Adam called every living creature, that was the name thereof.

And Adam gave names to all cattle, and to the fowl of the air, and to every beast of the field; but for Adam there was not found a help meet for him.

The land creatures were made as a help, as servants, for man. Although none was a help *meet*, all were a potential help for Adam. They were then all his servants, and he was perfect master of them, for he was able to name them all - a mark of his uncontested authority.

But none was a help *meet*, as divine Providence well knew - none was *just right*. They filled a space, but they did not fit *that particular space.*

Therefore:

Gen.2:21-24

And the Lord God caused a deep sleep to fall upon Adam, and he slept: and he took one of his ribs, and closed up the flesh instead thereof; and the rib, which the Lord God had taken from man, made he a woman, and brought her unto the man. And Adam said, "This is now bone of my bones, and flesh of my flesh: she shall be called Woman, because she was taken out of Man. Therefore shall a man leave his father and his mother, and shall cleave unto his wife: and they shall be one flesh."

Many people, both married and single, will identify with the following: You are the only person in existence. It seems there is no other human being to accompany you in the entire world. In fact, the surface of the earth is destitute of that other person. There is no one. The animals are inferior as company. You are the only person on the earth. Your case seems hopeless.

You go to sleep, without much hope, and alone. You wake up to see the person who has been missing. You can see him/her, with your eyes - a miracle.

Countless people identify in part or in whole with Adam's experience. Shouldn't we be encouraged by it? Shouldn't we be encouraged when we consider the remarkable way in which marriage was and is brought about? A partnership begun on such pleasant and - it could be said - almost *supernatural* terms, has the potential to have something new and supernatural in it every day from its inception onward. Marriage is a great institution. Having begun with a miracle, it should be assisted with a miracle every day, overcoming all obstacles. Marriage is the first institution of human society (unless we count speaking with God as an institution) and it has a stamp of approval - a one hundred per cent guarantee from its Maker.

We are introduced to the original and incomparable Genetic Engineer. The rib is obviously not an entire rib, for men are not wanting one rib; presumably, it is speaking in medical terms of a specimen of bone and various tissues from an auspicious anatomical site. From this surgically removed fragment, the Master Craftsman "made" in the sense of "builded" a woman.

Were it not that the scriptures emphatically rule out the possibility of any modern individual coming into existence without a father and mother (Honour thy father and thy mother! *Ex.20:12*) we could almost imagine our modern technology manufacturing individuals by the same methods.

We have nothing to fear in regard to the true cloning of people. It cannot be done by man. The Almighty never yet gave a command that cannot be obeyed. Honour thy father and thy mother! Clones have only one parent. (The so-called "cloning" of humans has not been cloning in the true sense. It has been nothing more than embryo splitting, a simulation of the natural process of identical-twin generation.)

The anaesthetized body and the idea of tissue transmutation may well be a pointer to events surrounding the advent of the first parents of animal species. Some forms of hibernation go close to complete anaesthetization; and in very broad terms, it is as easy to transmute the component cells of a given organ from those of one species to those of another as it is to transmute the component cells of one organ to those of a different organ within an individual animal.

Life appears in some degree suited to transformation, organ by organ, across species. A human body could function on some internal organs of a pig, if it could be induced to accept them. This question of species transformation awaits advances in medicine. But no advance will come close to this achievement of the First Genetic Craftsman. The medical implications are profound, almost imponderable.

The implications in terms of spiritual meaning have long been at least partly understood. The animals were a help, but they were not a help *meet.* They fell short of true partnership. The woman was "bone of [his] bones, and flesh of [his] flesh." She was a perfect and spotless bride. She was more than a help, more than a servant: she was a "help meet." She was one with her partner. In a sense, she was her partner. She was brought into being through the death (sleep) and bodily sacrifice (removal of the rib) of Adam. She was, in effect, his body.

The second Adam, the matchless Christ, seeing his sacrifice and death imminent, said to his disciples, "Henceforth I call you not servants . . . I have called you friends" *John 15:15*. The New Testament, sealed with his blood, makes men not only his servants but his friends, bringing mankind to a wonderful new possibility of status and relationship. "By a new and living way, which he hath set apart for us, through the veil, that is to say, his flesh . . ." *Heb.10:20.*

Nakedness

Gen.2:25

And they were both naked, the man and his wife, and were not ashamed.

The unmitigated happiness and contentment of the original couple was the contentment of innocence. It was not the product of character- building, of overcoming difficulties, of defeating sin and the powers of evil, of walking by faith. They saw God with the eye and spoke with him by mouth.

They knew no sin, pain, or setback, and did not comprehend the meaning of such. Their nakedness could occasion themselves no harm. Such was their almost childlike integrity they did not know there was such a state as nakedness.

Whatever the composition of the fruit of the tree of knowledge, it had the effect of changing a person who does not understand the meaning of nakedness to one who felt his nakedness keenly. Surely this is a profound concept.

Adam and Eve were in paradise. Did they understand they were in paradise? Could they understand paradise? Is paradise really paradise at all to someone who has never experienced anything but paradise? These concepts tax the comprehension.

Nakedness is only nakedness to those who know it to be such. The first couple did not know it to be such, because to them everything was right, and they were in a place where everything could only be right. Those who have no shame in public nakedness or unwonted public exposure now are either ill or are so motivated by despair that they throw off their outward protection as a sign of the loss of their inward protection. They are not innocent, unless they are Adam or Eve, and paradise is with us yet.

Public semi-nakedness, expected and ubiquitous in Australia today, is associated with a utopia - a utopia of family breakdown, personal disillusionment, and personal confusion. Scientifically conducted surveys of western youth in the twenty-first century reveal that a majority of males view males as human beings and females as *body parts!* Females may aim for happiness and acceptance as *body parts?* Is this a communal confidence trick? No child asks to be programmed in this way.

The public aim of Australia appears to be empty fulfilment of the appetite-who isn't plagued by that inner monster?-and children are programmed to see themselves as adjuncts in a frenetic search for something that can never be found. "The adults have lost the way - where do we turn?" Our programming of children and the environment in which we program children will become the world of tomorrow. Faith, calm assurance, respect of others, respect of self, respect of family, personal covering, and personal integrity? Stress, worry, throwing off personal protection – nakedness?

Man cannot help himself. We can be given help - and who doesn't need it?

Our original parents were fully innocent: and not only innocent; they had none of the "sin principle," the "body of this death" *Ro.7:24,* the "flesh," with which to contend. They had no inbuilt motivation to go astray. They possessed genuine free will. In them, the Tempter's sparks need fall on only wet tinder, which would not take fire. They were innocent; they were free; they were happy; they were in control. They were perfect. Did they know by experience that they were any of these things?

Gen.3:1

Now the serpent was more subtle than any beast of the field which the Lord God had made. And he said unto the woman, Yea, hath God said . . .

If this is paradise, what is a serpent doing in it and why is this serpent permitted to speak negatively?

The animal that spoke to Eve was no mean crawler, but the prince of the animals and the crown of the animal kingdom. It may have been the aptly named *Tyrannosaurus Rex* himself. Unless the Bible is speaking completely allegorically at this point.

The reader is invited to take whichever of the two paths, pure allegory or biological reality, he sees fit. The matter is of no ultimate importance. But he may find the path of allegory only and allegory alone even more difficult to reconcile with hard fact than that of literal zoological characters.

This topic warrants a volume to itself. Entire books are destined to come of it.

Biologists have a difficulty. Class *Reptilia.*

The Bible contains a narrative, almost too strange to take as literal if it refers to physical creatures, with Class *Reptilia* at the centre.

Biology has a difficulty and the Bible speaks into the very centre of that difficulty.

Something has happened to the reptile class. In evolutionary terms, it has almost been blown apart. The snakes are almost like a fragment of that explosion, wriggling their way to sudden notoriety in some obscure evolutionary corner, many of them not long before, or even at the same time, as man appeared. As such, the snakes could well be unique amongst all the animals, and the reptile class is unquestionably unique amongst all the classes.

The facts are a little scanty as yet, but this subject is nothing if not intriguing.

Extinction

Extinction in the geologic meaning of the term means an absence of discovered fossils. It is not intended to mean proven complete extinction, for a species can go on surviving, yet leave no fossils. This is shown by cases from the geologic record itself. It was vividly demonstrated when coelacanths, fish formerly thought to have died out with the dinosaurs, were caught by fishermen of the twentieth century. Instances are common, and are to be expected.

There is no conclusive proof, either way, of complete extinction of all dinosaurs before the times of earliest man. We certainly know these creatures are now extinct: we only have circumstantial evidence - failure to leave fossils - to suggest they were extinct seven thousand years ago. We may take our choice. The jury must remain out at this time. Other juries have been surprised before today.

Science would have no difficulty whatsoever with survival of small numbers of dinosaurs until the times of early man. To show that this is so, let us consult a world authority on the history of the Earth and solar system, geologic history, animal extinctions, and so on: "It is interesting to speculate how. . . [we may] . . . account for removal of such a dominant and successful race as the dinosaurs. The ancient Greeks could readily have credited Zeus with hurling a thunderbolt to remove the dinosaurs.

The Old Testament Jehovah, who drove Adam and Eve from the Garden of Eden, and barred their re-entry with a flaming sword, might have been equally dissatisfied with his reptilian creation. Given omnipotent powers, it would not be too difficult to direct . . . [an] . . . asteroid to wipe the slate clean, and so give the mammals their opportunity. However, a few survivors would have to be left, such as the serpent needed to tempt Eve[12]."

No problem; no difficulty. "A few survivors would have to be left, such as the serpent needed to tempt Eve." This well-qualified Australian scientist, recognized around the world as an authority on the history of the various planets, and especially the Earth and its past, understands enough of the Old

12 Taylor, S. R. *Destiny or Chance.* Cambridge University Press, page180, 1998

Testament to see that a dinosaur best fits the description of the serpent, and sees no problem in survival of a few of these creatures until the times of our early ancestors. (Touching on the matter of mass extinctions, theories from new parasites to magnetic pole reversals have been addressed to the problem of extinctions, none completely satisfactorily. An impacting asteroid is little better. Why would a body hitting the Earth result in the selective removal of some reptiles (the dinosaurs) and not others - crocodiles, iguanas, etc.? Why did it not have a greater impact upon the birds, which are essentially small, fragile, warm-blooded, winged dinosaurs? Extinctions are puzzling.)

Dinosaurs could easily have survived until the times of ancient humankind. We ourselves may choose. The evidence in favour remains circumstantial; the case against is little more than circumstantial.

If the biblical account of the Serpent has a technical, earthly component besides the obvious, supernatural meaning, then a reptilian animal that stood up and/or flew co-existed with earliest man. The creature must have been reptilian, so as to come within the ambit of the term, Serpent. It needs to have been a beautiful if not scintillatingly fascinating animal, its beauty and perfection making it the prince of God's earthly creation. (Thus it becomes an earthly shadow or type of Lucifer, the most scintillatingly and stunningly beautiful of God's supernatural creation). Not only eye-catching and attention-demanding (what creatures command more attention at bookstore or box-office than *Tyrannosaurus* & company?) but having an aura of subtle wisdom besides. The aloof wisdom of the small-braincase crow, as opposed to the friendly but dim-witted intelligence of the larger-brained ox. It must have flown, or habitually stood upright like man.

Are there any prizes for guessing which of God's creation fits this description? Fits it perfectly?

The only known reptilian creature, living or extinct, amenable to being commanded to go on its belly, is . . . the dinosaur.

All other members of the reptile class are already on their belly.

This happened at a time when, as both the geologic record and the scriptures tell us, gigantism was a widespread part of nature.

An attention-getting, beautiful, cunningly wise-witted prince of creatures, reptilian, that either stood upright or flew. An era of longevity and gigantism. What became of the reptile, and what became of those strong, long-lived people? What is the subsequent history of the Serpent, and what is the story of the people?

Trusting and Obeying

A central theme of God's Word is that trusting and obeying result in improvement of the human condition, whilst mistrust and self- willed aberration lead to degeneration. Another, lesser theme is the unimportance of animals in the overall scheme. Animals may be important to man, but are nothing more than an automaton, without the divine spark, and without final, eternal significance.

The fate of the dinosaurs is of no ultimate significance. The fate of mankind is of total significance.

The Serpent became a mouthpiece and an embodiment of the Cosmic Serpent, Leviathan and Lucifer became one. Just as the prince of angels, becoming lifted up in pride, was cast down to Hell, so Leviathan (known elsewhere as a dragon), prince of earthly creatures, was cast down and sentenced to crawl in dust. From this low, degraded station, the erstwhile prince of creation carries out a vicious underhand war against his one-time fellows and associates.

The war he wages is already lost. He has no ultimate power against those of true faith. The best he can do is follow the apostles of Christ like a chained dog, and proclaim, "These men are the servants of the Most High God!" (*Acts 16:17*) The way he can be overcome is to reverse the process, by which he first gained power here, and believe God first, believe God exclusively, believe God single- mindedly, and believe God no matter what our eyes, our ears, and our senses tell us. To trust, and obey, departure from which led to Leviathan's being cursed, the ground of which our bodies are formed being cursed and starting to die, the earth at large being cursed, and ultimately led to God's correctional judgments, such as the great flood.

The history of the Serpent? He became a venomous, hurtful snake - a serpent in the core meaning of the word. A messenger of pain, sickness and death; a cause of fear and suspicion. A creature always underhanded, always dangerous, never forthright and open. When opposed by superior force, it runs. It bites without intentional provocation on the part of the victim. It is loose in the world, now, in more ways than one. Is one of the ways in which it is at large, figuratively speaking, as a physical snake? Was this snake, technically speaking, once a dinosaur? *Tyrannosaurus,* perhaps?

Because God told Noah after the flood, "I do set my bow in the cloud, and it shall be a token of a covenant between me and the earth" (*Gen.9:13*), does not prove there were no rainbows prior to this time. Perhaps they were never so bright before this time, but logic suggests they would have existed, and the scriptural text does not forbid it. Likewise, just because God said to the Serpent, "On thy belly shalt thou go" (*Gen.3:14*), does not mean there were no snakes or snake-like creatures until this time; neither does it mean that all elevated reptiles instantaneously and universally became snakes. Some time may have been involved before all the elevated individuals became extinct.

If the scriptural account does indeed have a secondary meaning referring to flesh-and-blood animals, we could at least expect the following:

- A disruptive event in the history of the reptile class, exclusive to that class.
- Genetic information to the effect that snakes once possessed legs, and are a degenerate life form.
- Origin of at least one species of poisonous snake no earlier than Man.

These matters are of no ultimate significance, but to solve a dilemma faced by biologists, could we consult a world authority on the subject of reptiles and measure up his findings against the Scriptural account?

"It is surprising to discover that many modern biologists would claim that there is really no such thing as a 'reptile'! The reason for this apparent absurdity is as follows. The other terrestrial vertebrate classes - amphibians, birds, and mammals - are each, in an evolutionary sense, more 'real' than the reptilia."[13]

Requirement (1) fulfilled. A unique difference in the history of the reptiles.

"All snakes may be regarded as degenerated quadrupeds . . ." [Shine is actually quoting another zoologist at this point].

Requirement (2) fulfilled. Snakes once had legs.

---

[13] R. Shine, *Australian Snakes,* Balgowlah, N.S.W.: Reed Books, Aust., pages 28-33, 1991

"The first definite fossil snake is an Algerian species from the early Cretaceous period . . . Snakes are a much younger group, in geological terms, than most other reptiles. The fossil record of snakes is poor . . . Partly because of the scarcity of good fossils; the classification of snakes is a mess."

Requirement (3) fulfilled. "The fossil record of snakes is poor . . ." little better than that of man, in fact.

Quoting Shine again, "One writer suggested that much of the recent period of Earth's history should be called the 'Age of Snakes.'"

We have fossils of jellyfish, and even fossils of birds, but very few of snakes. Such as have been found are at or near the top of the geologic column. This can be said of few, if any, other life forms except man. We are indeed living in the 'Age of Snakes' - and man! We may well have once cohabited with elevated reptiles. There were then few snakes, none of which can be proved to have been venomous. We are now in the 'Age of Snakes,' and elevated reptiles have become extinct.

This then is the story of Leviathan or the Dragon, the Serpent. A story foreshadowed in the Bible, and shown to be technically meaningful by biology and palaeontology. It appears we may have begun to read the Serpent's story from the Bible, the rocks, and the laboratory.

The reader may take his/her choice as to the biologic detail. But how could negativism, how could anything contrary, whether spoken through a physical reptile or no, enter paradise?

Free Will

We have previously learned of how it may be helpful to visualize the eternal, the spiritual dimension, as having "air." For a being to have existence in that dimension, he must be able to "breathe." To enable breathing, he must have free will. He is living in the realm of moral considerations. In that realm, God is God - he is perfect truth, perfect love, he has total endurance, and so on - yet even he "knows good and evil" *Gen.3:22.* He can do no evil, but he knows good and evil. So, man, "made in the image of God," must be able to "know good and evil." The fact that he was created with free will implied that he would sooner or later exercise it. To exercise it necessitated his encountering the possibility of wrong.

Unless there is the possibility of wrong, there is no such thing as free will. It cannot be exercised.

If there is no such thing as free will, there is no eternity dimension. If there is no eternity dimension, there is no God.

If there is no God, there is no reality.

If God was to make man, then the scenario of *Gen.3:1* was inevitable. No matter who or what was the agent in presenting to man the possibility of a decision, the very existence of man meant that sooner or later he would have a choice. He would be exercising his inbuilt free will.

The serpent was not the cause of man's fall. The serpent merely presented mankind with an opportunity to exercise free will. Man was the sole cause of the fall.

One will now say, "If God knew man was capable of evil, why did he make him in the first place?" "Why am I thus?" *Ro.9:19.* "Nay but, O man, who art thou that repliest against God? Shall the thing formed say to him that formed it, why hast thou made me thus?" *Ro.9:20.* "Hath not the potter power over the clay . . .?" *Ro.9:21.*

We are what we are. We can be factious, and chafe; and to what purpose? No advantage in the clay complaining to the potter. How can that help the clay? The reality is the clay and the reality is the potter. The best path for the clay is to accept that it is indeed clay, and cast itself upon the potter's good care. Michelangelo made *David* and it is no use the marble or whatever the statue consists of complaining to Michelangelo.

Acceptance of what God has done, contentment with what God has done: this is our course. We have been created; from here we either go on by faith, or draw back, wither, and die.

Man's difficulties do not arise in the Devil, the serpent, or in any source outside himself. And to the person of faith, of sight, of character, there is no such circumstance as a difficulty - only a challenge, waiting to be overcome.

X. THE SERPENT

Gen.3:1-5

Now the serpent was more subtle than any beast of the field which the Lord God had made. And he said unto the woman, Yea, hath God said, Ye shall not eat of every tree of the garden? And the woman said unto the serpent, we may eat of the fruit of the trees of the garden: but of the fruit of the tree which is in the midst of the garden, God hath said, Ye shall not eat of it, neither shall ye touch it, lest ye die. And the serpent said unto the woman, "Ye shall not surely die: for God doth know that in the day ye eat thereof, then your eyes shall be opened, and ye shall be as gods, knowing good and evil."

Here is the classic case study of the methods to use to subvert a perfect society. This is the *modus operandi,* the signature in large hand of Satan's tactics when attempting to infiltrate a stable, a harmonious, in a sense, a Christian society. This is how he begins his infiltration of once- respected religious-based institutions in particular. Above all his other tactics, this is worthy of study.

For there can be little purpose in studying his obvious tactics. The obvious needs no explanation. The banning of the dissemination of truth, the exaltation of criminals, the sword of injustice, the rack, the stake, the inquisition, the all-pervasive conformism, the institutionalization of souldestroying quasi-religious superstition, the power-hungry elite: these need no explanation. Stalin, Hitler, Mao, the ayatollahs of autocracy—these we can understand. Only once the Devil gets sufficient control, he reveals his hand. It is the stage preceding his gaining of pervasive control that we should consider carefully. *Gen.3:1- 5* reveals his methods for this early stage. To receive benefit, we then need to apply our findings to our personal lives.

Toward the end of the twentieth century, various bodies, institutions, and departments of and within democracies such as Australia embarked upon a program of compilation of various statements and written expressions of motivating philosophy. These documents and statements were not a source of doctrine as much as a reflection of existing, underlying doctrine.

The underlying policy statement emanating from parts of more than one body or department, including segments within some education departments, was a paraphrase of *Gen.3:1-5,* all but word-for-word. And so it has been and will be throughout history, whenever people deliberately eliminate biblical/Christian doctrine from their own thoughts. Without the grace of God we are nothing but pathetic marionettes of "the god of this world." The immediate targets of this insidious deception include, of course, children - like Eve, open, innocent minds. The Adversary is not slow to exploit an opportunity.

The paraphrase of *Gen.3:1-5* as unwittingly compiled by non-Christian religious thinkers comprises variations on three main components: 1) a somewhat mesmeric, opiate-like phraseology (verbal manifestation of the fascinating subtlety of the hidden prompter); 2) a re-statement of "Yea, and hath God said . . ." ("Values-evaluation" or suchlike, by definition leading people to "talk around" the things God has said, rather than simply obey them); and 3) repetitive reference to self. ("Ye shall be as gods"). Stirring of the senses and sensuality. Appealing to self-importance. Directing the mind away from a solid foundation whilst subtly creating a mesmerizing, dulling atmosphere of peace and religious/philosophic correctness. Robbing a victim in a way that the victim feels is helping him.

Temptations

The Tempter captures people through their feelings and their physical, flesh-related senses. All too often he induces feelings of religious warmth, or feelings of camaraderie with the spirit of the age. There are few, if any, who do not know what it is to fall through obeying our senses or sensualities first, not last. There are few of us who have not at some time gone with the prevailing consensus, to our personal cost.

Our personal lives are a microcosm of the societies of which we are a part. Human societies, like the individuals comprising them, stand or fall on the same principles. So far as a people and a government adhere to the spirit and intent of God's word, so far they have success. So far as they ignore the divine precepts, so far they fall. The word of God speaks into every area of personal conduct and government administration.

Economics, trade, family and societal structuring, child rearing, personal conduct, health, industrial relations, immigration, defence, crime control, the environment, *ad infinitum.* Name any item or issue of private or public concern; God has spoken into that area. Rush to consult our senses or the spirit of the age on such matters, and more- than-likely consult ourselves into troubles. Consult God's word first and respond in the spirit of his words, and consult with ultimate success.

The Tempter knows his business. He has no difficulty in "leading captive at his will," *2 Tim.2:26,* any person or nation that is not focused on "the truth in Christ" *Ro.9:1.*

Our twentieth- and twenty-first-century societies, so mysteriously mimicking his whisperings to Eve, are fraught with examples of his cunning. Tragedies are not foreign to us. At the centre of these tragedies are people, people made in the image of God. People of inestimable worth. Liberty and tolerance themselves are under insidious threat. Freedom hangs in the balance. The great controversy between light and darkness continues unabated, with humanity at the centre of the spotlight.

The methods employed by the adversary are variations on the same old theme: ignition of pride and self-congratulation under cover of comfortable, quasi-religious misguidance. Put the subject to sleep, make him feel comfortable, pander to his ego, and propel him toward trouble whilst deceiving him as to his ultimate destination. "Ye shall be as gods." The appeal to pride and self-importance. "Yea, and hath God said?" Benumbing of sensitivity to truth, by jargon. "Ye shall not surely die . . . ye shall be as gods." The cunningly concealed, deadly sting. The lie.

Materialism

The first camouflaged pit that respectable, Christianized society tends to fall into is the deception of materialism. (*See Luke 12:15, 1 Tim.6:6-10, Pro.11:28,* etc.) Truly Christian societies tend to become wealthy and powerful; hence the likelihood of this trap, and the need to be alert and avoid it. "The iniquity of . . . Sodom, pride, fullness of bread, abundance of idleness . . . neither did she strengthen the hand of the poor and needy" *Ez.16:49.* "Fullness of bread . . . abundance of idleness . . . ." Our proper attitude to possessions is *Pro.30:8*: "Give me neither poverty nor riches."

The effect of prosperity upon western civilization has been both profound and potentially ruinous. We all too easily lose our roots and our reality. At times, we have witnessed an unhealthy drop-off in birth rates (*Pro.14:28*). We have erosion of societal cohesion through influx of peoples with incompatible ideologies. Children tend to be abandoned in a moral wilderness whilst suffering overprotection and overindulgence.

This overindulgence is being compounded by yet another sleight- of-hand by the Deceiver: the idea that children should receive a soft upbringing free of hard work and physical correction. (See *Eph.6:1-4; Heb.12:6-8;*

Pro.23:13, 14, etc.). One of his approaches is to point out that violence is wrong (but he does not point out it is only wrong in certain instances), and since violence is wrong, it is always wrong to use violence, even in its lawful and beneficial forms. Thus he makes Jesus Christ a sinner. (Christ employed righteous force on at least one occasion, and certainly lent moral support to forceful upholding of the law.)

By deceit, the seducing Serpent destroys the futures of multiplied thousands, and threatens the future of whole societies. Thirst for riches and power lie at the root of both militant (that is, extortionist) unionism, and a non-family based welfare state - "welfarism" *(see Luke 3:14; 1Tim.6:6; I Tim.5:16; 2 Thess.3:10-12*). The scriptures provide clear leadings toward a free-market economy with compassion and with family-based societal structures *Pro.11:26; Luke 15:11-24; Matt.20:1-15,* etc.

Obedience to the words of God, who desires us to "bear one another's burdens" *Gal.6:2*, and to "look not every man on his own things [situation], but every man also on the things of others" *Phil.2:4,* would lead men to know and consider policies helpful to all. Notice it says, "look **...every man . . .** on the things of others." Personal responsibility, not personal political agitation, to "pass the buck." It does not say, "look every politically correct **administration** . on the things of others." Socialism, the communal "cop-out"! Fake charity; Christianity by proxy! Throwing away common sense in favour of false security and false delusions about human behaviour, built on a mirage. There is a very good and logical reason why the Bible provides strong, sometimes severe guidelines for all areas of human existence. Overlooking the words of God in favour of a mirage harms *everyone.*

Is Australia building a house of freedom, or pulling down a house of freedom? "Every wise woman buildeth her house: but the foolish plucketh it down with her hands" *Pro.14:1.*

Co-Existence

The kingdom of God allows co-existence of distinctly different peoples because God is the perfect gentleman. Who is the antithesis of a gentleman, and how do his policies impact free and harmonious societies? As Benjamin Franklin's classic *Poor Richard's Almanac* has it: "Half a truth is often a great lie." How to set a course to avoid deception?

The Devil's equality is the equality of the lowest common denominator men will allow him to enforce. The lower, the better. The West saved the free world, only to discover that the price of liberty is eternal vigilance - and the enemy can be within. So far has western 'civilization' fallen into drunken torpor, it is embracing moral and administrative dunghills.

Multiculturalism imports supremacist cult division and violence, the antithesis of peace and equity, under the guise of tolerance.

Australia has been importing and incubating the death of democracy. Any philosophy (such as Islam) which gets itself to paradise by suppressing and even killing off the supporters of democracy is the death of democracy.

Extreme or militant environmentalism places objects, trees, and animals above human beings, taking away the liberty of choice of employment (and other activities) by public smear. This at the cost of the environment, under colours of improving the environment!

In extreme feminism, we see the classic smoke screen or snowstorm to cover a distressing fall-off in the privileges and prestige of females, doubled with an insidious attack on family structure and unity and freedom of the press. Women suffer most. And so the list goes on. "Civil Liberties," whilst a high ideal, has at times been an obfuscating cover for (amongst other crimes) a revived money- for-flesh, or slave trade, centred on exploitation of the female and even children for base gain. The female half of humanity is thereby given the "liberty" of being depicted as an exploitable object, the legitimate target of the corporate lust.

Same sex 'marriage' equality in its ultimate effect destroys every possible law and removes every possible safeguard. Every human being by definition loses equality and freedom under that tyranny of anarchy. "Land Rights," a laudable catch phrase, panders to superstitious nonsense and greed with culpable naivety, whilst making private land ownership more difficult, and potentially but not irrevocably damaging the people it is intended to help. "Children's rights," "animals' rights," *ad infinitum.* There is nothing new under the sun. The Adversary always attacks personal liberty - liberty to own land and goods; liberty to work, travel, and live according to personal preference; liberty of expression; liberty of worship.

To set people against people, to lade with superfluous burdens whilst not lifting a finger to help; to point the finger across an ocean of water or a gulf of culpable ignorance at others whose situation is different, or who have a greater load to carry; this is the *imprimatur* of the serpent. Are any of us free of it? Happy the man who is so.

The hidden prompter behind the serpent has not lost his touch. Neither has God's word lost its power.

Democracy

Thanks to the work of Jesus Christ, modern human beings have a privilege - democracy. It exists because of the mercy, favour, or grace of God, coupled with the sacrifices of our forebears. The hallmark of successful democracy is the rule of law, coupled with mercy, favour, and grace toward others. The Serpent is intent on seeing off democracy, permanently.

Obstacles may lie on the pathway, but far greater difficulties than these have been overcome in bringing us to this place in history. Jesus Christ is Lord!

Our problems are not popular movements, political parties, or others' policies. Our concern is to make Jesus Christ Lord in every corner of our personal lives. Divine Wisdom speaks into every corner of our personal lives, and into every corner of human society. Our calling is to appropriate a victory already won. Look steadfastly at the victory and ignore the serpent. But observe how the inveterate Deceiver operates -subtlety perfected!

Gen.3:6, 7

And when the woman saw that the tree was good for food, and that it was pleasant to the eyes, and a tree to be desired to make one wise, she took of the fruit thereof, and did eat, and gave also unto her husband with her; and he did eat.

The sinner knows what it is to be ruled by his hunger, his appetite, his lust, his personal feelings and inadequacies/insecurities. He knows what it is to be unable to resist the urge of the moment, the fashion of the day, the magnetic power of the herd. The person who is adopted into the family of God is still subject to such feelings, but he knows he can put a child-like reliance upon God in every circumstance, and by looking to what God has said only and to what God has said alone, he has a way forward. The battle is not always easy, nor successful. But "though he fall, he shall not be utterly cast down: for the Lord upholdeth him with his hand" *Ps.37:24.*

If Eve had put complete, childlike trust in God, looking only to the words he had spoken, she would not have fallen. In her was no dry tinder amenable to ignition from the Tempter's sparks. But then, she had no personal knowledge of the horror, the terror, and the degradation of sin. She was innocent in a sense we find difficult to visualize.

There is no more future in blaming our problems on the woman than there is in blaming them on the Devil. Nor is the woman to blame, even though she, "being deceived, was in the transgression" *1 Tim.2:14.* If I am sinful, I can blame it upon none other than myself. "By one man [Adam] sin entered into the world, and death by sin; and so death passed upon all men, for that all have sinned" *Ro.5:12*. Sin entered by Adam: I am Adam: all have sinned: I have none to blame other than myself.

The dialogue that ensued when Adam found his wife in a profoundly altered state we can only surmise. Whether he ate the fruit to follow her and perhaps try to bring her back, or simply out of desire to eat the fruit, we cannot say. The former seems possible. If so, this is an object lesson in the impossibility of helping others by sinking to their own level.

Gen.3:7-11

And the eyes of them both were opened, and they knew that they were naked; and they sewed fig leaves together, and made themselves aprons. And they heard the voice of the Lord God walking in the garden in the cool of the day: and Adam and his wife hid themselves from the presence of the Lord God amongst the trees of the garden. And the Lord God called unto Adam, and said unto him, "Where art thou?" And he said, "I heard thy voice in the garden, and I was afraid, because I was naked; and I hid myself." And he said, "Who told thee that thou wast naked? Hast thou eaten of the tree, whereof I commanded thee that thou shouldest not eat?"

The fig leaves as clothing are symbolic of man's attempts at self- justification. All our attempts at justifying ourselves do not even class as garments.

Adam sinned, and from now onward all men except one will be born sinners, with a "sin-principle" within them. It is not that we merely commit sin; we are sin. Adam himself immediately felt this and knew it. He felt it more and more keenly as the perfect God approached him. He had murdered no one; he bore enmity against no one; he was as near a perfect man as it is possible for fallen man to be. But hear his confession: "I heard your voice. I hid myself. I am afraid. I know I am naked." He may have disobeyed, but he retained a true conscience. He did not try to belittle the matter. He felt conviction of sin. He knew his nakedness, and he was afraid. We learn subsequently that God met him where he was and ministered to his need - the blood sacrifice that gave him real clothing (v.*21*).

See in *Gen.3:7-11* the total etiquette with which the Almighty is graced. God sees all things. He knows all things, even before they happen. Had he so chosen, could he not have seen Eve eat the fruit? Did he not know the exact place of our first parents' concealment? Could he not have appeared suddenly in their hiding-place, and bluntly accused them? But this is man's world, and the Almighty comes as a discreet guest. His discretion, his gracious, all-seeing wisdom, led him to approach our first parents in the precise manner they needed to be approached in this, their first great difficulty. "A bruised reed shall he not break, and a smoking flax shall he not quench" *Matt.12:20.*

Gen.3:12-19

And the man said, "The woman whom thou gavest to be with me, she gave me of the tree, and I did eat." And the LORD God said unto the woman, "What is this that thou hast done?" And the woman said, "The serpent beguiled me, and I did eat." And the LORD God said unto the serpent, "Because thou hast done this, thou art cursed above all cattle, and above every beast of the field; upon thy belly shalt thou go, and dust shalt thou eat all the days of thy life: and I will put enmity between thee and the woman, and between thy seed and her seed; it shall bruise thy head, and thou shalt bruise his heel. " Unto the woman he said, "I will greatly multiply thy sorrow and thy conception; in sorrow thou shalt bring forth children; and thy desire shall be to thy husband, and he shall rule over thee. " And unto Adam he said, "Because thou hast hearkened unto the voice of thy wife, and hast eaten of the tree, of which I commanded thee, saying, Thou shalt not eat of it: cursed is the ground for thy sake; in sorrow shalt thou eat of it all the days of thy life; thorns also and thistles shall it bring forth to thee; and thou shalt eat the herb of the field; in the sweat of thy face shalt thou eat bread, till thou return unto the ground; for out of it wast thou taken: for dust thou art, and unto dust shalt thou return."

If the serpent was to blame for mankind's predicament, justice would have apportioned the blame entirely to this unfortunate creature. Not so: in fact, if man had not fallen, the serpent may well have come away scot-free. Man's disobedience caused the serpent's curse, as well as his own. And although the heavy sentence was spoken by the Almighty, it might have been man's own voice, for he sentenced himself. No sooner did Adam touch the fruit than these heavy words were inevitable. We brought it upon ourselves. And where did the problem originate? What precisely set the curse in motion? "Because thou hast hearkened unto the voice of thy wife [a lesser voice than God's], and hast eaten of the tree, of which I commanded thee, saying, Thou shalt not..."

A failure of trust and obedience.

The ensuing curse needs little explanation. It is all too familiar to us.

Enmity

The enmity between the woman and the serpent obviously speaks of the Devil's enmity against Christ and His people. Encouragement here: "her seed . . . shall bruise thy head." "Behold, I give unto you power to tread on serpents and scorpions, and over all the power of the enemy; and nothing shall by any means hurt [in an ultimate sense] you" *Luke 10:19.*

Rule of the husband over the wife (v.*16*) is not a license to dictatorship but the establishment of order or hierarchy in family life. The scriptures give males the authority but also the responsibility. See how paradise has no rules or need of administrative strictures, but not so the fallen world. Already the female is placed in a role relative to the male, and both must fulfil their roles if the species is to survive. These roles are not so much a commandment but a state-of-being. They are intrinsically part of the normal male and normal female. Ideally this is a partnership rather than a master-servant relationship.

Observe (v.*16*), "I will greatly multiply . . . thy conception." This was spoken directly to Eve and to all women in general. This increase in frequency of childbirth was necessitated by the onset of death and disease. Being spoken personally and directly to Eve, it must mean Eve herself gave birth to a large number of children. This becomes significant further into the narrative, where the account superficially appears to give Eve only a handful of children, yet speaks as though the world was already becoming populated. This assurance that Eve had many children confirms our suspicions that the few that gain specific mention in the later narrative are important to the narrative, and those not essential to the account - a great number - are passed over.

When we think of all the pain and difficulty suffered down through the ages through childbirth and childcare, and think that a single act of disobedience by one person occasioned it all, then we begin to see the enormity of sin. Even in this the Victor over sin and suffering invites trust and faith: *1 Tim.2:15,* "She shall be saved in childbearing, if [she] continues in faith and charity "

We also may note in passing a matter relating to the female and her particular status. There is a temptation common to some who are second-in-command - a wish to become first-in-command. To chafe at being under. To vainly imagine that they can take the reins and get the glory themselves.

Delusions of grandeur. The danger of taking the reins of their own volition and being made to appear foolish thereby. The scriptures by examples do allow that a female in rare cases can rise to the leadership level of males. These cases are exceptional. (The scriptures also tell us that in times of moral weakness, women become our rulers.) The scriptures confirm a deep-seated difference between the sexes. Women tend to be ruled by their heart, and provision is made in the Law for this fact (e.g. *Num.30:1-16*). This is no discredit. But because the woman has been cast for the role of second-in-command, she may encounter the temptation to usurp authority; just as the male, being in the leading role, may encounter the desire to abdicate his necessary place of leadership.

The scriptures cover both possibilities, and in the case of the female, they employ strong phraseology specifically designed to evaporate false delusions. The language employed is not that of belittlement but of safety. Some have wrongly concluded that the Bible belittles woman, when in truth it gives her correct natural status, along with appropriate guidance and warnings, just as it does for the male. As St. Paul has it, the male-female relationship "is a great mystery." To understand it is to understand in some measure "Christ and the church" *Eph.5:32.* For woman to usurp authority or man to abdicate responsibility is to deny nature itself and deny Christ himself. Society must automatically dematerialize if this should happen.

Microbiological Matters

Turning to technical matters: v.*17-19* conceals a remarkable microbiological statement. We are "formed . . . of the dust of the ground" *Gen.2:7.* Our bodies are chemicals or minerals - ground, or earth. It has been deduced that physical aging is caused by imperfect reproduction of our body cells in their continuous replacement process. Older cells are continually being replaced by identical newer cells in our bodies, and it is in this replicating process that imperfections creep in, resulting in aging. Viruses - agents of sickness and death - may also play a part in this process of aging, by occasioning damage to some cells as they replicate. Viruses have no place on the tree of life; they are neither living nor dead, but are agents of death; they are neither animal nor vegetable, but are perhaps best described as mutations of mineral substances. So we age because the ground (or earth) of which we consist does not operate perfectly during cell-replication, compounded by the deleterious actions of viruses, themselves apparent mutations of mineral (or earth).

Read now the same message.

"Cursed is the ground [the dust of which our bodies are made] . . . ; thorns and thistles shall it cause to bud to thee . . . ; till thou return unto the ground; . . . for dust thou art, and unto dust shalt thou return." Amongst various venoms and death-agents presumably brought into effect by the curse, none are worse than these microscopic "thorns and thistles" which the curse brought forth or "caused to bud." The earth of which we were formed has risen against us.

Under the tree of life, life once ruled; but now the curse rules. The only life forms successfully mutating and improving themselves now are the agents of deprivation and disease. *The curse rules.*

For an accurate description of the reproduction and successful mutation of viruses, try "cause to bud." Cause to bud now, and cause to bud, and bud, down the hallways of time. Even the earth itself has risen up against us in revulsion against sin. "In the day thou eatest thereof, dying, thou shalt die."

The curse explains why life forms harmful to man and the environment seem to be getting stronger, whilst beneficial life forms go backward. In the case of viruses - our great enemies - did they entirely originate at the time of the curse, or were they already present in the earth, but outside the garden? An intriguing question, which the absence of any fossil virus remains fails to answer conclusively, viruses have no fossil record, but in the case of such minute structures, this does not constitute complete proof of absence. But at this point of time, the fossil evidence - or lack thereof - is in keeping with a view of worldwide virus origin contemporaneous with Adam's heavy sentence.

Gen.3:20-24

And Adam called his wife's name Eve; because she was the mother of all living. Unto Adam also and to his wife did the Lord God make coats of skins, and clothed them. And the Lord God said, Behold, the man is become as one of us, to know good and evil: and now, lest he put forth his hand, and take also of the tree of life, and eat, and live forever: Therefore the Lord God sent him forth from the garden of Eden, to till the ground from whence he was taken. So he drove out the man; and he placed at the east of the garden of Eden Cherubim, and a flaming sword which turned every way, to keep the way of the tree of life.

Eve was the mother of all living (v.*20*). Our first parents' complete genetic strength and diversity meant they were all peoples of all time. Adam married a product of his own body, his "daughter" by asexual reproduction. Adam and Eve's children may have gone through similar processes, although it is not mentioned: most probably brothers married sisters. We draw back from the thought, but those children would have been more different from one another than any couple marrying today. The pattern was set in Adam's marrying his "daughter" under divine approval. The scriptures tell us no more.

That God himself killed advanced animals for man's benefit destroys any notion of virtue in vegetarianism or of the sanctity of animal life. Animals only have value insofar as they are of value to man. This includes the most advanced. To preserve animals that are a real danger to human life, especially those that have taken human life, is contrary to divine command (e.g., *Ex.21:28*).

V.*21* is a forerunner of animal sacrifice, so central to Old Testament Law. Under the Old Testament, millions of animals were killed, and their blood was symbolically sprinkled between God and the stone tables of the Law. When Absolute Justice saw the blood sprinkled over the Law, he was able to spare his people from the requirement of the Law: death, disease, destitution. Since animals are of no eternal significance, how can their death be any protection for man? Does the blood of animals have any efficacy with Justice?

No, none. It was faith that lent the animal blood its saving virtue, faith looking forward to Christ, thereby making the animal's sacrifice Christ's sacrifice. Have *faith!*

An Act of Mercy

The barring of man from the tree of life (v.*22*) was an act of mercy. Man was afflicted in some degree with the same ailment as the Devil- rampant pride, making him suffer pernicious delusions of grandeur. The danger now was that instead of being the beneficent god of the Earth, he would try to be god on Earth in the evil that phrase entails. Imagine a Stalin, a Hitler, and a Nero, who would live forever. Emperor worship, with its corollary, the infallibility of popes and patriarchs, all the tendency in man to lord it over his fellows and equals, embodied in power-hungry demagogues who could neither die nor be killed.

It is a rare and precious person who possesses true leadership, a thoroughly humble spirit. Moses was the meekest man in the Earth (see *Num.12:3*), and one of the greatest. Humiliation need be no disaster, even if it cuts us off from physical strength. Pride is our greatest enemy, but we may take heart: "Those that walk in pride he is able to abase" *Dan 4:37.* No, we cannot go directly to some supernatural principle or process and eat fruit from it as a fountain of eternal youth. If we are to access a tree of life now, it can only be through the humble Christ, and even then our bodies will only become impregnable again after the final resurrection, when all possibility of evil has gone from the elect. See the wisdom of God.

V.*24* prompts the oft-asked question: if angels (cherubim) stand guard at the gateway of the Garden of Eden, where are they? Why can we not locate these angels? The question is worthy of an answer. *Genesis* employs some strange geographic terms.

Chapter 2:8: "The Lord God planted a garden eastward in Eden."

Chapter 2:10: "And a river went out of Eden to water the garden; and . . . it became into four heads . . . the third river is Hiddekel: that is it which goeth toward the east of Assyria."

In terms of Old Testament Bible geography, Assyria was far to the east. Go much farther east than Assyria, and enter *terra incognita.* It was almost at the edge of the map. And note: the Hiddekel "goeth toward the east of Assyria."

The Hiddekel went toward the eastern edge of the map, east of Assyria. The garden was *eastward* in Eden, meaning east in or of Eden. A river that went to water the garden went eastward of one of the more eastward-situated regions. And now, Chapter *3:24,* "At the *east* of the garden . . . Cherubim, and a flaming sword "

The garden was east in/of Eden, which was itself on the eastern extremity of the map (world), east of Assyria. If this was not sufficient, the angels are east of the garden (v.*24*).

Too many easts. East of east. East, repeated three times, a configuration sometimes meaning multiplied, multiplied. Multiplied easts. East of east? Where is east of east?

We have learned already of multiple meanings of Eden. Eden is a location on the world map. It also speaks of the whole world of former, happier times. It speaks of the reign of the Prince of Peace and the spread of peace to the four corners of the Earth.

The Garden of Eden - the garden eastward in Eden, always eastward; in Eden yet eastward of Eden; this garden still exists. The same garden is spoken of in *Rev.22.* It is Heaven, the eternal Paradise of God. This Paradise once touched the Earth, at a specific location. God, and two godlike human beings, possessed of powers we would now see as supernatural, enjoyed this *panacea,* this terrestrial utopia.

Once the "slightly lower than the angels" opened this utopia to the possibility of evil, Heaven withdrew back from the Earth. The two almost-angelic beings concurrently lost their more heavenly aspect. Man could no longer access the supernatural as he once did. Hence, he cannot access the translator, the tree of life. The species are locked to him. This is emphasized by the angels and the multi-directional sword, or barrier. Man will never make new species or tap a source of eternal youth.

Where do these angels stand? Where is the barring mechanism? It is to the east; as we have deduced, east of east. And who is the only one who can return from east of east, open the barrier, and fetch again utopia and perfection? *Ez.44:1-3:* "Then he brought me back the way of the gate [bar] of the outward sanctuary which looketh toward the east; and it was shut. Then said the Lord unto me; "This gate shall be shut, it shall not be opened, and no man shall enter in by it, because the Lord, the God of Israel, hath entered in by it, therefore it shall be shut. It is for the Prince; . . . he shall enter by the way of the porch of that gate . . . ." "For as the Father hath life in himself; so hath he given to the Son to have life in himself . . ." *John 5:26.* One man has had the authority to pass through those flaming swords. He is destined to return, and take his people "east of east."

XI. MALE-FEMALE RELATIONSHIPS

Gen.4:1.

And Adam knew Eve his wife . . .

There is only one document fully able to educate us for life. Some aspects of life can only be adequately spoken into by divine authority. Attempts at educating and enlightening a population in fields such as human relationships/personal conduct, outside Holy Writ, are an insult to the students, a fist shaken at our Creator, and a blow against human society. The Adversary laughs all the way to the penitentiary, the asylum, the rehabilitation centre, and the morgue. If Jesus Christ will not be Lord, the Devil soon will.

We know the scriptures speak into every aspect of human existence. In passing, could we investigate, by way of illustration, a little of its teaching on male-female relationships?

The scriptures embody *flexibility* within *certainty.* They allow the special case. They accommodate human variety. They credit people with the possibility of sanctified common sense. In matters of civil and criminal law, for instance, they will sometimes set down a law as though it is immutable (which it is), but in some other place give an example in which this law appears to have been diluted or even disannulled, by the counsels of God himself. (This because the law is a generality and the example is a special case, in which the perfect Judge sees all the circumstances and sees the heart.)

We can only speak in generalities here: but there will be exceptions to a general rule. One obvious conundrum is multiple wives - we shall not entangle ourselves in that can of worms.

The Old Testament Law, as it relates to male-female relationships, owns two classes of people involved in the male-female physical union: those who are married, and those in a relationship in which one or both of the parties is a criminal. The criminal penalty is death.

There is no such state as physical union outside marriage, or outside criminal behaviour (excepting the above-mentioned special case). Generally speaking, physical union constitutes either marriage or a capital crime on the part of one or both parties. In simple terms, physical union is profoundly significant, and to steal from its significance in any way is a very serious matter. Physical union is marriage, and marriage is not a light undertaking. It has profound, deep, and lasting effects upon the participants. It has profound implications for society, and for children's welfare within society.

Society stands or falls on the male-female relationship, and on the security of those involved in it. And "romance," strange though it may seem, goes hand-in-hand with the security feelings of the participants. There is no joy if failure is a real possibility. That is why true "romance" is only experienced fully by those with arranged marriages - particularly if the Everlasting and All-Knowing Father is undertaking the arrangements.

"Adam knew . . . his wife." Physical knowledge, or physical union, is marriage. This is a foundational, unchangeable principle. Special cases may arise, but the principle remains.

In terms of human behaviour likely to lead to stable marriage (lasting romance), the scriptures give many hints and directives, which we can but summarily touch on in passing. Since everything that does not come of faith is ultimately worthless, simple trust in God is the basis of success in anything.

1) "Arranged" relationships are likely to be successful, if higher Providence is involved in the "arranging."

2) We need to do our parts also, and seek and prepare ourselves for a partner. Faith prepares for what it knows will happen and patiently waits for it.

3) Feelings are not conducive to good matches, especially amongst younger people. Friendships formed in teenage years have a reduced chance of survival compared to those formed in later years. "Falling in love" is an encumbrance; impossible as this may seem to those afflicted by it, it is both a fever from which recovery can be fast, and a fly in the ointment of good matchmaking.

4) It is of no purpose imagining that it is possible to live with someone unless conversation is easy and amicable between the two. Begin by finding if communication is possible. Upon which topic to converse?

5) Sooner rather than later it is essential to testify to personal beliefs. This will lead to mutual trust or mutual exclusion. A common view of life is foundational.

6) As for personal conduct, generally it is best to run from anyone who is intentionally immodest, or displays excessive, violent, or uncontrolled behaviour. We should not imagine that someone

whom we cannot reform prior to marriage will necessarily be easier to reform subsequent to it.

7) Avoid going alone with or touching any member of the opposite sex unless you are fully convinced you are qualified to marry them, they are qualified to marry you, and such a union is correct, as of now, in the eyes of God. Within reason, avoid private conversation; avoid private association with any other than our life partner.

Each of these pointers is suggested by and is supportable from the Word of God. This is not to say that we are duty bound to slavishly observe them in meticulous detail. Faith and obedience are the overriding and deciding factors in all spheres of human activity and aspiration. But in this matter of the female-male relationship, we are provided with a complete example to follow in our first parents. They ever and only had eyes for the one God gave them. On his part, the Almighty made certain these two were made for each other. There were no others. Even now, wherever two people are in the will of God, there need be no others. Divine Wisdom does not make mistakes. We do well to become one with the Eternal Purpose for ourselves.

When society does not act in trust and obedience, it loses romance. In this matter of the femalemale relationship, we clearly see that the world is a liar.

The Legacy

Gen.4:1-24

And Adam knew Eve his wife; and she conceived, and bare Cain, and said, I have gotten a man from the Lord. And she again bare his brother Abel. And Abel was a keeper of sheep, but Cain was a tiller of the ground. And in process of time it came to pass, that Cain brought of the fruit of the ground an offering unto the Lord. And Abel, he also brought of the firstlings of his flock and of the fat thereof. And the Lord had respect unto Abel and to his offering: But unto Cain and to his offering he had not respect. And Cain was very wroth, and his countenance fell. And the Lord said unto Cain, Why art thou wroth? And why is thy countenance fallen? If thou doest well, shalt thou not be accepted? and if thou doest not well, sin lieth at the door. And unto thee shall be his desire, and thou shalt rule over him. And Cain talked with Abel his brother: and it came to pass, when they were in the field, that Cain rose up against Abel his brother; and slew him. And the Lord said unto Cain, Where is Abel thy brother? And he said, I know not: am I my brother's keeper? And he said, "What hast thou done? The voice of thy brother's blood crieth unto me from the ground. And now art thou cursed from the earth, which hath opened her mouth to receive thy brother's blood from thy hand; When thou tillest the ground, it shall not henceforth yield unto thee her strength; a fugitive and a vagabond shalt thou be in the earth." And Cain said unto the Lord, "My punishment is greater than I can bear. Behold, thou hast driven me out this day from the face of the earth; and from thy face shall I be hid; and I shall be a fugitive and a vagabond in the earth; and it shall come to pass, that every one that findeth me shall slay me." And the Lord said unto him, "Therefore whosoever slayeth Cain, vengeance shall be taken on him sevenfold." And the Lord set a mark upon Cain, lest any finding him should kill him. And Cain went out from the presence of the Lord, and dwelt in the land of Nod, on the east of Eden. And Cain knew his wife; and she conceived, and bare Enoch: and he builded a city, and called the name of the city, after the name of his son, Enoch. And unto Enoch was born Irad: and Irad begat Mehujael: and Mehujael begat Methusael: and Methusael begat Lamech. And Lamech took unto him two wives: the name of the one was Adah, and the name of the other Zillah. And Adah bare Jabal: he was the father of such as dwell in tents, and of such as have cattle. And his brother's name was Jubal: he was the father of all such as handle the harp and organ. And Zillah, she also bare Tubalcain, an instructor of every artificer in brass and iron: and the sister of Tubalcain was Naamah. And Lamech said unto his wives, Adah and Zillah, Hear my voice; ye wives of Lamech, hearken unto my speech: for I have slain a man to my wounding, and a young man to my hurt. If Cain shall be avenged sevenfold, truly Lamech seventy and sevenfold.

Our status and our current standing are reflections of our own actions and attitudes, and also those of our forebears. In some measure our religious development is the development achieved by our parents. If we are handed a rich legacy of godliness, we are very privileged. In *Gen.4*, we learn of a genetic line that inherited the opposite of godliness, and a miserable inheritance it proved to be. The father of this line killed his younger brother without provocation. He began by speaking with God face-to-face; he murdered his innocent and godly younger brother; he then turned his back completely on God (despite proffered mercies) and shut himself off from God and all good thoughts of him. As far as the record informs us, he never again regarded his Creator in any light other than as someone who had offended him and occasioned him personal trouble. As far as the record goes, none of his lineage was markedly better than himself. One of his descendants, Lamech (v.*19-24*), was a true reproduction of his progenitor; he descended to polygamy, and boasted to his wives of his prowess in murdering the young and (perhaps) innocent.

If we are far from God, or our progenitors were far from God, it was not God who moved. At some time, someone in our ancestry deliberately turned away. There is no greater inheritance than an inheritance of godliness (*Pro.13:22*), and it endures to *children's children.* There is no worse inheritance than idolatrous rebellion; the rewards of it are visited to the *third and fourth generation of them that hate me* (*Ex.20:5*).

See Cain complain that his punishment is too severe (v.*13*), even though it is not as great as the offense, and is a merciful amelioration of the normal sentence. See him turn his footsteps away from humane and god-fearing company. See him go to the land of Nod, which some interpret as *shaking* or *restlessness,* east of Eden, to far-removed regions where he spent his life in restless wanderings.

See his descendants follow in his mould until, in the person of his descendants, he finally receives the sentence from which only repentance and restitution could have saved him - the ultimate penalty. His line and his history apparently terminate with v.*24*, cut off, by the great flood or some other cause. "A man that doeth violence to the blood of any person shall flee to the pit; let no man stay him" *Pro.28:17*.

The mark of Cain (v.*15*) is something of a mystery and well may remain so. Its purpose we know; it stayed others from slaying him. Its nature taxes the imagination. Having no description of it and no living descendants who might display it, we could perhaps leave it lie, shrouded in mystery. God is able to protect people, even murderers.

Lamech's avenging seventy and seven-fold (v.*24*) stands in stark contrast to the spirit of Christ, who commands us to forgive [maintain a non-condemnatory attitude] not seven times, but seventy times seven.

Observe technologic skills such as manufacture of musical instruments and brass and ironware, amongst the very first peoples (v.*20-22*). As biology, as the fossil record, and as logic tell us, species do not struggle into being; they evidence suddenly, in full strength and diversity. Precisely as the scriptures relate. However, despite these earliest peoples' physical and mental power, their fossil or archaeological remains are bound to be few. As such, this paucity of surviving evidence could be mistakenly regarded as supporting human evolution, or upward development over time. In reality this lack of fossil remains supports the scriptural account. It supports it in a number of ways.

- Even though individual members of a society may be highly active and intelligent, time is necessary to the development of societies to the level where those societies can construct durable edifices by which to be remembered.

- The biblical account raises doubt in regard to the societal competence and cohesion of much of the early population.

This deficiency presumably hamstrung technologic and societal development.

- Both the Bible and the geologic record speak of "a world that then was" *2 Pet.3:6,* of strata of the Tertiary/Quaternary deposited in an environment much more salubrious than our own.

- A benign climate coupled with ample food supplies and physical robustness would provide little motivation to build as modern man does.

- The great flood was a type or a forerunner of the final judgment. Therefore it was specifically designed to obliterate the works of sinful man - everything not "of faith." Therefore little, if any, record of pre-flood society should exist. Such structures as they did build would have been partly destroyed, and their building materials and metal tools reworked by post-flood artisans.

There is some limited record of metal tools being found encased in stone, and some evidence of human footprints set in rock. But some rock can form quickly. If any archaeological record of those people exists, it is currently sketchy in the extreme. So, in one of those ironies of research, the same dearth of archaeological discoveries can be taken as supporting infinitesimally slow ascent from the ape, or the scriptural view!

Calling Upon God

Gen.4:25, 26

And Adam knew his wife again; and she bore a son, and called his name Seth: for God, said she, hath appointed me another seed instead of Abel, whom Cain slew. And to Seth, to him also there was born a son; and he called his name Enos: then began men to call upon the name of the Lord.

"Call unto me, and I will answer thee" *Jer.33:3.* Did men in the times of Enos begin to call upon the name of the Lord? The name above every name? Jehovah: I AM THAT I AM? By his name, *Jehovah- nissi,* The Lord is my banner, *Ex.17:15?* By his name, *Jehovah-jireh,* The Lord my provider, *Gen.22:14?*

By his name, *Jehovah-shalom,* The Lord send peace, *Judges 6:24? Jehovah-tsidkenu,* The Lord our righteousness, *Jer:23:6?* Men began to call upon the name of the Lord. Were they heard?

No one has yet called upon the Lord from an attitude of godly-fear without being heard. He hears before we call.

If the people of those times had gone further than *beginning* to call, the history of the world may well have been different; but insofar as we seek God, he will be found of us, as men found him then. "To this man will I look, even to him that is poor and of a contrite spirit, and trembleth at my word" *Isa.66:2.* "Look unto me, and be ye saved, all the ends of the earth" *Isa.45:22.*

Only three children of Adam and Eve are specifically named in the Bible, and one of them was murdered. Yet even by the time of this murder, the greater middle-eastern region was beginning to become inhabited. By the time Adam and Eve's son, Seth, had his own son (Enos), it could be said that "men" - many people - began to call upon the name of the Lord. God's words to Eve - "I will greatly multiply thy conception" - were found effective, as are all his words.

Gen.5:1, 2

This is the book of the generations of Adam. In the day that God created man, in the likeness of God made he him; male and female created he them; and blessed them, and called their name Adam, in the day when they were created.

The reference to Adam as though he was many people addresses the question of the lawfulness of intermarriage amongst his immediate children. It may assist in this concept to remove from the mind the thoughts and notions of incest and replace them with the idea of multiplied peoples marrying. "Male and female created he them: and blessed them, and called their name Adam, in the day when they were created." Adam was a multitude.

At this juncture it may be helpful to emulate the text we are studying, step back, and refresh our minds through contemplation of the overall historical perspective at this point in mankind's history. "This is the book of the generations of Adam [mankind]." Where are we in the flow of history? Where are we located? What can be seen around us? What lies ahead and behind, where are we going, and above all else, what year is this? What is the time compared to modern times?

This very question has exercised the minds of thousands, if not millions, and has all but generated its own academic discipline devoted to itself alone. When, how, did we first step out on mother Earth?

When? Why? What were we like then, when the world was fresh, when the streams were clear and snow-fed, when the mammoth, the mastodon, and, in Australia, the diprotodon, were our fellow travellers?

What purpose, what reason, what mechanism put us here? When? Why? How did it happen?

The same communicating Power that is now translating the primordial energy-pulse into the visible print we are reading, translated mineral structure into simple plant structure - perhaps even simpler than the simplest plants we yet know. Into that structure he communicated animation, life. And so all life appears to come from mineral (and water is a mineral), yet it has step-by-step been communicated, over time, upward, ever upward, by the communicating power. Known by the ancient Greeks as the *Logos,* known now also by the Name above all Names.

At the acme of geologic history, the communicating power communicated a part of itself to the highest tip of its animated mineral series. The tree of life, growing from the throne of God, reached up to the throne of God, and God touched its highest tip with the royal sceptre. The tip became the crown.

On Descending from Animals

We shall now destroy the concept of the evolutionary origin of man by genetic descent from animals. We shall destroy it on the evidence of the fossil record. We shall destroy it on the basis of common sense. We shall destroy it on the basis of everyday observation. We shall destroy it so that it never rises again as a scientific force. We shall do all this by consulting common sense and the Bible. To do it, we shall require only the jawbone of an ass and a source of higher Inspiration.

To Darwinist dogma: present your reasons!

The challenge to this body of unsanctified, self-opinionated spider webs is now the challenge of Sennacherib to Hezekiah: Go to now, and give pledges; and I for my part will provide a squad of horses, if you for your part can put riders on them. Set up Truth beside this icon, and see if *Dagon* has anything but his prostrate stump remaining to him by morning. "Associate yourselves, 0 ye people, and ye shall be broken in pieces . . . Take counsel together, and it shall come to naught; speak the word, and it shall not stand . . ." *Isa.8:9,10.*

This unsanctified obscurantism in theoretical human ancestry does not have one brick standing on top of another. "Sanctify the Lord of hosts himself; and let him be your fear, and let him be your dread . . . To the law and to the testimony: if they speak not according to this word, it is because there is no light in them" *Isa.8:13, 20.*

We shall now proceed (by the help of Divine Wisdom) to build, step-by-step, precept upon precept; a factual, scientific foundation of understanding in human history. In this, the reader is invited to turn detective, and by application of logic and some simple facts, decipher his own ancestry for himself. The matter is not complicated. The great and gracious God chooses to give us some inkling of our ancestry - we are important to him. People, people's ancestors, people's family lineages are important to the God who knows the number of hairs on our heads. God loves us! We are important! We matter!

Like all good detectives, we need to lay the foundation of our case in solid, unshakeable facts.

We shall endeavour to lay this foundation under four main heads:

- Species (and mankind) arise with their individual members fully developed.
- As a species, we have been here a comparatively short time.
- Our historical record prior to 5000-4000 B.C. has been all but obliterated.
- By understanding the likely cause of this truncation we can begin to understand ancient history

First Head

Species, and therefore mankind, arise as a group of competent, fully developed individuals. No matter what mechanism of species generation is postulated, geologists are in no doubt that once a species becomes a species here on Earth, it is a complete species. They are obliged to believe this because their observations give them no choice. One cannot seriously contemplate the fossil record or the world around us without coming to the same conclusion.

Certainly, apparent linking or halfway creatures leave their record in the rocks, like harbingers of new species to come, or desperate strivings of natural selection to produce that for which the changing environment is calling, but which only an all-knowing Provision can supply. Some of these natural-selection attempts, or halfway "stop-gaps", are bizarre in the full sense of the term. Certainly they are strong circumstantial evidence in favour of species evolution. And there is an abundance of them.

Some of the celebrated "ape men," so central to evolutionary prognostications, may well fall within this category. Natural selection sensed an empty, man shaped space and valiantly tried to fill it. Natural breeding programs such as these certainly have produced weird, novel, and almost entertaining oddities. On top of this, there is nothing to stop new species from drifting toward some other or some older life form, at least in external shape. So some "ape men" could have been apes, and some could have been men.

Inbreeding or selective line-breeding amongst an isolated or morally deranged fringe-group of humans could effectively simulate a return to an ape-like species. And moral derangement has at various times, especially earlier times, been a sad feature of our now-fallen species. Institutionalized human sacrifice, institutionalized line-breeding, annihilation of anything or anyone that is different - fallen man does not always have a pretty record.

But to return to more pleasant topics: oddities, bizarre oddities, weird oddities, "halfway" oddities - the geologic record has its share, and strange it would be if it did not. It is this very ability to produce oddities that keeps species viable. But species themselves, whatever their origin, do not struggle onto the world stage. Consult the geologic record for confirmation of this unshakeable fact! They explode onto the world stage, and they enter upon it in full genetic maturity, in full potential diversity, with initial zest and competitiveness that can be all but startling to the observer.

From the initial simple, simple, plant-like organisms seeding the earliest rocks prodigally with traceable carbon element to all the animal phyla leaping into reality at the Precambrian/Cambrian interface, to the sudden and startling *debut* of the flowering plants in the Cretaceous - species activate with vitality, with zest, with remarkable initial output.

Species actuate on the Earth fully developed, genetically complete. From observation of fossils, it could reasonably be said, with some qualifications, that the earlier individuals of a species are as robust, as competent, as capable, as any that follow. Or more so. This is a generalization.

Generally speaking, our earliest human ancestors - whether they originated as apes or no - were as robust, as competent, as capable, as any of us, their descendants. Or more so. To suggest otherwise is to confound the evidence of the entire fossil record, not to mention observable genetics and other witnesses besides. Our ancestors of long ago - our human ancestors - were physically, mentally, and intellectually a match and probably much more than a match for anyone living today. Evolution has no choice but to concur in this fact, (which it does, albeit reluctantly). This overall physical and mental competence did not necessarily translate into societal cohesion or competence.

Our earliest human ancestors were individually a force to be reckoned with. They were quite capable of leaving a record of themselves, at least in some measure.

This fact throws grave doubts on any proposal for an extended timeframe for our ancient history.

Second Head

We can have been here for a limited time only. From the fossil record, new species tend to fill their ecologic niche quickly and actively. Unless something strange has happened in our case, we should quickly have overspread the Earth, and overspread it with evidence of our presence. The most primitive of peoples at least crack rocks and leave bones and tools of various types to be buried. And there is no reason to believe earliest man would have been as primitive as some of the isolated fringe- groups that followed, of whom there exist ample modern examples. If mankind has been here for any time at all, and he has displayed similar expansionary behaviour to other species, where is the record of it? Of all the species, man is above all likely to leave a rich fossil record.

Had he been here in any numbers for anything approaching (say) a million years, surely he would have cracked every rock and filled recent strata with his bones and other remains. Where is the evidence? Think of what man has done to the Earth's surface in five or six thousand brief years. What would he have done in five or six *hundred thousand* years?

Remember, species do not begin weak and grow strong; if anything, the reverse. So either something completely out of the ordinary has happened to our species or we are relatively recent arrivals. And just as the scriptures confirm that species should manifest in full power, without an initial transition stage, so do they advise us of our own very recent beginnings here. Mankind is as recent as the Earth is ancient. (See *Ps.102:11, 25; Job 8:9,* etc.) See the internal consistency of the biblical model.

It would be a brave man, basing his estimate on the sound witness of the fossil record, who would give us more than twice the five or six thousand years for which we have archaeological records. Ten thousand years would surely be generous. "We are but of yesterday" *Job 8:9.*

But what happened that we leave little or no archaeological (or fossil) record before approximately 4000 B.C.?

Third Head

Mankind's historical record prior to roughly 5000-4000 B.C. has been largely obliterated. The backward-leading trail of historical information terminates as though at a steeply-sloping, rapidly darkening drop-off, somewhere in the region of 5000 to 4000 B.C.

We have now come to our first major signpost.

From now onward, we can begin to unravel ancient history. For here, at this signpost, this rapidly darkening drop-off in recorded history, at about 4000 B.C. or beyond - here is our first unifying consistency of science, of ancient history, of the scriptural historic account.

There was a "world that was" (*2 Pet.3:6*). The scriptures own that man has lived in two worlds, the modern world, and a "world that was." This first world was peculiar for water and the abundance of it; it was noteworthy for long life and gigantism: and it was terminated through a water-related event which revisited in part conditions of the formative early Earth (see *2 Pet.3:3-7*). By faint but definite association, the text distantly implicates "the waters above the firmament" in this terminating event. (The Earth standing "out of the water and in the water" - two waters.) As such, this text is probably the only one in the whole Bible to revisit those ancient and original "waters above the firmament." From a technical point of view, this is noteworthy.

As we have already learned, the geologic record likewise speaks of a "world that was." It should not be confused with the Earth generally throughout geologic history, but realistically describes the middle latitudes and perhaps some other parts of the Earth prior to and shortly after man's arrival. This world was topographically younger but similar to ours; the actual surface conditions, the environment, were quite dissimilar to ours. To stand upon it, to see and experience it, was to stand in a different world. Not that the whole globe was necessarily then a near-utopia, but the middle regions, away from the icecaps, were idyllic. The remarkable attributes of this lost world were its abundance of water and health-giving environment. Certainly, the atmosphere was different in some significant way.

That world has terminated in favour of our modern environment and climate.

Something led to its termination.

The record of human history was likewise mysteriously truncated, cut off. The Bible implies the two are linked.

So we can perhaps now tie an actual geologic event to an historical event. If so, we are poised to begin untying the knot of ancient history.

What was the geologic event?

Fourth Head

As we go backward in human history, the record suddenly, inexplicably, tapers off and all but dies. Something major and sudden happened in history. It was not evolution; evolution is the antithesis of sudden, dramatic events. Evolution would demand a steady, progressive tapering off of the historic record. Like progressive development of new species, it cannot have what does not exist.

There is no more evidence of evolution in the abrupt blanking-off of history than there is evidence of it in the abrupt appearance of new life. The Bible comes to the rescue, and implies a blanking off of history, and the fossil record concurs, by speaking of a fundamental change in atmospheric conditions during man's period of tenure. Something, deeply significant to history, changed the world environment.

The potential implications roll down like an avalanche.

This avalanche sweeps everything off to expose the foundations. When we finally are able to see the foundations, we will find them infinitely preferable to the obfuscating, impenetrable maze the avalanche takes away.

For our purposes, the dating methods capable of surviving the projected world-changing event unscathed are the old faithful radioactive-decay methods. This is a generalization, but true for our purposes.

The "old faithful" methods have proved useful in their place. They are best suited to dating volcanic and metamorphic rock of substantial age. With some qualifications, generally, the older the rock, the more accurate the date. And like all chemical dating methods, the results are somewhat selective and are only accepted if they are believed to harmonize with an overall theory of origin of the specimen being tested.

These standard and proven methods are by definition at a disadvantage at the small end of the time-scale. Their potential for inaccuracy tends to expand as the present is approached. Obviously they are also susceptible to the intellectual bias of the interpreter. Some of these methods are employed at the small end of the time scale, in limited applications. For current purposes they may be set aside.

This leaves relatively newer methods, of which 14C is the most tried and tested, while electron-spin- resonance and a family of luminescence methods are under development. There are others besides, but for our purposes, these will suffice; and to a greater or lesser degree they *assume an unchanged atmospheric environment!* The one most tried and tested, upon which the existing web of human pre-history has largely been woven, 14C, *relies entirely upon an unchanged atmospheric environment!*

The other, above-mentioned newer methods rely on radiation coming up out of the Earth, as well as that penetrating the atmosphere from above, and thus are somewhat less subject to atmospheric variations. And there are one or two less-used methods, not mentioned here, that theoretically could survive a dramatic atmosphere change unscathed. Just to be confusing, one of these utilizes uranium - but is not the uranium-lead method used for old rocks. For current purposes we may overlook lesser details, and go to the nub of the matter. The nub of the matter is that if there have been dramatic events implicating the Earth's atmosphere and environs within the last few tens of thousands of years, most chemical dates in that period require re-evaluation.

The entire evolutionist story of truly ancient humankind is predicated upon an idea that species struggle into existence slowly and the atmospheric envelope of the Earth has remained effectively constant. Where does objective observation obtain an entry into this imbroglio? Could we undertake an unbiased assessment?

14C is produced in the atmosphere as a secondary result of incoming radiation from space. Quantity of said incoming radiation is governed by events far off in space, by magnetic fields and effects surrounding the Earth, and by thickness and composition of the atmosphere. Therefore the quantity of this cosmic radiation need not be constant, and could vary from almost zero to excessive, depending on circumstances. The atmosphere of man's earliest times was such as to induce gigantism and its corollary, long life. Undoubtedly, our atmosphere has changed in some ways over time.

Production of 14C in the atmosphere is a balanced or equilibrium- seeking process. It is analogous to pouring water into a permeable container. When the level in the container is initially low, a sudden and ongoing inflow results in a rapid rise in level, followed by an adjustment period during which the level fluctuates a little before finding a steady equilibrium. 14C today is displaying this fluctuating, equilibrium-seeking behaviour. Its rate of production in the atmosphere was measured at almost twenty per cent higher than its rate of disappearance, at the time of the method's inception. Subsequent problems with the method led to arbitrary compensation factors having to be applied. Arbitrary adjustments of up to five hundred years have been found necessary for some dates - and these correctional factors are only known for the past 5000 to 4000 years, the period of time over which such methods can be calibrated against artefacts of known age!

A reasonable assumption seems to be that the container has recently received an inflow, and is now finding equilibrium. If the event or events that terminated "the world that then was" also markedly increased radiation from space - highly likely, since it was an atmospheric/ environmental event - this would logically account for the inflow.

It would be intriguing to analyse the 14C method and other newer methods, to attempt to discover their total message. Perhaps they could lead us directly to the precise date of the projected event we are pursuing. Such a study is beyond our present purposes. It may also be unnecessary. If this projected event or events had a profound effect upon the atmosphere and environment, some trace or signature of it must lie in the earth somewhere.

Some organisms are environment-responsive. Corals, for example. Perhaps some sort of event is written into coral growth. Perhaps through study of the growth-history and current distribution of organisms such as these, not only a time but an inkling of the locus and geographic extent of any such event could be garnered. When we consider it, much of the world's coral is in the Australasia- Pacific region, which is a part of the world less likely to be inhabited by early man, and therefore, less likely to be impacted by the event . . . but our current purposes lie elsewhere.

Climate Research

Update: Climate research is providing new information relating to carbon in the atmosphere.

Climate has no effect on the "old faithful" radioactive decay methods. 14C is a special case.

Calibration even back past the pyramids is being attempted; yet it relies upon a series of assumptions not fully shared by other methods. Our atmosphere is not a closed system. Our atmosphere needs to have been closed within reason for tens of thousands of years into the past. 14C (and other methods calibrated against it) has the potential to be technically accurate, yet the results can be perplexing. If Australia really was populated by humans for anything like the tens or hundreds of thousands of years suggested, we should right now be wading in stone artefacts ankle deep. Mathematics does not lie. Has our atmosphere within reason been a closed system, going back fifty and more thousand years? And, seriously, how are these events so accurately dated, *if carbon is used,* if the system was not closed, within reason?

"A University of Colorado at Boulder-led research team tracing the origin of a large CO_2 increase in Earth's atmosphere at the end of the last ice age has detected two ancient "burps" that originated from the deepest parts of the oceans.

The new study indicated carbon that had built up in the oceans over millennia was released in two big pulses, one about 18,000 years ago and one 13,000 years ago, said Thomas Marchitto and Scott Lehman of CU-Boulder's Institute of Arctic and Alpine Research, who jointly led the study. While scientists had long known as much as 600 billion metric tons of carbon were released into the atmosphere after the last ice age, the new study is the first to clearly track CO_2 from the deep ocean to the upper ocean and atmosphere and should help scientists better understand natural CO_2 cycles and possible impacts of human- caused climate change.

The team analysed sediment cores hauled from the Pacific Ocean seafloor at a depth of about 2,300 feet off the coast of Baja California using an isotopic "tracer," known as carbon 14, to track the escape of carbon from the deep sea through the upper ocean and into the atmosphere during the last 40,000 years. Extracted from the shells of tiny marine organisms known as foraminifera - which contain chemical signatures of seawater dating back tens of thousands of years - carbon 14 is the isotope most commonly used to radiocarbon date organic material like wood, bone and shell."[14]

"Some 41,000 years ago, a complete and rapid reversal of the geomagnetic field occurred. Magnetic studies of the GFZ German Research Center for Geosciences on sediment cores from the Black Sea show that during this period, during the last ice age, a compass at the Black Sea would have pointed to the south instead of north.

Moreover, data obtained by the research team formed around GFZ researchers Dr. Norbert Nowaczyk and Professor Helge Arz, together with additional data from other studies in the North Atlantic, the South Pacific and Hawaii, prove that this polarity reversal was a global event. Their results are published in the latest issue of the scientific journal *Earth and Planetary Science Letters.*

What is remarkable is the speed of the reversal: "The field geometry of reversed polarity, with field lines pointing in the opposite direction when compared to today's configuration, lasted for only about 440 years, and it was associated with a field strength that was only one quarter of today's field," explains Norbert Nowaczyk. "The actual polarity changes lasted only

[14] ScienceDaily, 11 May 2007

250 years. In terms of geological time scales, that is very fast." During this period, the field was even weaker, with only 5% of today's field strength. As a consequence, Earth nearly completely lost its protection shield against hard cosmic rays, leading to a significantly increased radiation exposure.

Besides giving evidence for a geomagnetic field reversal 41,000 years ago, the geoscientists from Potsdam discovered numerous abrupt climate changes during the last ice age in the analysed cores from the Black Sea, as it was already known from the Greenland ice cores. This ultimately allowed a high precision synchronization of the two data records from the Black Sea and Greenland.

The largest volcanic eruption on the Northern hemisphere in the past 100,000 years, namely the eruption of the super volcano 39,400 years ago in the area of today's Phlegraean Fields near Naples, Italy, is also documented within the studied sediments from the Black Sea. The ashes of this eruption, during which about 350 cubic kilometres of rock and lava were ejected, were distributed over the entire eastern Mediterranean and up to central Russia.

These three extreme scenarios, a short and fast reversal of Earth's magnetic field, short-term climate variability of the last ice age and the volcanic eruption in Italy, have been investigated for the first time in a single geological archive and placed in precise chronological order."[15]

Whether dated correctly or no, events such as these do not inspire confidence in dating methods which presume a reasonably steady state in our atmosphere and environs over the past fifty to one hundred thousand years. A major disturbance leading to flooding would scarcely be out of place amongst these events!

---

[15] ScienceDaily, 16 October 2012

We have been attempting to proceed on the basis of logic and observation. If something momentous occurred to change the environment and disrupt history, then logic and observation should be able to deduce the cause and nature of the event.

What was the event?

Could we rehearse the clues we have been given?

It caused a profound change in the Earth's atmospheric and surface environment.

It involved water in quantity. It was a world event (although specifically aimed at the world then inhabited by man). It involved a partial return to conditions applying at the Earth's formation. And the "waters above the firmament" were implicated (refer to *2 Pet.3:3-7*).

What could cause a partial return to formative Earth conditions? Substantial reduction in centralized gravitational pull downward. How to achieve it?

Pass a body close to the Earth. What sort of body?

One largely made of water (ice). "Waters above the firmament" - comet(s).

Evidence?

Inevitability of such an event in a solar system such as ours. Modern examples of it. Both Jupiter and Saturn have drawn comets into/around themselves in the past *two centuries.* Saturn's rings probably consist predominantly of water ice, and are a relatively recent phenomenon.

Evidence from the Earth's past, such as snap-frozen mammoths and temperate forests buried under permafrost. Something has been at work, something that had periodic, sudden, and profound effects upon the environment.

The great flood, one of the most disbelieved stories in the whole Bible, was a natural phenomenon statistically inevitable in a solar system such as ours.

Alarmist opinion has us smothering in CO_2 bye-and-bye; fortunately the same opinion-source has not been gazing at the solar system and thinking, else we would be dragooned into funding sufficient nuclear warheads to blow apart the imminently-arriving next comet. Like true clones, it is not going to get here. Take it from the God who makes and propels them.

Without reference to and respect of the One who made the worlds, man of necessity refers to and references the god of this world, with all the best intent his misguided efforts tend toward the very predicament that the Babel dispersion was designed to forestall. World despotism. There once was a time when peddlers of conformist superstition, with state authority, charged expecting women money for the use of Mary's cloak to help the birth. Some recent policies for helping the environment, society, or whatever, are disturbingly reminiscent of Mary's cloak. As well to apply Peter's old boat anchor as some of the conformist, finger- pointing, power-seeking, money-grabbing non-science now in the public eye. Shun superstition!

We shall leave precise dating of that signal and sad event of long ago to those whose business it is. A major point to be gained is that *it can be dated.* It can be dated by means at man's disposal. Therefore, man can trace his own history back as far as the flood. We are about to return to the biblical account of history, and we need to know this fact. We need this fact, because the Almighty does not encroach upon man's territory. If man can date it, divine wisdom will leave it to him to date, just as he leaves the discovery of the order of appearance of life forms to him.

A Historical Timeframe

But where man cannot date, there we may find an historical timeframe set out for us by inspired revelation. It seems likely that man will never be able to date pre-flood history. The Bible, by its own internal evidence, does not date the flood. (Volumes have been written about this, and are available for consultation; for example, Professor. A.E. Wilder-Smith observes that the genealogy between Noah and Abraham is expressed in a format implying it is not intended for determining dates. "It looks as if Moses knew that his table was incomplete and that he therefore deliberately avoided his usual custom of totalling the years[16]." He also advises that an excellent analysis of the question was undertaken by Professor William Henry Green, of Princeton Theological Seminary, and was published, quote, "nearly eighty years ago.")

Our upcoming *Gen.5* genealogy differs slightly from other Bible genealogies. It is more numerically detailed and exhaustive than any other. By an extension of logic, it may therefore be intended for determining the true age of the species, once the flood is dated. Then again, considering the experience of others in relation to genealogies, perhaps we should avoid coming to conclusions.

Perhaps. Nevertheless, at this point in the biblical narrative, as Adam and Eve and their immediate offspring step out into the world, we may be reasonably confident it is only thousands of years ago, not tens of thousands. If the *Gen.5* genealogy is indeed chronological, the flood is roughly 1500 years in the future. After the flood, mankind will need to recover from a population-reduction to eight, develop socially to the level of building communal brick edifices (the tower of Babel), undergo scattering and language-differentiation into clans (to forestall one-world

[16] Professor A.E. Wilder-Smith, in *Man's Origin, Man's Destiny.* Telos International, page 111, 1974

religious despotism), then again recover to the point where middle-eastern clans become the builders of the Sumerian and Egyptian cultures, which of course begins the flow of clearly-defined history, 5000 B.C. or soon thereafter. Ample room is available between the flood and settled, recorded civilization for a rapid ice age, Neanderthal Man, and most other human groups, assuming none pre-date the flood, which was designed to largely obliterate the record.

Returning to *Gen.5*, at this particular point in history, probably no more than six to ten thousand years ago, mankind, having recently debouched onto the wide stage of the Earth at large, like a gambolling new calf, is spreading on every side with almost superhuman verve and vitality. He is rapidly colonizing southern Europe and Asia, North Africa, and is looking farther afield. In time, he may perhaps build craft that will accidentally or intentionally take him across the Atlantic to the Americas, or beyond. He is physically strong, long-lived, outsize, comparatively disease-free, and physically and intellectually capable. He is setting out from the Middle East with no deserts to cross.

Gen. 5

This is the book of the generations of Adam. In the day that God created man, in the likeness of God made he him; Male and female created he them; and blessed them, and called their name Adam, in the day when they were created. And Adam lived an hundred and thirty years, and begat a son in his own likeness, after his image; and called his name Seth: and the days of Adam after he had begotten Seth were eight hundred years: and he begat sons and daughters: and all the days that Adam lived were nine hundred and thirty years: and he died. And Seth lived an hundred and five years, and begat Enos: and Seth lived after he begat Enos eight hundred and seven years, and begat sons and daughters: and all the days of Seth were nine hundred and twelve years: and he died. And Enos lived ninety years, and begat Cainan: and Enos lived after he begat Cainan eight hundred and fifteen years, and begat sons and daughters: and all the days of Enos were nine hundred and five years: and he died. And Cainan lived seventy years, and begat Mahalaleel: and Cainan lived after he begat Mahalaleel eight hundred and forty years, and begat sons and daughters: and all the days of Cainan were nine hundred and ten years: and he died. And Mahalaleel lived sixty and five years, and begat Jared: and Mahalaleel lived after he begat Jared eight hundred and thirty years, and begat sons and daughters: and all the days of Mahalaleel were eight hundred ninety and five years: and he died. And Jared lived an hundred sixty and two years, and he begat Enoch: and Jared lived after he begat Enoch eight hundred years, and begat sons and daughters: and all the days of Jared were nine hundred sixty and two years: and he died. And Enoch lived sixty and five years, and begat Methuselah: and Enoch walked with God after he begat Methuselah three hundred years, and begat sons and daughters: and all the days of Enoch were three hundred sixty and five years: and Enoch walked with God: and he was not; for God took him. And Methuselah lived an hundred eighty and seven years, and begat Lamech: and Methuselah lived after he begat Lamech seven hundred eighty and two years, and begat sons and daughters: and all the days of Methuselah were nine hundred sixty and nine years: and he died. And Lamech lived an hundred eighty and two years, and begat a son: and he called his name Noah, saying, This same shall comfort us concerning our work and toil of our hands, because of the ground which the Lord hath cursed. And Lamech lived after he begat Noah five hundred ninety and five years, and begat sons and daughters: and all the days of Lamech were seven hundred seventy and seven years: and he died. And Noah was five hundred years old: and Noah begat Shem, Ham, and Japheth.

Repetition of the phrase "and he died" is perhaps an emphasis of the irrevocability of divine statements. "In the day thou eatest thereof thou shalt surely die" *Gen.2:17*. The people whose names are listed lived so long, it must have seemed they were immortal; but at last that unhappy word was fulfilled. This repeated notification of death stands in contrast over against the record of Enoch (v.*24*). Enoch "walked with God," v.*22*. To walk with someone is a two-fold activity. It is impossible to do so unless both parties are agreed - more, unless both parties are made compatible to one another. It necessitates effort on the part of both, yet it is ease and safety. It requires ongoing commitment, yet it is ongoing relaxation. The two are individuals, yet the two are one. The two have been made one. "I am the vine, ye are the branches . . . Abide in me, and I in you . . . Take my yoke upon you."

A fragment of Enoch's message to his countrymen is preserved by Jude (*Jude 14, 15*). From it a conclusion seems unavoidable that his fellows were almost universally set against God in speech and attitude, and that Enoch, as well as Noah, endeavoured to save them from "opposing themselves" *2 Tim.2:25.* Those who shine when surrounded by flesh- minded, hardened people shine brightly indeed. It may be that this remarkable man walked with God and had no other companion with whom he could walk, so God took him to give him an everlasting companion. Whether or not, the Almighty will maintain a church, even in the bleakest times; when the church is small, it often shines the brightest.

See how faith should be a family affair. Lamech seemed to have some premonition that his new son, Noah, although a helpless infant, would do good service for mankind (v.*29*). So it transpired; and it was not only Noah but in some measure the combined faith of himself and his progenitors that achieved so much for mankind.

The Falling Away in Longevity

Gen.6: 1-4

And it came to pass, when men began to multiply on the face of the earth, and daughters were born unto them, that the sons of God saw the daughters of men that they were fair; and they took them wives of all which they chose. And the Lord said, "My spirit shall not always strive with man, for that he also is flesh: yet his days shall be an hundred and twenty years. There were giants in the earth in those days; and also after that, when the sons of God came in unto the daughters of men, and they bore children to them, the same became mighty men which were of old, men of renown. "

Even before the great flood there began an incipient falling away in longevity (v.*3*). This is in keeping with the biologic observation of decreasing, rather than increasing, vitality of species over time. In our case the cause was ultimately non-biological; the biologic result itself came into effect because of the imperfection of man's heart - our inner man, our spirit. See here the contrast between the outworkings of virtue and the outworkings of vice. Those retaining virtue were as the "sons of God." Their bodies, their countenances, were visibly affected by inner virtue, physically distinguishing them from their graceless fellows (v.*2*). Unfortunately their virtue did not always extend to wisdom in marriage. Intermarriage of the two lines sealed the fate of that world (v.*2, 5*). Or perhaps the expression "sons of God" refers to the inner spirit of man, which divine Insight looking into sees as either a consecrated image of himself, or a marred image, disfigured by evil.

The intriguing theory that "sons of God" refers to some variety of supernatural beings cannot be entirely discounted, but they would perforce have needed to have been secret beings, for they find no mention in scripture. It is apparent from the text that sexuality was a property of the "sons of God," and the only eternal beings mentioned in scripture which possess sexuality are human beings.

V.*4*, "There were giants in the earth," covers gigantism in general throughout nature. It need not refer solely to *Homo sapiens.* Since gigantism was a feature of the biologic world about the time of earliest man, the narrative is altogether scientifically correct. Some modern animal species had members approaching even twice normal size in times past - most expressed gigantism in some measure. For example, at certain times the continent of Australia was host to outsize kangaroos, emus, wombats, platypi, marsupial lions; most of the continent's unique fauna expressed remarkable size at some time. The fact that man can grow outsize is confirmed by his genes, which occasionally throw a giant even now.

Giant has a second meaning in scripture. It implies obstacles and seemingly impenetrable difficulties. Obstacles to personal and societal functioning and progress. Mountains barring the way. Trouble is ahead.

XII. THE GREAT FLOOD

Gen.6: 5-8

And God saw that the wickedness of man was great in the earth, and that every imagination of the thoughts of his heart was only evil continually. And it repented the Lord that he had made man on the earth, and it grieved him at his heart. And the Lord said, I will destroy man whom I have created from the face of the earth; both man, and beast, and the creeping thing, and the fowls of the air; for it repenteth me that I have made them. But Noah found grace in the eyes of the Lord.

There is a long-standing dichotomy of opinion regarding the geographic extent of the great flood. Was it global or local? Strange though it may seem, its extent probably presents more of an interpretational challenge than its cause.

The likely cause is neither obscure nor controversial. With an intelligent application of mathematics, astronomy, and some attention to detail and adjustment, circumstances surrounding the cause should focus relatively easily. Whether or not the same is true of the surface extent awaits more investigation. Was it global or local - or, in some sense, both?

What have the scriptures to say?

The Reader is as good a judge as any.

If the language employed is taken as being addressed to Noah, that is, speaking of the heaven and earth as it was to the peoples of the time, then it may have been non-global.

Conversely, if the language is taken as fully global, beyond the ken of those involved, the event was in keeping with the language - fully global. There is at least one other option, embodying elements of both.

It was as described to Noah and the people of the time, and it was also true in a fully global sense, but only in a figure.

Thus where it says, "all the high hills, that were under the whole heaven, were covered," all the elevated regions inhabited by man were covered, with total loss of life; all hills everywhere were covered in some sense, but without total loss of life. Where it says, "all flesh died," all flesh, perhaps even including flesh of fish, died in the regions known to man; *some* of all flesh died elsewhere. All flesh died in the sense of representatives of every species dying.

Agreeable with this third option is the distribution of the Earth's fauna. The unique faunas of the Polar Regions, of the Australasian region, of parts of the Americas, and elsewhere, are not suggestive of recent origin at Mt. Ararat, but of partial survival at the fringes of a great catastrophe. (The Bible itself tells us that all flesh of every type everywhere certainly did not die - there were no aquatic creatures in the ark.)

Under this interpretation, the animals that came to Noah - he did not need to muster them quite as Samson mustered his foxes - were cooperatively selected by God and accepted by Noah as being "all flesh." "All flesh" as presented to Noah. Under this model, one purpose of taking birds and animals into the ark would have been to provide stock for use during and immediately after the event. Whatever; the reader may be his own judge.

Gen.6:9-22, & 7, & 8, & 9:1-17

These are the generations of Noah: Noah was a just man and perfect in his generations, and Noah walked with God. And Noah begat three sons, Shem, Ham, and Japheth. The earth also was corrupt before God, and the earth was filled with violence. And God looked upon the earth, and, behold, it was corrupt; for all flesh had corrupted his way upon the earth. And God said unto Noah, The end of all flesh is come before me; for the earth is filled with violence through them; and, behold, I will destroy them with the earth. Make thee an ark of gopher wood; rooms shalt thou make in the ark, and shalt pitch it within and without with pitch. And this is the fashion which thou shalt make it of: The length of the ark shall be three hundred cubits, the breadth of it fifty cubits, and the height of it thirty cubits. A window shalt thou make to the ark, and in a cubit shalt thou finish it above; and the door of the ark shalt thou set in the side thereof; with lower, second, and third stories shalt thou make it. And, behold, I, even I, do bring a flood of waters upon the earth, to destroy all flesh, wherein is the breath of life, from under heaven; and every thing that is in the earth shall die. But with thee will I establish my covenant; and thou shalt come into the ark, thou, and thy sons, and thy wife, and thy sons' wives with thee. And of every living thing of all flesh, two of every sort shalt thou bring into the ark, to keep them alive with thee; they shall be male and female. Of fowls after their kind, and of cattle after their kind, of every creeping thing of the earth after his kind, two of every sort shall come unto thee, to keep them alive. And take thou unto thee of all food that is eaten, and thou shalt gather it to thee; and it shall be for food for thee, and for them. Thus did Noah; according to all that God commanded him, so did he. And the Lord said unto Noah, Come thou and all thy house into the ark; for thee have I seen righteous before me in this generation. Of every clean beast thou shalt take to thee by sevens, the male and his female: and of beasts that are not clean by two, the male and his female. Of fowls also of the air by sevens, the male and the female; to keep seed alive upon the face of all the earth. For yet seven days, and I will cause it to rain upon the earth forty days and forty nights; and every living substance that I have made will I destroy from off the face of the earth. And Noah did according unto all that the Lord commanded him. And Noah was six hundred years old when the flood of waters was upon the earth. And Noah went in, and his sons, and his wife, and his sons' wives with him, into the ark, because of the waters of the flood. Of clean beasts, and of beasts that are not clean, and of fowls, and of everything that creepeth upon the earth, there went in two and two unto Noah into the ark, the male and the female, as God had commanded Noah. And it came to pass after seven days, that the waters of the flood were upon the earth. In the six hundredth year of Noah's life, in the second month, the seventeenth day of the month, the same day were all the fountains of the great deep broken up, and the windows of heaven were opened. And the rain was upon the earth forty days and forty nights. In the selfsame day entered Noah, and Shem, and Ham, and Japheth, the sons of Noah, and Noah's wife, and the three wives of his sons with them, into the ark; they, and every beast after his kind, and all the cattle after their kind, and every creeping thing that creepeth upon the earth after his kind, and every fowl after his kind, every bird of every sort. And they went in unto Noah into the ark, two and two of all flesh, wherein is the breath of life. And they that went in, went in male and female of all flesh, as God had commanded him: and the Lord shut him in. And the flood was forty days upon the earth; and the waters increased, and bear up the ark, and it was lift up above the earth. And the waters prevailed, and were increased greatly upon the earth; and the ark went upon the face of the waters. And the waters prevailed exceedingly upon the earth; and all the high hills, that were under the whole heaven, were covered. Fifteen cubits upward did the waters prevail; and the mountains were covered. And all flesh died that moved upon the earth, both of fowl, and of cattle, and of beast, and of every creeping thing that creepeth upon the earth, and every man: all in whose nostrils was the breath of life, of all that was in the dry land, died. And every living substance was destroyed which was upon the face of the ground, both man, and cattle, and the creeping things, and the fowl of the heaven; and they were destroyed from the earth: and Noah only remained alive, and they that were with him in the ark. And the waters prevailed upon the earth an hundred and fifty days. And God remembered Noah, and every living thing, and all the cattle that was with him in the ark: and God made a wind to pass over the earth, and the waters assuaged; the fountains also of the deep and the windows of heaven were stopped, and the rain from heaven was restrained; and the waters returned from off the earth continually: and after the end of the hundred and fifty days the waters were abated. And the ark rested in the seventh month, on the seventeenth day of the month, upon the mountains of Ararat. And the waters decreased continually until the tenth month: in the tenth month, on the first day of the month, were the tops of the mountains seen. And it came to pass at the end of forty days, that Noah opened the window of the ark which he had made: and he sent forth a raven, which went forth to and fro, until the waters were dried up from off the earth. Also he sent forth a dove from him, to see if the waters were abated from off the face of the ground; but the dove found no rest for the sole of her foot, and she returned unto him into the ark, for the waters were on the face of the whole earth: then he put forth his hand, and took her, and pulled her in unto him into the ark. And he stayed yet other seven days; and again he sent forth the dove out of the ark; and the dove came in to him in the evening; and, lo, in her mouth was an olive leaf pluckt off: so Noah knew that the waters were abated from off the earth. And he stayed yet other seven days; and sent forth the dove; which returned not again unto him any more. And it came to pass in the six hundredth and first year, in the first month, the first day of the month, the waters were dried up from off the earth: and Noah removed the covering of the ark, and looked, and, behold, the face of the ground was dry. And in the second month, on the seven and twentieth day of the month, was the earth dried. And God spake unto Noah, saying, Go forth of the ark, thou, and thy wife, and thy sons, and thy sons' wives with thee. Bring forth with thee every living thing that is with thee, of all flesh, both of fowl, and of cattle, and of every creeping thing that creepeth upon the earth; that they may breed abundantly in the earth, and be fruitful, and multiply upon the earth. And Noah went forth, and his sons, and his wife, and his sons' wives with him: every beast, every creeping thing, and every fowl, and whatsoever creepeth upon the earth, after their kinds, went forth out of the ark. And Noah builded an altar unto the Lord; and took of every clean beast, and of every clean fowl, and offered burnt offerings on the altar: And the Lord smelled a sweet savour; and the Lord said in his heart, I will not again curse the ground any more for man's sake; for the imagination of man's heart is evil from his youth; neither will I again smite any more every thing living, as I have done. While the earth remaineth, seedtime and harvest, and cold and heat, and summer and winter, and day and night shall not cease. And God blessed Noah and his sons, and said unto them, Be fruitful, and multiply, and replenish the earth. And the fear of you and the dread of you shall be upon every beast of the earth, and upon every fowl of the air, upon all that moveth upon the earth, and upon all the fishes of the sea; into your hand are they delivered. Every moving thing that liveth shall be meat for you; even as the green herb have I given you all things. But flesh with the life thereof, which is the blood thereof, shall ye not eat. And surely your blood of your lives will I require; at the hand of every beast will I require it, and at the hand of man; at the hand of every man's brother will I require the life of man. Whoso sheddeth man's blood, by man shall his blood be shed: for in the image of God made he man. And you, be ye fruitful, and multiply; bring forth abundantly in the earth, and multiply therein. And God spake unto Noah, and to his sons with him, saying, And I, behold, I establish my covenant with you, and with your seed after you; and with every living creature that is with you, of the fowl, of the cattle, and of every beast of the earth with you; from all that go out of the ark, to every beast of the earth. And I will establish my covenant with you; neither shall all flesh be cut off any more by the waters of a flood; neither shall there any more be a flood to destroy the earth. And God said, This is the token of the covenant which I make between me and you and every living creature that is with you, for perpetual generations: I do set my bow in the cloud, and it shall be for a token of a covenant between me and the earth. And it shall come to pass, when I bring a cloud over the earth, that the bow shall be seen in the cloud: and I will remember my covenant, which is between me and you and every living creature of all flesh; and the waters shall no more become a flood to destroy all flesh. And the bow shall be in the cloud; and I will look upon it, that I may remember the everlasting covenant between God and every living creature of all flesh that is upon the earth. And God said unto Noah, This is the token of the covenant, which I have established between me and all flesh that is upon the earth.

There was a "world that was" *2 Pet.3:6.* This was our world, yet it was not our world. It was our Earth, new and fresh, with our mountains, our seas, and our own human kind. Yet it was a different environment, populated by animals and peoples with a difference, under a climate and an atmosphere not the same as ours. "The world that then was."

A world of water; a world peculiar for water; a world in some ways governed by water. A world engineered so that the substrate under our feet harmonized with the atmosphere and environs above our head in a union altogether salubrious. A world that perished, that no longer is such a harmonizing, health-giving microcosm of water. A world that is now, by comparison, a system of deserts. A world of shortened stature and shortened lives, of animal extinction, and of extremes of temperature. An environment so far removed from its Eden-like origins as to constitute a different world.

What Happened?

2 Pet.3:5, 6: "By the word of God the heavens were of old, and the Earth standing out of the water and in the water . . ."

Here is reference to the formation of the Earth and space. In *Gen.1,* the Earth is said to have coalesced or been "gathered together" from the waters. Likewise the other bodies in space. Waters in the scriptures has a twofold meaning. Under the one expression it means unformed, behaving as water; and it means water, H_2O.

This two-fold meaning is carried through to the text of *2 Peter.*

This is fertile ground.

"Being overflowed with water" does not necessitate an overflowing with water, H_2O, only or alone. It would be quite true to the scriptures to postulate the presence of other fluid substances, such as various atmosphere gases, in or besides H_2O. Thus, gas or gas-charged water, snow, or various emulsions, are compassed by this text. Water, H_2O, in vast quantities is implied, but not to the exclusion of other unstable substances. This immediately opens a door to conjecture. Gas, in or under bodies of water, can lead to spectacular effects. The exploding brewed drink is an instance of it. Within our times, lakes have erupted through the action of expanding gases at their bottom and destroyed all breathing animals on the hills above them. The production of stupendous quantities of liquid and gaseous hydrocarbons under lakes and oceans is a feature of the geologic past.

Another possible link to events surrounding the origins of the Earth relates to the concept of the primordial waters which were "above the firmament [sky]" of *Gen. 1*. At first glance, the waters above the firmament, which were utilized in production of the stars, planets, etc., appear to have been mostly non-H_2O waters. There is little H_2O in sun or stars. But recently, we have deduced the likely presence of H_2O water in space, and at times it travels close to the Earth.

<u>Comets Revisited</u>

These interplanetary passengers are now thought to contain a high proportion of H_2O, as ice. Interplanetary icebergs with the dimensions of cities. Other ices, such as dry ice (frozen C02), frozen methane etc., and some earthy mineral matter are believed to be incorporated. So it is now widely believed that comets are a mixture of frozen gases and liquids, with some rock or rock dust incorporated. If so, these travelling ice blocks surely have potential. Did they play a part in the events that led to various climate changes and mass extinctions in the past? Were they employed in re-supplying the atmosphere with necessary compounds?

Could the Earth/moon have captured quantities of them?

Encased in the ice of the northern hemisphere are evidences of catastrophic events.

Thousands of frozen animals with temperate vegetation in their digestive tracts, even in their mouths! No less mystifying are reliable reports of a frozen temperate forest intersected by oil wells in Alaska. This frozen (not petrified) forest lies at depth under the permafrost. Here is proof of temperate conditions quickly changing to polar conditions. The event(s) involved much more than a climate inversion; an unusual precipitation of super-cooled, emulsified ice, preceded by destructive winds, dust, grit, and partly salty, partly muddy, flood rains seems the best way to explain the condition of the fossils.

There is every reason to believe those regions were struck by a prolonged blast of gritty air, then by intense muddy rain, and then by falling ice particles so cold as to snap-freeze large animals in seconds, some in standing position! In the process, forests were levelled, and vegetation and animals, including birds, were jumbled together. The largest and strongest of the animals survived until encased in super-cold, dirty ice particles falling like fine hail - rhinoceros and mammoth frozen as they stood, their air-passages full of grit, their stomach enzymes rendered inoperable by instant freezing, their bodies entombed in ice in association with jumbled vegetation, animal remains, and mud. Dry ice and its vapour, CO_2, and perhaps other gases/ ices besides, were almost certainly involved in the catastrophe. Large tracts of the northern hemisphere suffered baptism by ice. The ensuing climate change was long-lived, although the evidence shows a subsequent partial northward contraction of ice-forming conditions.

Enquirers into 14C dating may be intrigued to learn that unedited dating results of some of these remains give a good 10,000 years age difference between the head and tail of some of the animals, and make timber inextricably tied into the same fossil deposits a solid 20,000 years younger than the animal frozen in the same tomb! As we have already deduced, any chemical date under the scenario of catastrophes such as these must be regarded with extreme caution. So we are reduced to applying logic.

To date, no human remains have been thawed out of the jumbled mud and vegetation, nor found huddled amongst the larger frozen animals. This dearth of human or humanoid activity scarcely concurs with the notion of prolonged human evolution over time. It could be taken as suggestive of an event pre-dating mankind altogether. Others will see it as an aspect of the great flood, and they may well be correct. We shall err on the side of conservatism, meaning that until proven human remains are thawed out of these deposits, we shall take them as pre- *homo sapiens.*

Improved dating and enlightened fossil study will eventually decide the question. Whether these frozen remains are a product of the flood event, or whether they precede the flood by some millennia, we may nevertheless discuss their implications so as to gain some idea of the events of ancient history. For the moment we will regard them as the signature of a possible comet-related event, this particular freezing event or events pre-dating man.

What possible scenario other than that linked to intimate contact with a comet could result in perhaps a quarter of the Earth's surface being blasted by abrasive winds, deluged with muddy, somewhat salty rain, showered with ice (including dry ice) colder than any normally found on its surface, then snap freezing, when, before, it was temperate? The whole scene is surely suggestive of volatile, space-chilled ice blocks falling into ponds or just falling to pieces. Compared to events such as these, a water-related atmospheric trauma such as the great flood begins to appear anticlimactic. Either a part of the play now showing, or an encore.

Waters Everywhere

Let us give reign to our imagination. It seems quite likely that some dramatic events - events which may have periodically been repeated during the Earth's history - helped trigger an ice age sometime before man's arrival here. One such event resulted in near-instant polar conditions over part of the northern hemisphere. In the long-term, events such as these may have helped either sustain or usher in a period of utopian conditions here on Earth, so that gigantism and long life were features of our early world.

Sometime later, another event or events caused water and water-like substances to (as it were) rise up and rain down over much or all of the globe, leading to substantial if not total death amongst various land and air creatures, and total extermination of man, except for those enclosed in a liferaft. Waters everywhere, rampant.

The dimensions of the enclosed raft, chest, or ark, are uncertain, but a reasonable assumption in relation to the length of the cubit employed in measuring it gives it the size of a small ocean liner. It was therefore capable of housing many, if not all species of land creatures and birds living at the time, provided the animals concerned were in a cooperative and semi-hibernating state. The biblical language employed implies a global catastrophe, but at the same time places the emphasis on the removal of mankind; it may or may not have been totally global in terms of the animals, but it certainly achieved its purpose in relation to man.

As a vessel, the ark was designed purely to float and nothing else. We may assume it received *special divine care and protection;* nevertheless, it was not designed for strong turbulence or to withstand impact, and we may therefore infer that the waters it rode upon were not excessively turbulent. (This does not prove that there was no turbulence anywhere in association with this event.) From the description, it was sealable, or airtight. Or close to it.

The waters it rode upon achieved great height. "The mountains were covered" *Gen.7:20.* Perhaps not all mountains, but those in the world as known to man at the time.

No amount of rain, of itself, could achieve such an effect. The waters themselves rose up.

Since no fish were in the ark, the waters rose up in such a way as to permit partial survival of the various species - salt and fresh. Heavy rain of fresh water may have played a part in preserving fish, especially the freshwater varieties.

The waters rose up in such a way that animal carcasses floated off and were not buried in quantity, or were not buried in a way that would lead to fossilization. Or perhaps were corroded through the action of strong vapours and chemicals. (There are no widespread sedimentary deposits rich in both human and animal remains. This particular flood seems to have left little provable record of itself in the rock-strata. Its record lies in a changed world environment.)

As we have learned, *waters* and *rain* need not refer to pure H_2O, and could in fact refer to anything the ark could float on - so long as fish and vegetation could survive. And these waters did not cause massive erosion or burial! Surely, then, they must have been of reduced weight. Is there any other way to reduce the weight of water than by gasification or by gravitational pull away from the Earth upward?

Did any signs of impending doom precede the deluge? "For as in the days that were before the flood they were eating and drinking, marrying and giving in marriage, until the day that Noah entered into the ark. And knew not until the flood came, and took them all way . . ." *Matt.24:38.* It was seven days between Noah's entry into the ark and the onset of the deluge. Thus it is not impossible that some signs or portents did manifest during that seven-day period between his entry into the ark and the onset of disaster. If so, the population at large either did not realize the full significance of these portents, or did not have the moral courage to mend their course. Some forewarning seems possible, if not likely.

At the beginning of those seven days, might the observer of the night sky have observed a pinpoint of soft, white light? Did the pinpoint grow, night by night, until at the last it was a thick haze, obscuring the light from the brightest stars, and by day shadowing even the sun itself? Did an incoming comet enter into orbit of the Earth itself, fixing itself like a silent rider above the clouds?

The "fountains of the great deep" most likely refer specifically to the deep waters of the Mediterranean Sea, but could refer to some or all great and deep expanses of water, anywhere. (The Mediterranean is the "great deep" of bible lands, but there are two schools of thought as to whether the language is worldwide or "man's worldwide." It could be both! It could be speaking specifically of a local event, whilst shadowing a larger event!) The flood was initiated and sustained through the "fountains of the deep" being disturbed or "broken up," and this was effectively co-incident with "the windows of heaven" being opened.

Both these events took place at the conclusion of those fateful seven days, during which Noah waited faithfully in the ark, and the "longsuffering of God" waited longingly for man to repent. Some sort of intense rain, coupled with disturbance of deep waters, then continued unabated for forty days. The remainder of the flood was basically the "winding- down," the aftermath of this intense, forty-day meeting of the waters on land and in the atmosphere.

The clear turning point came five months after the flood's inception, and a peculiar wind marked this turning. *Gen.7:24&8:1:* "And the waters prevailed upon the earth an hundred and fifty days. And God remembered Noah . . . and God made a wind to pass over the earth, and the waters assuaged . . ." Was this peculiar air-movement a return of part of the atmosphere, which, like some of the waters, had risen up toward a now-dissolving satellite comet?

It took a full year for the flood's effects to subside to the point where man could once again profitably venture abroad in Middle Eastern lands. By this time, vegetation had already begun to regrow (the olive leaf).

Whether it was global or only partly global, this event implicated vast quantities of rainwater. From whence came this rainwater, and whence did it depart? A tidal surge we can understand, but whence came sufficient fuel to supply forty or more days of solid rain? Even if the rain fell on but a part of the globe, the reservoirs were gigantic.

Could it have come from space?

It is not completely fanciful to suggest a procession of comets, breaking up around the Earth, and their remains falling as some sort of hail or rain. However, the volumes required are vast. The rain was constant and sustained.

Source of Water

The easiest place to find a sustained source of water is on the Earth itself. The Earth has its own water-budget. When the ice-sheets extend, the sea-level drops, and vice-versa. For example, the nature of certain undersea landforms very strongly suggests an approximate thirty-meter rise in sea level during or immediately before the times of earliest man. And around that time there was a reduction in the size of the ice-sheets. It is reasonable to conclude the ice melted and raised the sea level. Whether this was before or after our arrival is not certain. There are no proven signs of human activity on the land that has been drowned, so the obvious conclusion is it was not long after our arrival, if not before.

The quantity of water bound up in the ice caps means that melting and freezing of the ice sheets could periodically alter the level of the world's oceans by up to one hundred meters or more!

The Earth's water is stored in two obvious reservoirs: the oceans, and the ice-sheets. There is another vast, but hidden reservoir - the rocks themselves, and an obvious, but lesser reservoir - the atmosphere above us. These last two may be ruled out as major supply-sources of the deluge: the rocks because of inaccessibility, and the sky because of insufficient capacity.

And ice- sheets, unless they could be fragmented and blown into the atmosphere, are too slow- melting to supply the fuel for a forty-day deluge.

We can go back to a space origin, with its inherent difficulties, or we can postulate some sort of water "volcano," or water eruption. The eruption/ eruptions would need to be associated with atmospheric conditions that converted a rising spray of water into some sort of rain. Reduced gravity and gasification would almost certainly play a part in the process.

What could cause a huge water fountain or water "volcano"?

Moving into the realms of pure conjecture: reduced weight, triggering the rise and expansion of gas through a body of water. Ice and snow lying in great thickness on top of the body of water might also contribute by providing a seal, which cracked in some places to permit pressurized exit. The loose snow could be sucked up as an emulsion.

One way or another, the waters rose, and they also fell. They did not behave in precisely the same manner as our rains and tides. Rains and tides as we experience them could not cover even our low hills. The great flood cannot be envisaged in everyday terms. Something caused fluid substances to go up on land. They stayed on land for five months. And it took a concerted air-movement to start them back to their normal locations.

In the process, there was little or no mass burial of carcasses or timber in a manner conducive to fossilization; and in at least one place, the waters rose with an enclosed but rather frail life raft safely riding above. Enclosed, and from the language used, all but airtight. Certainly watertight on all surfaces. (There was a window, which the narrative indicates was opened only when necessary.)

This is describing a particular, physical event, which took place on this Earth, within the history of mankind, probably about 7000 to 6000 years ago.

Preceding this traumatic, water-related event, segments of the northern hemisphere had swung from a temperate to a polar climate, an event which, in some way or other, may have happened more than once in the Earth's history.

Could this sudden climate change have been triggered by a comet impinging on the Earth's atmosphere? Did the comet trigger sudden movements of dust, powdered ice, and frigid air, followed by onset of polar conditions over large areas of the northern hemisphere? Could a fragment of this rubbly ice block have fallen into what is now the Arctic Sea, or some other body of water, perhaps fresh water? Could this chunk, so rich in frozen gas, have been preserved by a cold overburden of water, and finally, ice, until its mother-body, in the fullness of time, returned, stalled in orbit above the Earth's atmosphere, and so reduced the pressure of overburden by its gravitational pull, allowed its daughter to turn to gas, split the overlying ice, and propelled a fountain of waters (mixed with some ice and snow) into the upper atmosphere and thence southward over the regions inhabited by man? With other deep bodies of water rising up likewise in response to their reduced weight and propelling effects of the reduced pressures on naturally- occurring gases formed in their depths?

A buried comet may be fanciful, and a satellite comet keeping pace with the Earth improbable, but then, the whole history of the Earth is a series of improbabilities. Details aside, all the raw materials for the event described in the scriptures existed - and exist even now.

Cloud Phenomena

"The mysterious 1908 Tunguska explosion that levelled 830 square miles of Siberian forest was almost certainly caused by a comet entering the

Earth's atmosphere, says new Cornell University research. The conclusion is supported by an unlikely source: the exhaust plume from the NASA space shuttle launched a century later.

The research, accepted for publication (June 24, 2009) by the journal *Geophysical Research Letters*, published by the American Geophysical Union, connects the two events by what followed each about a day later: brilliant, night-visible clouds, or noctilucent clouds, that are made up of ice particles and only form at very high altitudes and in extremely cold temperatures.

It's almost like putting together a 100-year-old murder mystery," said Michael Kelley, the James A. Friend Family Distinguished Professor of Engineering at Cornell who led the research team. "The evidence is pretty strong that the Earth was hit by a comet in 1908." Previous speculation had ranged from comets to meteors.

The researchers contend that the massive amount of water vapour spewed into the atmosphere by the comet's icy nucleus was caught up in swirling eddies with tremendous energy by a process called two- dimensional turbulence, which explains why the noctilucent clouds formed a day later many thousands of miles away.

Noctilucent clouds are the Earth's highest clouds, forming naturally in the mesosphere at about 55 miles over the Polar Regions during the summer months when the mesosphere is around minus 180 degrees Fahrenheit (minus 117 degrees Celsius).

The space shuttle exhaust plume, the researchers say, resembled the comet's action.

A single space shuttle flight injects 300 metric tons of water vapour into the Earth's thermosphere, and the water particles have been found to travel to the Arctic and Antarctic regions, where they form the clouds after settling into the mesosphere.

Kelley and collaborators saw the noctilucent cloud phenomenon days after the space shuttle Endeavour (STS-118) launched on Aug. 8, 2007. Similar cloud formations had been observed following launches in 1997 and 2003.

'Following the 1908 explosion, known as the Tunguska Event, the night skies shone brightly for several days across Europe, particularly Great Britain - more than 3,000 miles away.'

Imagine counter-rotating eddies with extreme energy. Once the water vapour got caught up in these eddies, the water travelled very quickly - close to 300 feet per second.

Scientists have long tried to study the wind structure in these upper regions of the atmosphere, which is difficult to do by such traditional means as sounding rockets, balloon launches and satellites.

Our observations show that current understanding of the mesosphere-lower thermosphere region is quite poor . . ."[17]

A global scale flood will not happen again. *Gen.9:14,15,16:* "And it shall come to pass, when I bring a cloud over the earth, that the bow shall be seen in the cloud: and I will remember my covenant, which is between me and you and every living creature of all flesh; and the waters shall no more become a flood to destroy all flesh. And the bow shall be in the cloud . . ."

It is unlikely but not impossible that in the times between man's creation and the flood, atmospheric conditions were such that rainbows were not seen in the high clouds. "The world that then was" was environmentally

[17] ScienceDaily, 25 June 2009

different to ours. But the language of *Genesis* is not necessarily of a new rainbow.

Could it be that the cloud that brought the great flood was indeed a feature of space, and therefore not of our normal cloud-type; and what is actually being said is, "I will never again bring a destroying cloud- type over the Earth that is incapable of displaying a rainbow" - just as a comet would not show a rainbow, but normal rain clouds do have rainbow-potential?

Covenant Faithfulness

God is a God of covenant faithfulness. "After this I looked, and, behold, a door was opened in heaven . . . and, behold, a throne was set in heaven, and one sat on the throne . . . and there was a rainbow about the throne . . ." *Rev.4:1-3.* A covenant bow of refulgent beauty, about the throne of God. *Ps.97:2:* "Righteousness and judgment are the habitation of his throne." *Ps.89:14:* "Justice and judgment are the habitation of thy throne: mercy and truth shall go before thy face."

Mercy and truth go before his face. Covenant faithfulness, mercy, truth, justice - attributes of divinity, the aura of God's throne. Judgment is his necessary but strange or foreign work, and he delights to show mercy and constant faithfulness in spite of every obstacle.

In Noah, we see a man after his own heart, who was faithful to his own generation despite all rebuffs, whose perseverance in well-doing led to the continuance of mankind at a time when man was on the brink of extinction. To such a man, the Almighty shows his covenant faithfulness in elevated splendour.

The purpose of history has been for God to separate to himself a people of covenant faithfulness like Noah. A people and a church who will turn their backs on the dying mirage that is this world, and give their undivided attention and loyalty to the Creator of this world. A people, or a church, typified by Noah, who chose to go into a prison-like, confined ark where God was, rather than stay in a gay and glittering world where God was not. A people and a church typified by the bride, Rebekah, who, when asked, "Would she go with this man?" replied without hesitation, "I will go" (*Gen.24:55*).

A church of whom no finer example is the foreign Moabites, declaring with covenant faithfulness: "Entreat me not to leave thee, or to return from following after thee: for whither thou goest, I will go: and where thou lodgest, I will lodge: thy people shall be my people, and thy God my God: where thou diest, will I die and there will I be buried: the Lord do so to me, and more also, if ought but death part thee and me" *Ruth 1:16,17.*

The sign of every true marriage is the rainbow. The aura of the Covenant bow is about God's throne, and about God's people. God's people are a committed people, faithful to each other and faithful to God.

There is a complete contrast between this charitable attitude of commitment and the prevailing world attitude before the flood. Mankind was clever, physically strong, and healthy. Food was relatively easy to obtain. Clemency of the environment meant clothing manufacture was a lesser task than in later times. There was industry; there was prosperity. Despite these advantages, almost universal amorality prevailed. Murder was regarded as a sport, and likewise marriage - if it could have been called such. In the scriptures we have a record of one man who composes prose to describe to his wives how he had murdered a man, speaking of the event as though it was nothing but a pleasurable pastime (*Gen.4:23,24*).

Water was ubiquitous and abundant, and perhaps the unwanted were regularly drowned out-of hand, like so many lesser animals. The factor finally sealing the fate of that world was intermarriage between the faithful, moral line and the amoral line (*Gen.6:2*). Following these intermarriages, amorality became ubiquitous. The people became blinded, numbed to reality, morally and spiritually destitute, seeing only the need for their own empty gratification. Man became totally possessed of the pride of the Serpent, a pride that sees only itself and destroys anyone or anything standing in its way. Maltreatment of the weaker and of the innocent is of no small moment in the divine reckoning. "Enter not into the fields of the fatherless: for their redeemer is mighty; he shall plead their cause with thee" *Pro.23:10.* It was a small thing, a thing *of no moment at all,* to dispose of the unwanted in those times, whether by drowning or some other way.

Marriage was likewise trodden underfoot as a mere aside to the pursuit of self-gratification - with all the misery that this entails. And so it was a righteous thing with God that those peoples were drowned, just as it shall be a righteous thing that the world following, which murdered Christ and burned many of his followers, shall be terminated by fire. But although the Almighty will sift the peoples of the Earth, "yet shall not the least grain fall to the ground" *Amos 9:9* He had a plan for Noah, and he likewise has deliverance for all his people; "those that make a covenant with him by sacrifice" *Ps.50:5.*

The final rolling of the heavens together like a burning scroll, accompanied by a loud noise, *2 Pet.3:10,* is yet another technical reference to an actual astronomical event. It is no longer a mystery as to how every human being will be resurrected in some sort of personal, bodily form. Bodies are information - and we know who has the files!

If the righteous scarcely are saved, and the just are needing mercy, where shall the ungodly and the sinner appear? May the name of the Lord, *Jehovah Our Righteousness*, be our refuge into which we run, just as Noah went into the ark, and the Lord shut him in.

XIII. QUESTIONS OF CLIMATE, SEA LEVEL, AND THE FUTURE

The big question about global warming? Why did a debate ever begin!

We may put global overheating to rest almost *instanter.* Personal overheating - not so quickly.

The geologic record ends the global warming scare. The scale of greenhouse gases is colossal, the time frame is colossal, the only explanation is colossal - a colossal plan for a sun - earth system. The plan involves a mechanism which functioned for more than four thousand million years and is functioning today.

The word of God is one with measurements and observations. In advance of the measurement and observation!

Recall, *Gen. 1:14* says *"And God said, Let there be lights in the firmament of the heaven to divide the day from the night; and let them be for signs, and for seasons, and for days, and years"*

"Let them be for ... signs ... ". Information. Information feedback.

Recall, *Ps. 19:1-5. "The heavens declare the glory of God; and the firmament sheweth his handywork. Day unto day uttereth speech, and night unto night sheweth knowledge. There is no speech nor language, where their voice is not heard. Their line is gone out through all the earth, and their words to the end of the world. In them hath he set a tabernacle for the sun, which is as a bridegroom coming out of his chamber, and rejoiceth as a strong man to run a race.*"

Information, information transfer, constant, all-pervasive.

Recall Kepler, placing the sun at the centre of the solar system. Thinking God's thoughts after Him. The sun is a 'type' of God. *Mal. 4:2:* "But unto you that fear my name shall the Sun of righteousness arise with healing in his wings..."

Recall, Christ commanded the weather. *"Peace! Be still!"*

And Christ is the sun, by 'type'. The Son of righteousness happens to be the sun of righteousness. The sun is therefore linked to our weather. Christ is God. God is the father. Adam, "that red earth" *(Hebrew)* is a son of God. Therefore, by 'type', the sun and earth are like a father and son, walking together. As a father receives feedback from a son and adjusts accordingly, so does the sun receive information feedback from Earth, and adjusts accordingly.

How can something that is 99.9% of the solar system adjust itself to something that is comparatively nothing?

The father and the son are figuratively holding hands. In a way that enables the son's needs to be met without causing major change to the father.

Global Warming being a semi-current topic, technical details follow-- this collation of comments gives a broad picture:

Not many people will dissent from the consensus fact that within human history, the Arctic region went almost ice-free long enough to facilitate the deposit of wave-formed 'beach ridges', and a quarter of the planet's land surface turned (mostly hot) desert. CO_2, by ice-core analyses, being *lower* than today. (Ice core estimates of palaeocarbon are readily available on-line.) Here are a couple of uncontroversial references. There are many more. These references blow human control of climate to smithereens.

"As recently as 5,000 years ago, the Sahara—today a vast desert in northern Africa, spanning more than 3.5 million square miles—was a verdant landscape, with sprawling vegetation and numerous lakes. Ancient cave paintings in the region depict hippos in watering holes, and roving herds of elephants and giraffes—a vibrant contrast with today's barren, inhospitable terrain."[18]

"Recent mapping of a number of raised beach ridges on the north coast of Greenland suggests that the ice cover in the Arctic Ocean was greatly reduced some 6000-7000 years ago. The Arctic Ocean may have been periodically ice free."[19]

Going on past trends we are, or at least, were, in a warming phase as of last time we looked at the climate gauges. But, within human history, the same thing has happened in various regions. The Arctic went almost ice free. The Sahara and the Middle East, with other regions to boot, turned burning desert. And so on. No discernible cause. Carbon? By ice core -- if we may rely on ice cores -*lower* than today.

The only existing, objectively documented driver of climate is solar effects. Solar effects, not the sun *in toto.* (The sun *in toto,* by measurement, has not significantly changed its raw infra-red light transmission through Space whilst we experienced the recent warmer weather (warmer here

18 Jennifer Chu, "Research points to abrupt and widespread climate shift in the Sahara 5,000 years ago (April 5, 2013)", on Phys.org

19 Geological Survey of Norway. "Less Ice In Arctic Ocean 6000-7000 Years Ago." ScienceDaily. www.sciencedaily.com/releases/2008/10/081020095850.htm (accessed 7 April 2018).

in Northeastern Australia, anyway)--it seems raw solar electromagnetic radiation does not necessarily tie directly to our temperature.

Hence: *Long term variations in solar activity and their apparent effect on Earth's climate*[20].

Sunshine from the Danish Met. Inst. - Abstract

The varying length of the 11-year cycle has been found to be strongly correlated with long-term variations of the northern hemisphere land surface air temperature since the beginning of systematic temperature variations from a global network, i.e. during the past 130 years. Although direct temperature observations before this interval are scarce, it has been possible to extend the correlation back to the 16th century due to the existence of a series of proxy temperature data published by Groveman and Landsberg in 1979. Reliable sunspot data do not exist before 1750, but we have been able to derive epochs of minimum sunspot activity from auroral observations back to 1500 and combine them with the direct observations to a homogeneous series.

Comparison of the extended solar activity record with the temperature series confirms the high correlation between solar activity and northern hemisphere land surface air temperature and shows that the relationship has existed through the whole 500-year interval for which reliable data exist.

A corresponding influence of solar activity has been demonstrated in other climatic parameters. Thus, both the date of arrival of spring in the Yangtze River Valley as deduced from phenological data and the extent of the sea-ice in the Atlantic sector of the Arctic sea have been shown to be correlated with the length of the sunspot cycle during the last 450 years.

[20] K.Lassen, Danish Meteorological Institute, Solar-Terrestrial Physics Division, Lyngbyvej,100, DK-2100 Copenhagen (2), Denmark, 1998

Conclusion

70-90 years oscillations in global mean temperature are correlated with corresponding oscillations in solar activity. Whereas the solar influence is obvious in the data from the last four centuries, signatures of human activity are not yet distinguishable in the observations.

Introduction

Variations in the activity of the Sun greatly influence the physics of the upper atmosphere. Thus, magnetic disturbances, occurrence of auroras at low latitudes, sporadic ionization above -80 km altitude, and...

Note on the supposed negation of Lassen's statistics. This supposed negation roughly coincides with the advent of satellite measurements. Lassen himself is reported as acknowledging, as faulty, his own conclusions regarding lack of human imprint...only since (roughly) 1980! My comment was framed in response to this supposed partial recanting by Lassen, and the (correct) assertion, "...solar irradiance up to the present time continues to move in a direction opposite that of temperature."

And so it did--possibly, if not certainly--throughout geologic history. As it is doing right now, if measurements of infra red light by satellites are meaningful. As the 'climate scientists' could have discovered before they made one model and one fool prediction. The 'faint early sun' conundrum as a glaring instance kicks it off. No dispute. Stars such as our sun, a far as is known, radiate at a rate 1/4 to 1/3 less than their long term average until they reach a substantial age. Yet -- no sign of a frozen early Earth. There are of course logical theories and, elsewhere, on-line, I personally point out how it can very easily and obviously be explained. No rocket science involved. And no need for strong early 'greenhouse' effects. I am somewhat embarrassed when I find myself 'hogging' comment pages. There is so much deliberate and non-deliberate misunderstanding. Irresponsibility in some high places. In Australia, climate 'experts' made the Commonwealth Scientific and Industrial Research Organization a standing joke. One expert went so far as to declare near everlasting relentless heat and drought over the inland, whereupon it rained so much over Australia, world sea-level actually fell by a slight but detectable amount!

"The Maunder Minimum, also known as the "prolonged sunspot minimum", is the name used for the period starting in about 1645 and continuing to about 1715 when sunspots became exceedingly rare, as noted by solar observers of the time."[21] (The Maunder Minimum is the 'mini ice age".)

Skipping over to *Hyperphysics*[22]*:* "The solar output is very nearly constant. The range of variation is about 0.2%, so reproducible that it is often referred to as the "solar constant". But there are other aspects of the Sun's activity that are not constant, as indicated by the changing sunspot activity. An early indication that the Sun's variability in ways other than total output had something to do with climate was the "Maunder Minimum". The researcher Maunder found that during this cold period between 1645-1715 there was very little sunspot activity, and this discovery led to the naming of the phenomenon after him. It suggested that solar activity was coupled to climate and led to tabulations of sunspot number as an indication of solar activity.

---

[21] Wikipedia, The Free Encyclopedia, s.v. "Maunder Minimum," (accessed April 2018), https://en.wikipedia.org/wiki/Maunder_Minimum

[22] R Nave, Correlation of global temperature with solar activity, (accessed May 2018) http://hyperphysics.phy-astr.gsu.edu/hbase/thermo/solact. html

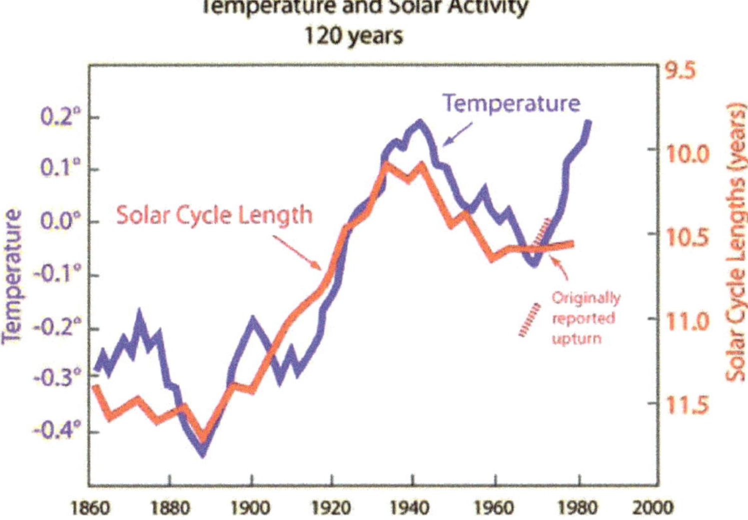

This illustration is a sketch of data from Durkin, based on data published by Friis-Christensen and Lassen. The end of the solar data has been altered in response to corrections of their data. This correlation between solar activity and temperature has been critiqued by Schneider and others, so it is an active area of investigation..."[Explanatory insert. Repeat: "...published by Friis-Christensen and Lassen. The end of the solar data has been altered in response to corrections...an active area of investigation..." The 'corrections' were made, only in deference to revolutionary, post-1978, *satellite* data! Read on...]

Skipping back to *Wikipedia*[23]*:* "Space-based observations of solar irradiance started in 1978... When going further back in time, one has to rely on... sunspots... [other proxies are mentioned]."

I am not a physicist, and I am assuming "solar irradiance...measured by satellites" is a measure of raw infra red light transmission somewhere in

---

[23] Wikipedia, The Free Encyclopedia, s.v. "Solar Constant", https:// en.wikipedia.org/ wiki/Solar_constant, accessed May 2018

Space. "The solar irradiance is the output of light energy from the entire disk of the Sun...It is looking at the Sun as we would a star rather than as an image."[24]

Anyone awake?

We have just now documented glaring circular reasoning on the part of 'climate experts'. Up until 1978, Solar activity was estimated using proxy variables, especially, but not entirely, the number of sunspots. Since 1978, solar irradiance has been measured up in Space - by satellites.

So, no surprises, Lassen and the Scandinavian and Chinese statistics, gathered prior to 1978, published 1998, do not measure solar irradiance by satellite, but by proxy.

The proxies are real world indicators of our climate! They flatly contradict the amount of light striking a given area of receptor on a space probe somewhere. Obvious conclusion? Climate, temperature especially, is not directly proportional to the reading of a light receptor out in Space. Lassen and the Scandinavians were correct in their observations. Half a millennium thereof! Maunder and the ice skaters on the Thames were not missing their faculties of observation.

Lassen, Maunder & co. concluded a link between temperature and solar activity, yes. The solar activity simply did not equal measurable light radiance at some point in Space. If I am correct about 'solar irradiance' and satellite measurement. Scarcely surprising, is it, since physicists remain mystified by sunspots![25]

---

24 Brian Dunbar, "Solar Irradiance", *National Aeronautics and Space Administration*, https://www.nasa.gov/mission_pages/sdo/science/solar- irradiance.html, updated on Nov. 27, 2017

25 "The Role of Sunspots and Solar Winds in Climate Change", *Scientific American,* accessed April 2018

So, your 2000 Lassen quote simply means there is a lot more to climate and 4 thousand million years of life on Earth than the heat being absorbed by a measuring device in a satellite at some place between us and the sun. This Lassen business sounds suspicious, if you ask me. His original work is proved correct. No surprises to discover his conclusions are being proved correct by sensitive magnetometers and weather stations right now!

"The results presented suggest that the observed secular variation of the Earth's magnetic field owes its origin to the ocean flow. Data analysis exhibits striking temporal correlation between the intensity of the North Atlantic oceanic circulation and secular variation in Western Europe; this explains, in particular, the geomagnetic jerks, and the recently discovered correlation between secular variation and climate. Spatial correlation between ocean currents and secular variation is also strong..."[26]

Repeating: "...geomagnetic jerks, and the recently discovered correlation between secular variation and climate." I mention this in other comments. The sun is not a conventional fireball. It is a quantum category, ongoing event! In combination with Earth's unique planetary features and the solar system's unique features, we can begin to understand climate.

On-line answer to Milankovitch Cycle Climate: Some self proclaimed experts really are excelling themselves. Quote: "Past climate change was primarily due to Milankovitch cycles. [Orbit related]"

Don't spoil a good story with facts! Facts. (Yes, Milankovitch is a big word.)

Our sun, from all the evidence and from physics, would have gone through a 'faint early sun' epoch.

---

[26] Ryskin, G., Secular variation of the Earth's magnetic field: induced by the ocean flow? New Journal of Physics, 11 (6), 2009

Heat output down by one third to one quarter. No evidence of a frozen early Earth. Look it up.

Common knowledge.

Orbit changes kept us warm?

Much later, post 'faint early sun', came a seeming (geologic evidence is seldom clear-cut) 'snowball Earth'.

Orbit changes kept us cold?

After the seeming 'snowball', complex life suddenly teemed in the waters, then, on land. Five major extinction events, causes unknown (although carbon starvation is likely), two of the most devastating being recorded in stratigraphic association with severe climate traumas and other geophysical events. Not necessarily ice ages by any means.

Caused by? Orbital changes?

Geologic history at large was not marked by clear cut hot-cold events on a clockwork system. "The fascinating occasional climatic fluctuations that we call ice ages have occurred only at rare intervals throughout the geologic record."[27]

On-line answer to "We can also see a clear link between CO_2 levels and many of the 5 major extinction events..." Geology does not possess one single atmospheric "fossil" which realistically could give certainty of past global temperatures or CO_2. Ice cores of course are more hopeful but go back no farther than 800,000 yrs. Hopeful -- not certain.

---

[27] Taylor,S.R., Destiny or Chance: Our Solar System and its Place in the Cosmos, Cambridge University Press, page 186, 1998

Palaeocarbon -- more and more difficult to estimate back into the past; pure guesswork mostly. Try vegetation that responds to CO_2 levels in the air in some visible manifestation? Try chemical proxies such as boron isotopes? Need to assume even distribution of boron in the oceans, even distribution of ocean pH, and no leaching or chemical alteration over time.

Palaeotemperature is based on proxies of various types and of course temperature at one fossil site does not give global temp.

Palaeo sea level can be estimated in the instances where deposits known to occur at a fixed ocean depth can be identified and their height relative to land can be determined. That is, assuming, the land did not sink relative to the sea, and not vice versa!

So tell us how, quote: "...we can study the paleoclimate and see a clear link between greenhouse gas levels and temperature and sea levels."

"We can also see a clear link between CO_2 levels and many of the 5 major extinction events..." Certainly! The two most significant stand-out mass extinctions followed hard on the heels of sequestration of massive quantities of carbon as geologic deposits. It only sticks out like a sore thumb. The Permo-Triassic extinction followed the Carboniferous and the End of Cretaceous followed the Cretaceous. *Creta,* chalk. CaCo3. And circumstantial evidence allows atmospheric carbon starvation as possibly or even probably being at the root of all mass extinctions. Let's not miss the astonishing message of the geologic rock column!

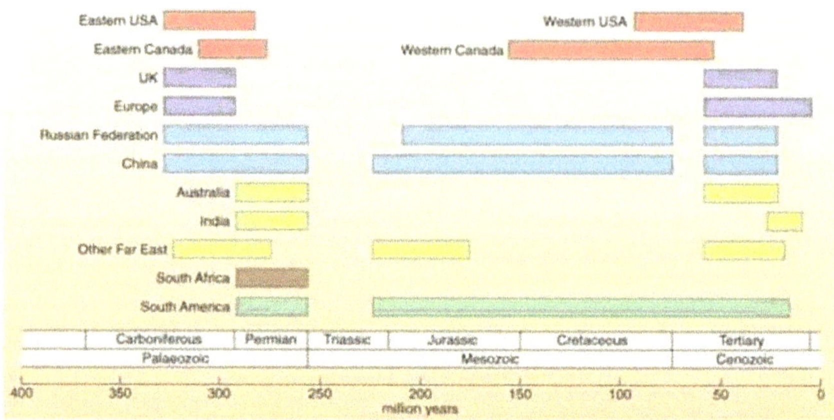

Image taken from OpenLearn 4.5 Global distribution of coal

The end of Permian and end of Cretaceous are the times of most severe and second most severe mass extinction, respectively. The discontinuance and partial discontinuance of coal - as shown above -- why? -- coal being compressed vegetation - why was vegetation scarce following the end of Permian and Cretaceous? Was scarcity of vegetatable matter caused by shortage of atmospheric CO_2?

"The carbon of sedimentary rocks was nearly all derived from CO_2 that once existed in the atmosphere[28]: If we estimate the total amount of carbon buried in sedimentary rocks, therefore, we should get a figure indicating how much CO_2 has existed in the air at one time or another. Rubey's calculations indicate that the amount of buried carbon exceeds that in the present atmosphere, oceans, and organisms by a factor of about 600 times[29]. Even if some of the analyses and estimates of volumes on which the calculations rest are greatly in error, the figure would still be startlingly large. Beyond any reasonable doubt, the amount of carbon now in the air is only a tiny fraction of the amount that has existed at some time in the geologic past. This result can be interpreted in several ways.

---

[28] Krauskopf, "Introduction To Geochemistry", McGraw Hill, 1967

[29] Rubey, W.W., Geol. Soc. America Bull.,vol.62, pages 1111-1147, 1951

One extreme possibility is that the atmosphere at some early period was very dense, consisting chiefly of CO_2 at a partial pressure of about 12 atmospheres, and that the activity of plants plus the deposition of carbonate sediments has gradually reduced the amount to its present low value, 0.0003 atmospheres [since risen to 0.0004]. This is an unlikely hypothesis, for it would mean that we are living at the very end of the history of life on our planet. Some CO_2 is returned to the air by respiration, rock weathering, and organic decay, but the amount is too small to make up for the carbon that is being steadily removed as precipitated carbonates and organic matter buried with sediments. A rough calculation of the carbon balance indicates that CO_2 in air will fall to a level too low to support plant life within a few centuries, unless some other source of the gas is available. Since the geologic record gives indisputable evidence for the continuous existence of multicellular organisms for at least 600 million years, and of unicellular life for at least 2 billion years [since extended to 4], the CO_2 content of air cannot have dropped far below its present figure for a long time. And it is scarcely believable that the present 0.0003 atmospheres [more precisely, 0.0004] has been reached only now after 2 billion years of steady depletion."

Four thousand million years plus, over which time our planetary atmosphere was host to something of the order of enough carbon (bonded into gases) to account for something like 12 entire Earth atmospheres worth of CO_2.

That's how much carbon went into the ground and the waters.

It follows that re-supply of carbon, to sustain life, was always a priority. Mass extinctions following deposition of coals and limestone, were all but a geologic certainty. New carbon could only have been supplied from Space or by volcanic eruption.

Climate governed by carbon gases immediately becomes a joke, invoking fairies twiddling inlet valves and extraction systems. Every day.

On-line, in answer to proclamations of, "We have the science."

The Science

Once upon a time, there was a planet with very high I.Q.

It decided to grow some plants. After this, it decided to grow some animals. All these living things relied upon atmospheric carbon. The planet took care of the plants and animals for four thousand million years -- never allowing atmospheric carbon to fall so low as to cause total annihilation. You see, the atmospheric carbon must have come from Space -- as did the entire planet. And, perhaps, from time to time, more carbon gases arrived from Space. Frozen carbon gases in comet - like bodies? The planet knew it needed carbon, because it kept on burying the carbon in rock strata and in the waters. Carbon would run out if the planet could not find a source replacement. Perhaps it *did* go very close to running out -- five mass extinctions must have worried the planetary I.Q. lots, eh? Every mass extinction could have been triggered by shortage of carbon.

The planet collected carbon from Space (perhaps) and fired up its gas -emitting volcanoes, so life survived. This planet had brains.

It processed something of the order of the equivalent of twelve of its atmospheres pure CO_2 in sequestering the carbon estimated to exist in rock strata and water.

Being ambidextrous and ambi-generally, and, well, perhaps, ambitious (?), the planet supplied its plants and animals, collecting from Space, re-cycling with its volcanoes. Chug chug puff puff.

Whilst concurrently it governed its climate so nothing really bad happened. Bad. You know. Like the moon. Mars. Venus. *Ooh* so much carbon dioxide. Naughty planets! Those nasty asteroids killed their bunny rabbits.

On-line response to, "The earth will heat up *a la* blackbody radiation until outgoing radiation equals incoming." This is where this whole biz is unbelievably unbelievable. You obviously know something of physics etc. I am no physicist, but any amateur sees right through this charade -- once we get to the logical root of the question.

"The earth will heat up *a la* black body radiation until outgoing radiation equals incoming." Slow down a mo. I could download a mountain here to show that, in the Earth's past, CO_2 and temperature don't appear to do what alarmists claim they do. But go direct; consider the meaning of 'blackbody'. Ideally, it applies to something like a homogeneous metal ball, swinging around a point source of heat, such as a glowing lamp.

So, since the Earth is not a simple ball, and the sun is not a simple lamp, 'blackbody' calculations will necessarily need to factor in the not-simple features, such as gas and water shrouding. Assuming we can approximate the shrouded Earth to a 'blackbody' -- not simple, but theoretically possible -- then your statement would be relevant -- the non-co-operative geologic record notwithstanding. In fact-- I am sure you would concur -- 'blackbody', as you have noted, would give an 'exposed' body such as our moon, or Mercury, a rather hot and cold time. Heat goes in, heat must either come out, or the body becomes heated.

Where is the hidden rider?

The sun produces heat which can be employed in 'blackbody' calculations but the sun is not 'blackbody'. It is stellar nuclear fusion not replicated on Earth and not tested in any laboratory. The mechanism of heat transfer within the sun is magneto- plasma transmission, *besides* electromagnetic radiation. The mechanism by which the sun heats its corona is dominantly magnetic -- Alfven Waves. Not 'blackbody' transmission in the sense of a pin head being heated by a candle.

'Well!' we say. The sun provides heat. Even if in more ways than one!

Problem: No existing measuring device can measure heat transfer via magneto - plasma waves. So we cannot say how much heat we are receiving!

Second problem: The Earth is not only shrouded by various gases and liquids. Earth is notoriously shrouded by perhaps the strongest magnetic field of any planet of the solar system. (Note: planetary magnetic field 'strength' has a somewhat relativistic meaning.)

So, we are shrouded by a magnetic field. Which itself is intimately associated with subatomic plasmas. And which continuously interacts with the solar field. And it also interacts with our gaseous shrouding.

We cannot measure the total heat incoming. We cannot measure the total heat outgoing. And, suddenly, a whole family of palaeoclimate and today's climate data begins to make sense. And, no-one need be surprised to discover ice cores, human history, and the geologic data making asses out of people who claim to understand climate!

Play God, play the fool.

<u>The Scientific Method, Applied</u>

The scientific method stands upon a created universe. Galileo: "Mathematics is the language with which God has written the universe". Re-affirmed by Einstein: "What I'm really interested in is whether God could have made the world in a different way; that is, whether the necessity of logical simplicity leaves any freedom at all." Faraday, esteemed a genius by Einstein: "<u>The Bible, and it alone, with nothing added to it nor taken away from it by man, is the sole and sufficient guide for each individual, at all times and in all circumstances</u>". Balance these startling assertions against these men's advice to keep an open and unbiased approach - and we have three certainties. 1) If it is scientific, it may be expressed mathematically. 2) The Word of God is the final and foundational authority. 3) We may draw rational conclusions - about a rational universe.

Climate alarmism fails on every count. We live on a rationally created planet more than four thousand million years old. Atmospheric CO_2 must have always been present, since carbon-reliant life was always present. Minimum required? Possibly 0.0002 atm.? - But higher is necessary for complex life. Simultaneously and concurrently, climate must have never exponentially run on to extremes, causing extermination. By estimation of geologic deposits, over that incomprehensible time, of the order of 12, repeat, of the order of 12 atmospheres CO_2 or its equivalent were sequestered in our strata and our waters. Carbon is non-renewable other than by re-supply from Space or from the Earth below. Volcanism being an obvious source.

This is the story for carbon - a minor greenhouse gas. Carbon, supplied by comets and volcanoes, certainly could not have remained steady! So if our climate is governed by carbon gases, where is the mathematical expression of climate science which proves rate of carbon gases emission from volcanoes is proportional to the temperature adjustment requirement of the globe?

Further, even if, by some surreal co-incidence, carbon was finely tuned into the system - were water vapour, ozone, nitrous oxide, and all other greenhouse gases concurrently fine tuned to the system? More: did the sun mysteriously act unlike other observed stars and decide to not fluctuate in output at any time?

Fairy tale science. Unmathematical, unempirical.

Four thousand million years, every fear of 'climate science' a certainty---exponential runs, CO_2 evaporating from the waters, extensive ice cap melts, triggering, through isostasy, massive volcanism, more CO_2, more heat input, triggering more melting, more atmospheric carbon... then, at length, carbon runs short...the world begins to freeze...on and on...The one certainty of geology. This planet was doomed. Like the billion other blasted ruins of Space.

"Heaven is my throne...Earth...My footstool...Out of whose hills thou mayest dig brass." We live in a rational universe.

What mechanism kept the planet from ruin? The Bible specifically links magnetism and climate (*Job 38:24*) and concurrently makes the sun the main control. Einstein was puzzled by our magnetic field and thinking people remain puzzled. All conductors in motion within a magnetic field generate electric current and thus set up a secondary field. Therefore, our circulating oceans (salt water is conductive) contribute to our magnetic field. Oceanic circulation is influenced by the shape of the ocean basins and...climate. Atmospheric circulation presumably is interlinked. The geomagnetic record shows an undeniable, mystifying link between palaeo climate and frequency of magnetic field reversal[30]. New discoveries about the sun point to a possible mechanism of temperature moderation... Empirical, mathematical, rational. The sun is in control and we feed back our requirements. Geologic history makes sense.

---

[30] Jacobs J.A., "Reversals of the Earth's Magnetic Field", Adam Hilger Ltd., Bristol, 1984

Attempt to Draw the Outline, Climate Moderation

Life has existed on Earth 4 thousand million years. Carbon dioxide content of the air must never have been substantially less than 0.0003 atmospheres, to sustain life. (Currently 0.0004 atm) Carbon gases may have been added to the atmosphere from space (dry ice and methane comets) and via volcanoes. Carbon is constantly being removed from the air by going into solution in the seas, to be buried in calcareous sediments, and by being buried as coal. (Total burial over 4 thousand million years was roughly equivalent to 12 atm. pure carbon dioxide.) Assume carbon gases do warm the planet. Assume they kept it from becoming too cold. Either full scale runaway global freezing or heating would have exterminated many species currently on Earth.

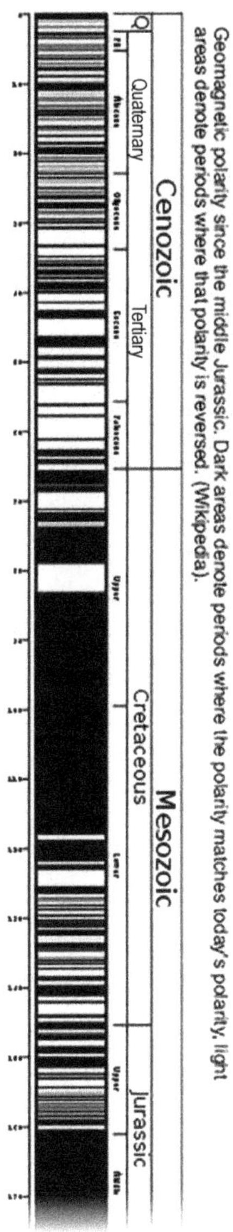

Geomagnetic polarity, late Jurassic to Present. Dark, polarity as at present; light; reversed. (Wikipedia; modified.)

What stopped the carbon gases from making it too hot? They must have been metered in extremely precisely, to sustain a liveable temperature, whilst not falling below the level required for plant life. Their concentration cannot have fallen below the minimum required for life during the existence of the planet. It is impossible to conceive of such precise metering by volcanoes and comets. A separate temperature correctional mechanism must have been built in. Assume the minimum carbon required for life also serves (through greenhouse effect) to stop total global freezing. Therefore there is no need to build in a low temperature stop - only a high temperature stop.

Assume such a stop (whatever its fine details may be) is built into the system, and involves our magnetic field.

Our magnetic field is in some sense climate driven. Assume a certain category of magnetic field activity, perhaps in some instances culminating in full reversal, invariably initiates a cooling effect. This effect for sake of argument could have to do with cloud formation or perhaps amelioration of some of the sun's input. It need not be total or abrupt in its effect and might taper off over time. Alfven Waves, instruments of heat transfer sensitive to magnetic field change[31], need not be ignored when considering the possibilities.

The strength and duration of the effect could be influenced by the forcefulness of the reversal or attempted reversal event? -- A simple process, perhaps varied in some measure as regards to its strength and duration, but always tending towards cooling. It is triggered at least in part through global warming altering atmospheric and oceanic circulation, which in turn triggers magnetic field changes, sometimes leading to reversal. Data are sketchy at best but we need not visualize reversal as a rigid, inflexible process.

There are reasons to suspect that no two reversal events are precisely the same - just as no two weather fronts are precisely the same. A cause-effect link between climate, carbon and the geomagnetic field is inescapable. The two best documented periods of muted reversal (one appears in the column in the previous page) were associated with obvious climate change and carbon. The older was during the **Carbon**iferous-Permian, the younger during the **Creta**ceous (Latin, chalk). Massive coal seams are associated with the first; limestone with the second.

---

[31] en.wikipedia.org/wiki/Alfven_wave

Conceptually, Alfven waves possess similarities to sound, which propagates through substances such as air; and radio, which propagates through the seeming void of Space. They are slower than radio/light but under rare circumstances may approach the speed of light. They exist wherever a magnetic field permeates 'plasma' of atomic fragments. The sun therefore features Alfven waves. In fact, much of the heat we receive from the sun is transmitted via magnetic action. The 'plasma' of the corona is closer to us than the sun, yet parts of it are much hotter than the surface of the sun.

The Earth, on the receiving end of the sun's output, also produces a magnetic field which passes through magnetically active substances (of our atmosphere). The sun's and Earth's fields continuously interact. The properties of our atmosphere are related in some ways to its temperature and composition. Therefore, carbon gases of our atmosphere potentially influence the magnetic interplay between sun and Earth. Oxygen itself possesses magnetic properties. These properties change according to the compound into which oxygen may be bonded.

Our (circulating) oceans are also influenced by temperature and dissolved substances - including carbon dioxide. They actively contribute to our overall magnetic field - what proportion, is unknown. In times past, their circulation may have been strongly modified through earth movements. Going on the geologic evidence, ocean basin shape and therefore ocean basin shape change have played an integral part in geomagnetic field behaviour, in climate, and in the story of life.

If information feedback via atmospheric change is insufficient to the purpose, do the oceans act as a back-up to trigger magnetic field re- action to trip the thermostat? Could the effect be to reduce the solar radiation headed our way via magnetic transmission? The potential suitability of Alfven waves to this purpose lies in their propagation according to the characteristics of the magnetic field via which they are travelling.

Thus, magnetic field excursion/reversal here on Earth does not expose us to ruinous solar activity - on the contrary, it is part of a mechanism which ameliorates certain forms of solar activity in relation to the Earth. Events leading up to excursion/reversal need not be entirely pleasant (?) but, from the geologic record and the Scriptures, there is no reason to propose entirely ruinous global destruction as an adjunct of such events.

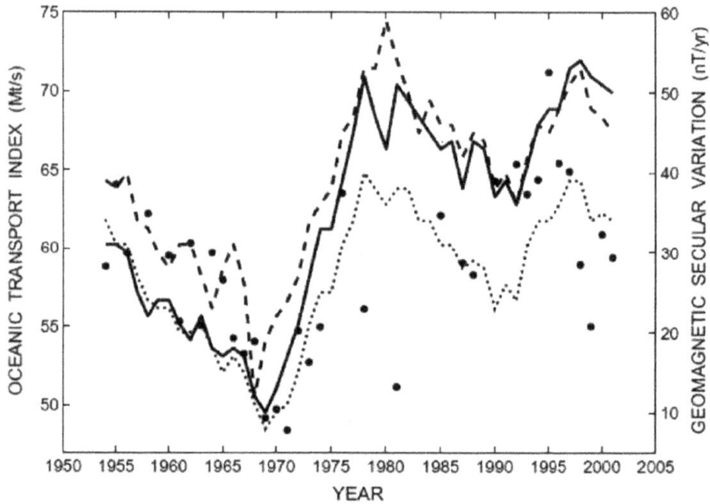

Does ocean flow cause the geomagnetic jerks? Comparison of oceanographic and geomagnetic data shows that the trend in secular variation is closely correlated with the trend in the ocean-flow intensity. Points - the oceanic transport index, a measure of intensity of the North Atlantic gyre circulation (Curry and McCartney 2001; data absent in some years, especially between 1979 and 1984). Lines - secular variation of the geomagnetic field (differences between successive annual means, east component) at three observatories in Western Europe: solid line - Eskdalemuir, dotted line - Niemegk, dashed line - Chambon la Foret (World Data Center for Geomagnetism 2007). It is seen that the hitherto unexplained geomagnetic jerks of 1969, 1978, 1991, and

1998 (De Michelis and Tozzi 2005) are correlated with sharp changes in the trend of the ocean-flow intensity.[32]

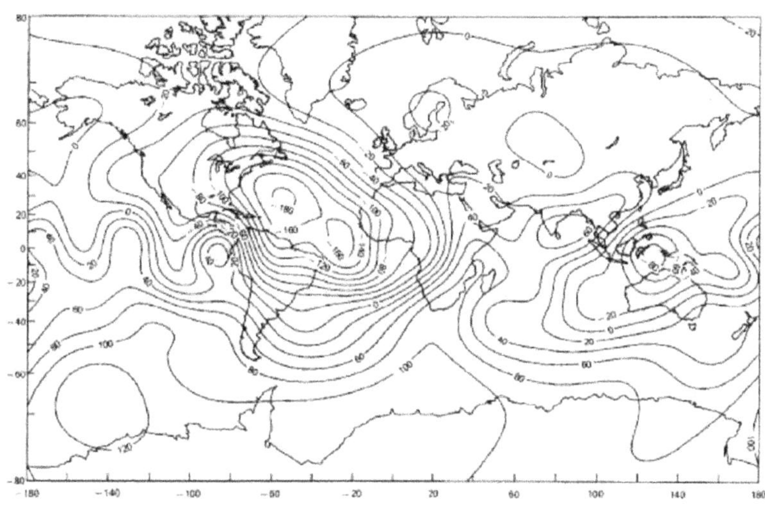

World chart of geomagnetic secular variation at 1980, Units are nT/yr; Mercator projection. Three local maxima (by absolute value) stand out as the key features of the chart; they are located east of Florida, east of North Brazil and south of the Philippines. Each of these maxima is associated with a major western boundary current: the Florida Current, the North Brazil Current and the Kuroshio, respectively. Not only the spatial correlation is strong, but also agreement is good between the local rates of secular variation and the order-of-magnitude estimates based on the currents' total transports. [33]

"The results presented suggest that the observed secular variation of the Earth's magnetic field owes its origin to the ocean flow. A numerical simulation using the induction equation of magnetohydrodynamics and

32 Ryskin, G., Secular Variation of the Earth's Magnetic Field: Induced by Ocean Flow? *New Journal of Physics,* 11 (6). Figure 1, page 18, used by permission, 2009

33 *reproduced from figure 42 of Langel, R. A., "The main field Geomagnetism" vol 1, ed., J. A. Jacobs (London: Academic) pages 249 - 512,1987*

the ocean flow field yields secular variation in rough agreement with observations. Data analysis exhibits striking temporal correlation between the intensity of the North Atlantic oceanic circulation and secular variation in Western Europe; this explains, in particular, the geomagnetic jerks, and the recently discovered correlation between secular variation and climate. Spatial correlation between ocean currents and secular variation is also strong...The current consensus is that the main field is generated by the hydromagnetic dynamo in the Earth's fluid outer core. Secular variation has been taken as evidence of motion in the core since the time of Halley (1692). Halley thought that secular variation, the westward drift in particular, was caused by differential rotation of a magnetized solid core, separated from the 'external parts of the Globe' (also magnetized) by a "fluid medium." Contemporary theoretical studies use the westward drift to estimate the characteristic large-scale velocity in the outer core, and to conclude that dynamo action is possible. If secular variation is caused by the ocean flow, the entire concept of the dynamo operating in the Earth's core is called into question: there exists no other evidence of hydrodynamic flow in the core."[34]

Ryskin is not suggesting our magnetic field is generated by ocean circulation. (Ocean circulation nevertheless must generate some magnetism.) Ocean circulation is related to climate and climate is related to ocean circulation. Immediately, we see an opportunity for information feedback. Is climatic information fed back to the sun via our magnetic field? How do magnetic events such as reversals, here on Earth, come into the picture?

Christ's words regarding future events, especially involving the atmosphere, suddenly begin to come into focus -- *Matthew 24; Mark 13; Luke 21.* Such detail would not be retained unless for a definite purpose. Late in time, as recorded in three Gospels, atmospheric phenomena on a scale never

---

[34] G. Ryskin, *New Journal of Physics*, 11 (6), "Secular variation of the Earth's magnetic field: induced by the ocean flow?" http://dx.doi. org/10.1088/1367-2630/11/6/063015, accessed 7 August 2009

previously witnessed by man, probably associated in some way with climate change and perhaps increased earthquake activity will catch the attention of mankind.

Recent studies of seabed drill cores suggest an association between rapid climate change, volcanic activity, and magnetic field fluctuation.

Volcanic activity is associated with earthquake activity. Claims of a statistical link between volcanism and climate change have also recently been published.

"Among others pieces of evidence, we have observations of ash layers in the seabed and have reconstructed the history of volcanic eruptions for the past 460,000 years," says GEOMAR volcanologist Dr Steffen Kutterolf, who has been with SFB 574 since its founding. Particular patterns started to appear. "There were periods when we found significantly more large eruptions than in others" says Kutterolf, the lead author of the Geology article. After comparing these patterns with the climate history, there was an amazing match. The periods of high volcanic activity followed fast, global temperature increases and associated rapid ice melting."[35]

This association between rapid climate change and volcanism is based upon assumptions and cannot be proved beyond doubt. A possible trigger for volcanism could be weight shift from ice caps to sea water and vice-versa.

The words of Christ do not specify such an association but can be taken as implying that such a link could exist. His words appear more definite in the case of tying future atmospheric, and, therefore climatic effects, to our magnetic field *Luke 21:25-28,* etc. (These predicted events need not be in strict chronologic order: and, *signs* refers to information, which

---

[35] Helmholtz Center for Ocean Research Kiel (GEOMAR), "When the ice melts, the Earth spews fire," ScienceDaily, http://www.sciencedaily. com /releases/2012/12/1212191335 51.htm, accessed 23 December 2012

from *Gen.1:14* we deduce implicates planetary magnetism and light.) The purpose of including these descriptions and implications in the Bible can only be to advise mankind that they need not prove fatal. Take heart; God is sovereign. Go on, without faltering, to the end. A ruined, a doomed, and an antagonistic world need not deter us: "look up, and lift up your heads; for your redemption draweth nigh [in cosmic terms]" *Luke 21:28.* We are here for a reason - warts and all.

The world will end at the command of God, not by a mischance of Nature nor through destruction by man himself. Startling future atmospheric phenomena are not the end of the world. They could well be an aspect of climate control!

Parting Thoughts

It seems certain that during Man's presence on Earth, injection of carbon greenhouse gases into the atmosphere never occurred on a more massive scale than during the past century. Atmospheric carbon gas levels have recently increased by something like one third, with no hint of a fall in rate of increase.

It seems certain that during the entire history of Mankind, Earth's magnetic field never changed as it has changed during the past century. It may be helpful to understand that Earth's magnetism shows every indication of being the sum of the magnetism of an unknown number of magnetic field generators. The more generators that align in the same orientation, the 'stronger' the overall field. The overall field has 'weakened' significantly. The north pole in particular has been wandering at increased speed.

During the past century, global temperature and global climate did not change at anything approaching the rate of change of either greenhouse gases or the location of magnetic north.

We have adduced evidence that this is as one might well expect, given geophysics and the geologic record. And, most tellingly - given logic and the word of God.

What does the future hold?

Another book of this size again would barely introduce the topic.

As we have surmised, the word, "signs", as employed in *Genesis 1,* by definition implies information technology of various categories and sophistication. Total sophistication. The level of sophistication calls on planetary magnetism, magneto-plasma energy transfer, stellar nuclear fusion, that superlative information carrier, light...the quantum character of the hydrogen bond...Only the Creator of heaven and earth could understand these things --- geomagnetism, nuclear fusion, climate, species as information programming outcomes...all interrelated! The visible and invisible "powers of heaven" *(Luke 21:26).*

All the factors known to physics - covered by this term, the "powers of heaven" - all the cosmic forces interrelate and interplay with each other. For instance, sudden movement of a massive body light years away from us billions of years ago theoretically can influence our planet today. Or, as another example: light shines on us from the sun and stars - but if, *en route,* the light passes through a magnetic field? The light may become altered in some way. For instance it may become polarized. Another possibility is twinning of its spectral lines. Cosmic forces interact. These are "powers of heaven" —which can give the appearance of being shaken.

"Men's hearts failing them for fear, and for looking after those things which are coming on the earth: for the powers of heaven shall be shaken." Luke 21:26.

Jesus Christ spoke these words. In doing so, he referred back to *Genesis 1.* Only the creator of heaven and earth could possess such information.

"And there shall be signs in the sun, and in the moon, and in the stars; and upon the earth distress of nations, with perplexity; the sea and the waves roaring;

Men's hearts failing them for fear, and for looking after those things which are coming on the earth: for the powers of heaven shall be shaken" (Luke 21:25,26).

This same man, Jesus, Creator and Lord, says, *"I have loved you with an everlasting love." (Jer.31:3). "Fear ye not therefore!"(Matt.10:31).*

As for the future that has future - Abraham was the "friend of God" *2 Chron. 20:7, Isa. 41:8.*

But he was not the friend of God! He is the friend of God! *Mark 12:26, 27: "Have ye not read in the book of Moses, how...God spake unto him, saying, I am the God of Abraham, and the God of Isaac, and the God of jJacob? He is not the God of the dead, but the God of the living!"*

Jennifer MacRae, *Alive Magazine,* (August 2000).

"a very readable work . . . skillfully shows the scientific facts underlying what many in scientific and educational fields have written off as mere fable."

Darryl Stringer, BS, *The Queensland Baptist,* (December 2000).

"Although there is a great deal of science included within the pages of this book, the reader does not need to have a broad understanding of science, for Heywood has done an excellent job of simplifying the complex so that everyone can understand the various ideas . . . His goal is not to promote himself or his theory, but to see God glorified."

www.ingramcontent.com/pod-product-compliance
Ingram Content Group UK Ltd.
Pitfield, Milton Keynes, MK11 3LW, UK
UKHW062312290726
14090UKWH00018B/1024